Gandhi's Khadi

GANDHI'S KHADI

A History of Contention and Conciliation

Rahul Ramagundam

GANDHI'S KHADI

ORIENT LONGMAN PRIVATE LIMITED

Registered Office
3-6-752 Himayatnagar,
Hyderabad 500 029 (A.P.), INDIA
e-mail: orientswan@gmail.com

Other Offices
Bangalore, Bhopal, Bhubaneshwar, Chennai, Ernakulam, Guwahati, Hyderabad, Jaipur, Kolkata, Lucknow, Mumbai, New Delhi, Patna

First Published 2008
This paperback edition 2008, co-published with Gandhi Smriti and Darshan Samiti, New Delhi

ISBN 13: 978 81 250 3583 1
ISBN 10: 81 250 3583 4

Typeset in 11/14 pt. AGaramond

Typeset by
InoSoft Systems
NOIDA

Printed in India at
Glorious Printers
Delhi

Published by
Orient Longman Private Limited
1/24, Asaf Ali Road
New Delhi 110 002

For Gandhi's voiceless millions

To Mithlesh and Nitya Nand Singh, whose I am,
and Pritha, who is mine,
...for being so close and yet so far... during the course of this work

Contents

Preface

My formative years were spent with my paternal grandparents. They were first-generation migrants from a rural area to an urban location, part of Nehru's modern India that had burgeoning public sector units with townships for its workers. While my grandparents benefited materially from Nehru's developmental model, their thinking and habits were drawn from Gandhian idealism. They were simple people. And they always wore khadi. I remember my grandfather going to his workplace in khadi *dhoti* and *kurta* with an *angavastram* wrapped around his neck and a Gandhi *topi* on his head; he looked resplendent and fashionable. My grandmother didn't speak any language other than her own rural dialect and yet never felt incomplete in any way. She was tiny and tenacious, confident and cautious. She could write only two words: one, Sitaram, which while being an invocation of the name of God was also her husband's name. The other word was her own name Arti, which she sometimes had to write when my grandfather brought some bank papers for her to sign. She wrote "Sitaram" repetitively in discarded old diaries and asked her relatives, if someone happened to go anywhere near the Ganges, to immerse them in the sacred river. Her illiteracy however never deadened her sensitivity or fanaticised her religiosity. She was pained as she watched the demolition of Babri masjid in December 1992 on television. She was a highly religious woman who would keep many fasts and worship many gods. Every morning, after her bath, she would stand in the courtyard before a *tulsi* plant, with folded hands, and invoke Surya to bring happiness, first to each and every one in the universe and then, lastly, to her family and herself. Her material and moral sustenance came from two sources: the material from Nehru's confident India and the moral from Gandhi's ethics. This book is a tribute to the memory of my grandparents, habitual khadi wearers, who now departed, had sown the seeds of this work by their cultural convictions and material aspirations.

Some sixty years after it was wrapped up as a non-violent voluntary movement that transformed a commodity into a political symbol of assertion and autonomy, this interpretive history of the khadi movement is being written. In this time, khadi was appropriated by the newly independent state as one of its "developmental departments". This time-frame is important because it shows the apathy with which khadi, its ideology and its history were seen by India's state architects and development thinkers. But more than intellectual apathy, the absence of a serious, policy-oriented assessment of Gandhian socio-economic practices shows some deeper symptoms of the malaise in the making of the state and its priorities in India. Khadi, ironically, in its own lifetime as a movement, had lost its sheen and had been declared as an "old man's fad" bound to vanish along with his mortal remains.

"The East India Company", Gandhi said to Katherine Mayo on 17 March 1926, "came to buy, and remained to sell. It compelled us to cut off our thumbs. This is the history of how our skill was lost." The khadi movement was an attempt at reclaming a lost skill in a restricted colonial environment. It was a massive voluntary exercise. However, Gandhi's critics, including established Congress politicians, saw his effort as a futile attempt at revivalism. Gandhian ideology was perceived as "religiously oriented, backward-looking".

I began to look at the khadi movement with a curiosity to discover elements of an alternative development model. But as the research progressed, I discovered newer strands. I realised how massively it was organised on a nationwide scale. I also discovered the almost continuous ideological contestation that the khadi movement witnessed as Gandhi and his close followers determinedly pursued it. But the most important discovery was its importance in Gandhi's attempt to establish self-rule for the "dumb-millions". In many ways, khadi was central to the conversion of the Congress into a mass-based organisation. And, yet the Congress was most vehemently opposed to khadi's occupying a central position in the struggle for freedom.

The second-hand set of the 90 volumes of the *Collected Works of Mahatma Gandhi* that Delhi's Gandhi Peace Foundation (GPF) was about to sell to a junk dealer in the winter of 1995, which I bought at the princely sum of five hundred rupees, became the backbone of this work. The book is equally informed by my grassroots engagements, to which Rajagopal, the then Secretary of the GPF, introduced me. During 1995 to 2001, while studying at JNU, I was simultaneously engaged with grassroots activism on the livelihood rights of the adivasi people in Madhya Pradesh. Those years lent me the perspective to look at Gandhi's khadi movement, which in many substantive ways was the first social movement in modern India that brought poverty to the centre stage of Indian consciousness and made livelihood rights an issue of mass mobilisation.

This book, in the making as it was for the last ten years, has incurred many debts and belongs primarily to the friends whose unstinted support and unwavering affection helped realise this dream. Akhilesh Kumar, Saral Ganguli, Sobha Tiwari, and Samskruti were some of those friends who supported this long drawn academic struggle with their faith, love and understanding. Samskruti's irreverent questioning enriched many ideological and narrative enunciations. I feel deeply for Malay, with whom it all began, and Mamsi, who provided vital support as it progressed; unfortunately their patience ran out before the dream had run its full course.

But for my parents, Mithelesh and Nitya Nand Singh, whose love and affirmation were my strength, this work would not have been possible. They put their aspirations on hold to let me complete this work. My brothers Niraj and Rajiv have been pillars of strength.

My association with Pitamabar Bhatt of the KVIC, which gave me some financial support to undertake empirical research on khadi-producing institutions in Bihar and Haryana; Ragini Prem of the Banwasi Sewa Ashram; Y. P. Anand, the director of the National Gandhi Museum; late Som Bhai and Jailok Thakur, institutions in themselves in the khadi sectors of Haryana and Bihar, respectively, and many others were vital preparatory ground when I began to explore archival sources.

With gratitude I acknowledge contributions of libraries at JNU, GPF, Teen Murti, National Gandhi Museum in Delhi, Sabarmati Ashram at Ahmedabad, and the Sarva Sewa Sangh at Wardha. My thanks to the reviewer of the manuscript for his helpful suggestions all of which have been incorporated. My deep gratitude to my publishers, Orient Longman, Delhi, for their inputs.

Certainly, in this long engagement, I have incurred many more debts than I have mentioned. Margaret Chatterjee wrote in from Westminister College, Oxford: "a Ph.D. thesis on Khadi! I do not think Ph.D. level work would be worthwhile on it". It was an academic challenge to prove that the project was well worthwhile, viable, and much more.

DELHI RAHUL RAMAGUNDAM

1 Memories of a Moral Movement

Yeh charkha tope hai,
Barood Iske ban gaye gole,
Isi se Lunkashayar
Manchester ko udadenga.[1]

The very thing that was a cause of our slavery will open the door to our freedom.[2]

Weapons are made in adversity. They are not produced by competition among societies or cultures, for such competitions can generate in the societies mutually enriching and ennobling

[1] This spinning wheel is a cannon,
Yarn-balls are its ammunition,
With this we shall smash,
Lancashire and Manchester.
A nationalist song quoted in *Outlook* (Delhi), 18 August 1997, 150.

[2] Gandhi in a speech at the All India Spinners' Association meeting, *Khadi Jagat*, December 1941, in *Collected Works of Mahatma Gandhi*, hereafter *CWMG*, 75: 176.

experiences. Weapons are born of threats to survival. During India's mass campaign for freedom, a new weapon was forged from a threat-perception which arose with regard to the British textile industry. The new weapon was *charkha* with its product *khadi*, the handspun and handwoven cloth. Early nationalists blamed the British for the destruction of India's once flourishing cloth industry. They were the ones who demonstrated to Indians how "the English had sucked our life-blood".[3] Mohandas Karamchand Gandhi, too, inferred that it was not machines but machinations of the East India Company that had led to the decimation of India's craft-based cloth industry. Gandhi said in August 1925 to a Rotary Club gathering at Calcutta that the indigenous cloth industry "was made to die".[4] The Company's persecution was so cruel as to force Indian craftsmen to "cut off their own thumbs in order to avoid imprisonment".[5]

Khadi (from *khad*, Hindi for pit), made from handspun cotton yarn by weavers working over a pit, acquired emblematic status in the first half of the twentieth century during India's freedom struggle. Gandhi, largely acknowledged as the one who not just

[3] Gandhi was explaining the role that the early nationalists played in vitalising the consciousness of Indians (Parel 1997, 15). Foremost among the "early nationalists" was Dadabhai Naoroji whose Drain of Wealth theory was the first to draw India's attention to the baneful impact of imperialist rule.

[4] "Speech at Rotary Club", Calcutta, reported in *The Englishman*, 19 August 1925, *CWMG*, 28: 84. The cotton industry of Manchester acquired a folkloric imagery in India. Writing in 1909 in *Hind Swaraj*, Gandhi stated: "It is difficult to measure the harm that Manchester has done to us. It is due to Manchester that Indian handicraft has all but disappeared" (Parel 1997, 107).

[5] "Who Cut The Thumbs?", *Young India*, hereafter *YI*, 30 March 1921, *CWMG* 19: 487. Gandhi was referring to the regime of the East India Company when "spinning or weaving had become almost a crime". He believed that it was not the *gumastas* of the Company who had cut off the thumbs of the artisans but that the mutilation was self-inflicted.

established the fabric but also invested it with immense symbolism, saw khadi as heralding real freedom to the millions of poor and marginalised Indians. Gandhi's khadi campaign made Indians see in the "slender thread of cotton" the essence and the practical structure of *swaraj*.[6] Swaraj, in Gandhi's view, hung on a thread, the cotton thread spun on a charkha. For the non-violent army, the charkha was its arsenal. In the heydays of his friendship with Gandhi, Maulana Mohammad Ali had declared that yarn cones were the bullets with which India would win her swaraj.[7] Jawaharlal Nehru, though distanced ideologically from his political mentor, called khadi "the livery of freedom". Scholars too have eulogised khadi in similar lines. Bernard Cohn calls it a "uniform of rebellion", and for Susan Bean, khadi is the "fabric of independence".

Situating the Kernel of Khadi

Historically, the khadi movement was ideologically woven around the need to provide supplementary work to idle or underemployed rural-hands. As it was designed to cater primarily to a rural workforce, khadi required simple, comprehensible technology and a local resource-base for both its production and consumption. It was round this constructive ideology that a political movement was built. It had a practical dimension of being a subsidiary occupation for India's famished rural masses and a symbolic

[6] "Speech at Ellore", 3 April 1921, *CWMG* 19: 511.

[7] "Discussion with Nagpur Congress worker", 27 December 1939, *CWMG* 71: 64. Mahatma Gandhi's own language was full of allegorical references to war. "We are engaged in a spiritual war. During the late war our rulers attempted to turn every factory into an arsenal for turning out bullets of lead. During this war of ours, I suggest every national school and college being turned into a factory for preparing cones of yarns for the nation." ("The Secret of Swaraj", *YI*, 19 January 1921, in *CWMG*, 19: 240).

value of being a mascot of mobilisation for India's freedom struggle. Khadi was as much a material solution to the predicament that colonised India found itself in as it was a spiritual quest. The khadi movement was a campaign to establish a non-violent socio-economic order. But its achievement of this aim is contested.

Much of the historiography of the nationalist movement has adamantly skirted the significance of a constructive agenda, of which khadi formed a vital part, in building the liberation movement. Issues such as *swadeshi*, khadi, village-reconstruction, and other related concerns falling under the generic term of constructive agenda occupy a bulk of Gandhi's writings and speeches.

Yet, surprisingly, it is his political engagement that has remained the focus of scholarly work at the cost of marginalisation of his real-life vocation. Not much is available in scholarly analysis on Gandhi's constructive agenda in general and khadi in particular. For instance, Nanda's *The Making of a Nation*, which charts India's road to independence and which was published to commemorate the fiftieth anniversary of independence, does not have even one chapter dealing with Gandhi's khadi or the constructive work. Biographers, such as Stanley Wolpert (2001) and Rajmohan Gandhi (1995), while writing mainly on the life and legacy of Gandhi, ignore his constructive agenda. Except for the study of Srikrishnadas Jajoo, who was a protagonist of the khadi movement, there is no systematic study of the khadi movement as yet. Even Jajoo's work is only a chronological appraisal of the All India Spinners' Association (AISA), an organisation founded in 1925.[8]

In recent times, however, a spate of studies on different facets of the khadi movement has emerged. Emma Tarlo's *Clothing Matters* is an anthropological examination of an everyday dilemma

[8] Srikrishnadas Jajoo, 1962, *Akhil Bharatiya Charkha Sangh ka Ithihaas.*

of what to wear.[9] It explores the much discussed question of identity as it wrestles with individual understanding and cultural encrustations that go into clothing and the making of it. Her central theme is the significance of clothes in the making of individual as well as group identity. In doing so, she explores also the relationship between clothes and the wearer. Clothes define the identity of the wearer. Thus, it manifests a plethora of "multiple and conflicting" identities according to the kind, design, and fabric of the clothes that one wears. But in the Indian context, Tarlo obviates the possibility of an emergence of multiple and conflicting identities. A formal recognition of choice regarding cloth did not arise as a natural outcome of the presence of a reinvented khadi. The dilemma of choosing khadi or other cloth was enforced through a sustained campaign.

According to Bean, Gandhi used "his appearance to communicate his most important messages in a form comprehensible to all Indians".[10] In Tarlo's critique, Bean, with such deductions, fails to address the problem of intention and interpretation. Dress, as in other symbolic phenomena, is capable of signifying a variety of different meanings simultaneously. Often what was intended was not interpreted as it was meant, and therefore Gandhi explained his intention through self-edited journals and national tours. "If dress was truly capable of communicating his message clearly, there would have been little need for such explicit verbal explanations", Tarlo argues. Her own interpretation that Gandhi attempted to control the clothing of the nation by encouraging all Indians to wear khadi and all Indian men to wear the "Gandhi cap" is, to say the least, problematic. A national sartorial uniformity, she adduces, was the aim of Gandhi's khadi campaign. However, as she says: "He never obtained his objective of clothing the entire Indian nation

[9] Emma Tarlo, 1996, *Clothing Matters: Dress and Identity in India.*

[10] Cf. Tarlo; Susan Bean, 1989 "Gandhi and Khadi, the Fabric of Indian Independence".

in Khadi." Gandhi, undoubtedly, was ambitious about his khadi agenda and saw it as a means towards voluntary cooperation on a scale that was never witnessed anywhere in modern times. He regarded his contribution in resuscitating the charkha as vital and more important than his role in India's freedom struggle. He wanted posterity to remember him as one who refurbished the charkha into a political and economic weapon.

But, Gandhi's aggressive khadi campaign was not an attempt to produce a uniformly blended Indian, homogeneously dressed in white khadi. Instead, he was clearly creating a sartorial divide between those who clung to self-satisfaction and, by extension, loyalty to British imperialism, and those who acted in the interests of social well-being through suffering and self-sacrifice. He was well aware that the British ruled India not by their superior military power but by the active collaboration of the well-off Indians. The khadi campaign sought to divide Indians into two "classes"—those who believed in and wore khadi and those who did not. But Gandhi's "class division" was enforced non-violently, though it was not entirely free from coercion.[11] It provided mobility of passage from one "class" to another. His emphasis on

[11] Ideally, it was designed to be morally and not physically coercive. There was a tremendous amount of moral coercion involved in associating khadi with certain values. Krishna Das narrates an incident when Gandhi along with Mohammad Ali was in Allahabad during the non-cooperation movement. The Maulana was about to address the crowd when a man shouted that the Turkish cap worn by the Maulana was of foreign make. This created a ruckus which was, however, controlled when the Maulana said that though in shape it resembled a Turkish cap, it was made of khadi. Gandhi and other leaders tried to suppress such enthusiastic followers. Gandhi recalled the weapon of bonfire after such incidents where his zealous followers would strip anyone wearing foreign clothes which would then be consigned to the fire. It amounted to violence. Yet, in no small way, Gandhi himself fostered such an attitude. Krishna Das mentions an occasion when Gandhi was gifted a khadi dhoti to which he responded that it was hardly adequate to meet import substitution (Krishna Das 1928).

non-violence was intended to provide a possibility for the transformation of an individual's alignment. Wearing khadi in that sense was a transformative experience. One could change one's class affiliation through personal conviction and a change of heart. Khadi became an ideological pivot on which one's political and personal beliefs could be vindicated; one's clothing became an index of one's affiliations.

In a recent paper, Lisa N. Trivedi says that in a largely illiterate and multilingual South Asian context, Gandhi's khadi movement adopted a visual medium of expression to disseminate messages, forge a nationalist consciousness, and map the geographical and political boundaries of the newly "invented nation".[12] As Trivedi reiterates, nationalism in South Asia arose "without the benefit of a common written language and rising literacy". She says, "the nation in South Asia was popularly conceived in a discursive field in which visual medium and printed languages were mutually constitutive." "Print capitalism" and visual vocabulary together brought about the national consciousness. In substantiating her arguments, she discusses the role played by printed posters or line-expressions, slide-shows, and lantern-lectures and exhibitions in imparting a visual map of the nation in people's minds. Whereas posters were the printed form, lantern-lectures and exhibitions were the visual form in this communication package.

Such arguments erroneously assume that visual communication is the sole preserve of oral traditions and "illiterate" societies.[13] It assumes that "visual vocabulary" is only for those from an

[12] She begins with a critique of Anderson's "print capitalism" axiom and then ends up strengthening the same (Trivedi 2003).

[13] In fact, for the nationalist agenda, using exhibitions as a means of communication was nothing new. The empire builders themselves used exhibitions to disseminate imperial values by regularly holding the "British Empire Exhibition" in Britain. George Joseph, the then editor of Gandhi's *Young India*, wrote a pungent critique of the practice of sending dancing girls to London as part of the exhibition (Joseph 2003).

"illiterate culture". None of the images Trivedi produces is an example of isolated representation. On the contrary, images retell what written texts and oral speeches have already emphasised. Moreover, such arguments, although purportedly coming from a "third world" perspective, are misplaced and displace the main theme of the discourse, that of khadi's role in highlighting colonial exploitation and its centrality in forging the struggle for emancipation. Further, it is wrong to say, as Trivedi does, that Gandhi "regarded visual experience as a neutral and transparent kind of communication that was open to everyone". The truth is that the exhibitions were a contested terrain for different streams within the nationalist movement. It was important to control and manoeuvre the exhibition site and exhibits displayed therein, and thus messages transmitted from the visual display were not shorn of politics, and Gandhi was immensely aware of this. There are quite a few conceptual faultlines that cloud her narrative. The most important one is her erroneous understanding of the real motive of the swadeshi movement. Under Gandhi's leadership, it was not nationality alone but the motive of the producer and the nature of production that was significant, too. Thus, given India's existing material reality, the swadeshi movement was directed more towards the literate/middle-class population rather than towards the rural "illiterate" poor.

One of the most significant instances of the swadeshi movement's contribution towards mapping a national geography, though overlooked by Trivedi, was Gandhi's call to dump foreign cloth outside the national boundary; he advocated its export. He asserted that each commodity has its specific relevance according to the national context. Burma might choose something other than khadi to suit its national manufacturing context. Khadi, for Gandhi, was an economic and political imperative. Gandhi employed, as Bayly rightly observes, a symbolically charged moral language.[14] But his use of this moral language

[14] Cf. Tarlo, 63.

held immense political significance. This language tried to mould the latent "moral" beliefs of Indian society, but its purpose was very much secular. Gandhi's own sartorial metamorphosis was dictated less by spiritual than material concerns. It brought parity between precept and practice.

Therefore, Cohn's "clothes literally are authority" equation,[15] Bean's logic of "communication", Tarlo's unscrambling of "identity", and Trivedi's display of "visual vocabulary" articulate concerns that are not the kernel of issues surrounding khadi. They are scholarly productions derived from a virile imagination and not from the material reality of the movement. Such interpretations displace the core strand of the discourse, which holds significance not just in the contemporary but persists even in the present South Asian context. Khadi is a "third world" commodity. It was an attempt to make a dent in the "drain". The colonial economy compelled the colony to send raw material to the metropolis and then receive the "value added" commodity from the metropolis. Khadi was the reverse of this, as it began its career as a commodity of import substitution. In this context, Dipesh Chakrabarty's "Reading of the Use of Khadi/White in Indian Public Life" is of great relevance.[16] He explores the semiotic beneath the persistence of khadi as a political dress for Indian male politicians, explaining it as "the site of the desire for an alternative modernity". It was a desire brought to fruition by the contingencies of British colonial rule, and yet it nurtured an idea that was alternative to and autonomous of imperialism. What Chakrabarty is perhaps hinting at is the persisting relevance of the idea of khadi despite seemingly irresistible and irreversible global dynamics.

This book seeks to explore the history of Gandhi's khadi, the political fabric that was used to transcend the prevailing socio-

[15] Cf. Trivedi, 13.

[16] Dipesh Chakrabarthy, 2001, "Clothing the Political Man: A Reading of the Use of Khadi/White in Indian Public Life".

economic system and establish a parallel system, based on new socio-political and economic mores. It is argued here that khadi's core semiotic lay in its being chiselled into a commodity of resistance against colonial exploitation. Khadi was transformed by a sustained campaign into a commodity of conscious choice for the consumers. Its transformation gave the cloth a character but, ironically, it also stifled its growth. The ideological investment into the character of khadi gave birth to a moral consumer who preferred character to cloth. Such an exercise gave khadi a unique identity, a brand-equity, but also imposed a self-limiting variable on its wider acceptance as a commodity of general consumption. Being identified with a certain value system distinguished it from the plethora of commodities that were available for consumption, but its linkage between the outer manifestation and the inner being of the wearer restricted its commercial success. It became a fabric for exceptional occasions rather than a commodity of all times.

Khadi's commercial prospects, therefore, in some subtle way became imprisoned in its transformatory ambition. Gandhi hoped that by his swadeshi campaign he could transform the sartorial tastes of Indians. Implicit in such a hope was also an ambition to alter the inner being of Indians.[17] It was this twin aim that spawned confusion among the consumers and its messengers alike. Here, we are not suggesting that the campaign should have shunned its latter aim and concentrated its energy on its commercial prospects. We are merely hinting at a self-debilitating variable and, given the moral context of the Gandhi-led freedom movement, escaping from this context meant a paradigm shift in the character of the national movement.

[17] When Gandhi wrote a rejoinder to Katherine Mayo's *Mother India*, he rebuffed her for what he called a "Drain Inspector's Report", and yet he exhorted Indians to learn from indictments as they contained important lessons ("Drain Inspector's Report", *YI*, *CWMG* 34: 539). In his own assessment, as he wrote in *Hind Swaraj*, Indians were guilty of temptation that brought their fall.

Khadi was a passion for Gandhi,[18] and it remained so till his very end. It played a significant role in the struggle for freedom. Khadi was a cloth against colonialism and an idea against imperialism—freedom's fabric. Gradually it became a commodity that denoted what the entire Gandhi-led freedom struggle stood for. It came to symbolise liberation, not just from the exploitative colonialism but also from the market-driven techno-capitalism. It came to be identified with principles of social responsibility and neighbourly compassion. It stood for forging living bonds between the rich and the poor. It brought issues of social segregation, economic inequality, and political isolation into the agenda of the national struggle. It aspired to shape the content of freedom and determine the values at stake in post-independence rivalries over resource-use. It invested moral responsibility in the representative character of democracy. It gave character to politics as well as to protest. It was a road map to swaraj.

This book proposes to reinstate core issues of khadi to its rightful legacy. As yet, there is no historical study on the subject. A study of the khadi movement with its diverse symbolism and historical realism is an imperative today. Was charkha just a symbol of India's struggle against British imperialism? A weapon brandished to affirm her will for independence? Or was it a

[18] Gandhi was fond of narrating this story to his audience. "When the first railway line was laid, there was an obstacle. There was a deep trench. If that could be filled up the railway line could be laid. The engineer said: 'Fill up the trench'. It could not be filled up in any way. The men who were trying to fill it up got tired and asked, 'What shall we do now?' 'Fill up the trench,' was the reply received again. They tried but could not fill it up. They asked: 'What now?' Once more they got the reply 'Fill up the trench'. So again basketfuls of rubbish were dumped into it. At last the trench was filled. Stevenson, the engineer, became immortal. I also want to be immortal. So I tell you only one thing: 'Spin and wear khadi'." ("Letter to Kalyanji Mehta", 20 August 1925, *CWMG* 28: 96).

means to eradicate poverty and ameliorate the economic condition of the marginalised? Did it nurture political ambitions? Or did it desire only the well-being of the poor? For Gandhi himself charkha and khadi possessed multiple meanings. Khadi manufacture, Gandhi said at the beginning of his campaign, provided an immediate occupation until an alternative could be found for the millions who were idle for half the year. It represented simplicity and economic freedom and peace and non-violence. It became the "symbol of salvation" for the poor in India.[19] It was the greatest and the most extensive national industry. The charkha provided a thread that knit the whole country into one. Spinning created a "moral bond" between urban-educated and economically well-off Indians and the rural famished masses.[20]

The charkha encompassed a symbolic connotation which went much beyond the realm of economics. As the movement progressed, Gandhi ascribed more virtues to the cause of khadi than he had done earlier.[21] He emphasised khadi's spiritual characteristics: "There are many aspects of khadi; amongst them the spiritual one I hold uppermost and the economic one next."[22] The charkha became a "sedative for a troubled mind".[23] In 1931, while in London, Gandhi spoke of spinning as a "great exercise in patience".[24] "When your wife gets angry, just spin", he said

19 "Comments on a Letter", before 16 June 1925, *CWMG* 27: 243–44.

20 "Speech at Santiniketan", 31 May 1925, *CWMG* 27: 180.

21 Speaking to Louis Fisher in June 1942 on the idea behind the institution of "silence day", Gandhi said that at first the idea was motivated simply to protect himself from the incessant work and engagements. "Later of course I clothed it with all kinds of virtues and gave it a spiritual cloak." ("Interview with Louis Fischer," 6 June 1942, *CWMG* 76: 433).

22 "Message at the Miraj Khadi Exhibition", 28 September 1940, *CWMG* 73: 59.

23 "Notes: Why He Spins?", *YI*, 29 July 1926, *CWMG* 31: 223.

24 "Interview to the *Evening Standard*", 12 September 1931, *CWMG* 48: 1.

in an interview there. To a man whose active political life was interspersed with periods of incarceration, spinning taught him "patience, industry, simplicity".[25] Spinning was a protection against passion and anger. It was a shield against toxic emotions. "I feel that the spinning wheel has all the virtues needed to make one's life truthful, pure and peaceful and fill it with the spirit of service."[26] The spinning wheel was an "emblem of human dignity and equality", the "handmaid of agriculture", the "nation's second lung". Though Gandhi spoke of khadi's "unifying influence", the act of spinning was, at the same time, a socially subversive force.[27] In India, where Brahmins spun their own sacred thread and where the majority of its population were compulsorily excluded from the ritual of wearing the sacred thread, Gandhi by asking everyone to spin sought to implicitly undermine the influence of caste.[28] By spinning, either one became a Sudra, as it was alleged at the time, or a Brahmin. In either situation, caste was subverted in a subtle yet substantive way.[29] The spinning wheel, in Gandhi's vision, became a symbol of self-respect, self-reliance, and economic self-sufficiency.[30] Charkha, through Gandhi's advocacy, acquired a social and political identity that was capable of generating multiple meanings.

[25] "Myself, My Spinning Wheel and Women", *Daily Herald*, 28 September 1931, *CWMG* 48: 79.

[26] "Speech to Students", Dinapur, 21 May 1925, *CWMG* 27: 141.

[27] "Discussion with Nagpur Congress Workers", 27 December 1939, *CWMG* 71: 64.

[28] "Notes: What a Brahmin says", *YI*, 7 August 1924, *CWMG* 24: 524.

[29] In contrast, however, S. Ramanathan, a vehement critic of Gandhi's, wrote in 1947 that the "Gandhian movement for the revival of the charkha is but a gigantic attempt to reconstruct the caste system and its medieval economy." Ramanathan was also a leader of the Justice Party in Tamil Nadu and formerly an activist/office-bearer of the All India Spinners' Association (Ramanathan 1947, vi).

[30] "Orissa and Andhra", *YI*, 13 April 1921, *CWMG* 19: 566.

Commodity of Conscious Choice

Gandhi was accused of reviving a commodity reduced to a relic by the inevitable march of technology. For Gandhi, though tradition was the arsenal of the khadi movement, revivalism was not his objective; besides, he did not revive khadi but refurbished it to suit his needs. The notion of revivalism has a deceptive connotation—it is understood to be a re-enactment in the present of elements from the past. Society's enchantment with revivalism springs out of its disenchantment with the present. The past—distanced and overpowered—in contrast to the chaotic and convulsing present, seems calm and comforting. Revivalism therefore attains an imagined realm where order around societal norms and individual mores are established and replaces the perceived rank disorder of the present. Whereas the past is soothing, the present is perilously threatening. The past is not revived as it is; the present draws from the past only the legitimacy it needs in order to stand for itself. Thus the past, as it is, is of no consequence. Tradition, whose lineage extends to the past, is not so concerned with common practices of the past; it is sculpted by the present and is ever-generative. New elements go into the making of tradition, but, at the same time, it needs to have a history to draw legitimacy. Tradition, therefore, is the legitimate past. Tradition is like an overgrown tree, whose roots are entrenched in the past with its branches shaped by the present. Both the root and the branch, however, rarely have commonality in externals. It is in this framework of looking at the past from the vantage point of the present that makes a study of the khadi movement an experience in the present.

Was the charkha in its second occurrence a farce, having ended earlier in tragedy? Was Gandhi a revivalist in the sense that, convulsed by the present, he sought solace in the past? Being the legitimate past, tradition is often hankered after. Gandhi argued that India was lost as Indians did not know the charkha's significance: "We were self-contained, but without realizing its necessity." The destruction of the charkha, according to Gandhi, was the beginning of poverty in India. Its eradication therefore needed the charkha's reinstatement to its original pre-eminence. Although a medieval instrument of production, the charkha in its modern incarnation acquired entirely different meanings. Though the article was the same, it came to signify now freedom and unity as in the time following the advent of the East India Company, when it had come to signify slavery and mutilation. In his speeches and writings, Gandhi used powerful mythical imagery to legitimate charkha. It became the "Sudarshan Chakra", the destroyer of evil in the hand of God, and the "Kamdhenu", the mythical cow who gave milk plentifully. But his restorative attempts made many question the utility of the charkha. In Indian politics people were confounded by the "novelty and simplicity" of Gandhi's ideas.[31]

Simplicity, in the days when human advancement is measured by material morality, could be unsettling. It disrobes one off all the complex cultural encrustations that facilitate one's social acceptability; it dares the practitioner as much as the spectator; it exposes the vulnerable flanks of both to outside aggression; both of them had to prepare in anticipation of an attack. Gandhi's way of life was culturally threatening to educated Indians; his progressive simplification of life attacked their notion of distinction that separated them from the masses. He would wear only Indian garments stitched in Indian fashion; eat only five things in a day; travel third class by train; use only handspun and handwoven clothes and see greater beauty in them than in the colorful mill manufactures; wear minimal clothing as India needed all the clothes for its unclothed multitudes. He was so confident in his convictions that he went into Buckingham Palace without any change in attire. It was culturally threatening for someone like an over-clothed Jinnah, or Jayakar—the educated,

[31] "Letter to Mahadev Desai", 11 September 1921, *CWMG* 21: 46.

suave, and professionally successful.[32] It was not that Gandhi did not share these attributes, but he could gleefully expose his vulnerabilities that others were secretive about. In simple khadi garments, one would be no different from the masses and would be shorn of all sense of superiority. But this mannerism of Gandhi's was not confined to matters of clothing alone; it extended to the realms of interpersonal relationships, to politics, to struggle strategies, etc. It was innate in him; public and private spaces merged in him. All his momentous political moves were thought out in full view of the participating public, and the authorities were informed well in advance of his moves through his own letters. But Jinnah and Jayakar were courageous enough to reveal their abhorrence to simplicity and thus earned Gandhi's attention. There were others who adopted simplicity but made such a mockery of their acceptance that it imperilled the ideal. Khadi became in Gandhi's lifetime a livery of hypocrisy, of opportunism, of sham patriotism. All ideals unfortunately have the same fate as time erodes their sheen. Simplicity, too, the cardinal Gandhian ideal, which also formed the philosophical crux of the khadi movement, met the same fate that conceded victory to a Jinnah or Jayakar—the ideological forerunners perhaps of globalisation of the consumer palate in the Indian context.

How relevant is the study of the khadi movement in today's perspective? For many, the khadi movement, despite being an obsessive ambition backed by magnificent propaganda, was a failure. For some, khadi has undergone a metamorphosis what

[32] Mohammad Ali Jinnah is a well-known figures of the Indian colonial past. M. R. Jayakar was a Bombay lawyer who sporadically emerged to mediate between the Gandhi-led national movement and the government. Jayakar wrote a two-volume autobiography which is noted more for his critical observation on Gandhi and his politics. He was opposed to the nationalist embargo on law practice that was imposed in the wake of the non-cooperation movement.

with the fashion fraternity being mobilised to upscale the "brand". Others discover a congruity between khadi's continued existence in the shadowy shops called *bhandars* and Sarojini Naidu's remark that it took abundance to keep Gandhi in poverty. For still others, khadi, the fabric that was positioned as the cloth against colonialism, was pushed ahead and re-branded as a mascot for environmentalism. Khadi, at least in the Indian context, retains its association with the psychology of protest and activism.

In its material format, khadi's future is a prisoner of its past. It is trapped within the parameters born of the historical brand-building exercise. Manufacturing khadi was about providing work over a local resource-base. It is another matter that it never lived to fulfil its own ideological destination. If village artisans, mainly women, spun cotton yarn, either within the confines of their homes or in common community areas, then cotton slivers for the same came from centrally located units. Its consumption was mainly dependent on the effect of propaganda in urban areas. Khadi workers hoped that one day khadi would become ubiquitous and self-spreading. It hasn't happened as yet and neither is there any prospect of its happening in the future. Khadi therefore is at the threshold of being restructured and repositioned as a brand. Its position is unenviable—if it takes to commercial enticement, then it dilutes its equity that initially had gone into its brand-building, and, if it abstains, it decimates itself. But from the recent trends it is evident that it has taken the former path, focusing on attractive packaging and fashion apparels to increase consumption.

Gandhi's khadi campaign was a part of the national regeneration agenda that had come to be called "constructive work" as distinguished from the "political work" of the Congress. While looking through some ninety volumes of the *Collected Works of Mahatma Gandhi*, each over five hundred pages, I tumbled upon a theme that vindicated a possible reinterpretation of the national movement for independence. The national movement as led by Gandhi was not as much a political strategy to wrest power from the British as it was a movement for national reconstruction. Its road map was succinctly laid down in *Hind Swaraj*. Throughout his career, Gandhi attempted to inculcate in Indians the same curiosity that had first found expression in *Hind Swaraj*. How was it that India, with a population of thirty crore people, was enslaved by a few hundred mercenaries? The reasons he found were also the factors that had sustained India's continued subjugation. The indigenous culture had legitimised untouchability and other corroding and baneful influences. A combination of social and economic neglect had brought about political subjugation. Only a simultaneous struggle against these social and economic accretions could win India her freedom. As a reading of the *Collected Works of Mahatma Gandhi* reveals, if there were any causes that constantly occupied Gandhi's thought and action, they were the campaigns for the eradication of untouchability and the reinstatement of swadeshi in India's social and economic mores.

This work sets a temporal limit between 1915 and 1945 for historical exploration: the year 1915 is when Gandhi arrives in India from South Africa and 1945 is when khadi is given the last policy reorientations in its development before its agency is subsumed by the larger Gandhian umbrella organisation. It was my last few years of simultaneous association with academic research and non-political grassroots activism that equipped me with the intellectual sensitivity and ideological conviction to revisit the history of the independence movement with tools that were marginalised in the contemporary political demagoguery and yet held its own importance.[33] Gandhi's khadi is an instrument whose historical capacity, contemporary symbolism, and future potential are the subject of this book. It

[33] For details, see, Rahul Ramagundam, *Defeated Innocence: Adivasi Assertion, Land Rights and the Ekta Parishad Movement*.

is through the newly invented instrument of khadi that I revisit the tumultuous and contentious times of modern Indian history. In doing thus, I explicate the institutional forms and the ideological norms that endorsed the khadi movement. Further, contrary to the post-independence discourse that has coalesced Gandhi and the Congress into interchangeable personalities, one underlying theme of this book is to show points of cleavages between the Congress and Gandhi.

The book seeks to explore and widen the academic debate surrounding the forces leading to the finale of independence on 15 August 1947. Its frame of reference lies in the arena of people's politics and not in either the constitutional progress as initiated by the British rulers or the institutional agitation as led by the Indian National Congress. People's politics hereby mean issues and concerns that fed the constructive work and made Gandhi institute an alternative regenerative ideology and programme independent of the political ideology and programme as enunciated by the Indian National Congress. Gandhi was successful in sharpening the ideological conflict between those silently toiling for the constructive work and those haranguing for the political course. Yet, and that is the marvel of Gandhi's politics, he did not sharpen this conflict to breaking point.

The book had its beginning in my curiosity about the building of a political movement with a constructive ideology. I was curious about the internal dynamics of a political organisation that contends for power with the ruling British, but also attempts to build an alternative ideology of living by looking inwards. A considerable amount of "subaltern" participation in the politics of the day was a by-product of activities surrounding the constructive work, primarily khadi. How effective was Gandhi's khadi campaign in bridging the gap between the political contention for power and the subalterns' mere spectatorship in such struggles? How inclusive was it of subalterns in the elite's contention for political dominance? In other words, was Gandhi's khadi an instrument to keep the "subalterns" confined to the constructive work while the elite contended for power or did it further their inclusion?

In studying the khadi movement, we unravel the paradoxical nature of commodity-consciousness and its symbolic potency at the material plane. Do ideas permeate and transmute the material world or does the material world shape the contours of ideas, or was it a dialectically interactive process between the two? How is the growth of consciousness interlinked with mass mobilisation towards achieving certain political aims? Can a communal manufacture of a commodity mediate a reconciliation of existing socio-economic cleavages? Can commodity-consciousness fight a culture of consumerism? The aim of the study is to bring into being an authentic exploration into the agency, agendas, and activism with regard to khadi.

A combination of archival exploration and anthropological study informs the present work. This study depends considerably on Gandhi's *Collected Works*, including his edited weeklies such as *Young India*, *Harijan*, and *Navajivan*. The study also draws from publications of the All India Spinners' Association (AISA), such as *Khadi Guide* and its *Annual Report* (since 1926), and from contemporary regional and national newspapers, reports from provincial khadi organisations, and government intelligence gatherings. There are writings by prominent khadi workers and also well-chronicled opposition that Gandhi faced on the ideology underlying khadi. Critiques by Gandhi's colleagues and sympathisers come under three categories: those from individuals, from insiders, and from institutions. Each category has left a rich source of written material that is yet to see historical light. Under the institutional category were his socialist opponents and opponents from the scientific community such as Visvesvaraya. *The Servants of India*, a journal brought out by Gokhale's society, was constantly censorious of Gandhi's khadi arguments. M. N. Roy pilloried the khadi movement by asserting that it was a sheer "waste of energy".[34] Among the insiders were those who once worked with Gandhi but later differed with his khadi agenda. These were the people who had once administered khadi institutions. Among them were people such as George Joseph,[35] S. Ramanathan, and others. Ramanathan was secretary of the Tamil Nadu branch of the All India Spinners' Association; he later wrote a pungent critique of the khadi movement and termed it a "superstition of recent origin".[36] Among the individual critics, the prominent people were Tagore, Chittaranjan Das, Aurobindo Ghose, and Jawaharlal Nehru. Nehru's ideological opposition to Gandhi is fairly well documented but those of the others are less known. The book draws insights from their critiques.

The scholastic analysis of Gandhi's economic thoughts had begun to appear in his own lifetime, and as he gained in domestic stature and international recognition, many appeared to interpret his "message" for wider journalistic and academic circles. Richard Gregg was an American with much experience in his own country, and he wrote many a volume on Gandhian economics. His *Economics of Khaddar* (1927) is an example of a work written with the purpose of making Gandhi comprehensible to a largely Western audience or those Indians who favoured a Western perspective. The book had an original perspective on the khadi movement. The *Economics of Khaddar* was given enviable publicity by Gandhi. He produced a lengthy review-cum-extract article in *Young India*. "The originality of Mr. Gregg's examination of the problem consists in his approach to it from the engineering aspect which is the title of the first chapter, and he has no difficulty in showing that the material prosperity of a country is increased not merely by accumulation of power or machinery

[34] "Waste of Energy?", *YI*, 21 August 1924, *CWMG* 25: 20–23
[35] Cf. George Gheverghese Joseph.
[36] S. Ramanathan, Pattabhi Sitharamyya, N.S. Varadhachari,1931, *The Superstition of Khadi, A Discussion*, 3.

but by the right use of it".[37] Earlier, Gregg had co-authored *Takli Teacher* with Maganlal.[38] Gregg would continue to write even after independence, this time more to make Nehruvian economists toe the Gandhian line. His *Which Way Lies Hope* (1957) and *A Philosophy of Indian Economic Development* (1958) were written with the fond missionary hope of influencing India's economic direction. Gregg's effort was to make the Western world comprehend the validity and practicality of the Gandhian programme.

Gandhi's *Collected Works* remains a vastly unexplored minefield of historical source material despite the severe but selective scholarly flogging it has borne since the inception of the project to collect and collate his written legacy into an archive of a hundred-strong volumes. He is quite generous with critics and lay correspondents in his writings. The editorial board of the *Collected Works* has omitted some names from Gandhi's letters. Was this done under state instruction? Who authorised the editorial department to undertake omissions with far-reaching consequences? Decisions may have been taken to leave out names that could lead to controversy or names of those involved in misdemeanours. The evidence from the *Collected Works* indicates that despite open defiance of *ashram* rules or occasional moral failures, Gandhi never shut off the culprit from his surroundings. He always desired amelioration. Given the moral background in

[37] "A Seasonable Production", *YI*, 12 April 1928, *CWMG* 36: 21.

[38] Maganlal K. Gandhi, and Richard B. Gregg, *The Takli Teacher* (1926). The *takli* was called "wheelless spinning" by Mahadev Desai whose article introduced the book. The book had chapters such as "The Takli Itself", "The Material for Yarn", "The Process or What is Done to the Material", "How the Process is Done?", "What to Do with Yarn after It is Spun", "Educational Value of the Takli", "Advantages of the Takli for Schools", "Use of the Takli to Adult", "Care of the Takli", "How to Make a Takli", "Historical Facts".

which people were interacting, how fair is the removal of names? When Gandhi himself openly discussed moral issues in public, how fair is it to remove names from his *Collected Works*? Was not Gandhi dead against the "sin of secrecy"?[39] From a historical perspective this moral battle has clear consequences for one of the most enduring lessons of Gandhi's life: can love and patience bring about the needed change of heart? By removing names of players, an attempt to conceal conclusions of the greatest importance was made.

[39] "My Shame and Sorrow", *The Bombay Chronicle*, 8 April 1929, *CWMG* 40: 209.

2 Morality of the Movement, 1915–22

MORAL RELEVANCE OF SIN, SINNER, AND SYSTEM

The year 1920 was a momentous one in the history of India. It was the year when Gandhi launched his signature politics with the call for the non-cooperation movement against the British. The call was motivated by the recent military atrocity in Punjab that had culminated in the Jallianwala Bagh massacre, the betrayal of the Islamic Khalifa by the Allies after the First World War—causing disaffection among the Muslims of India—and the promulgation of legislations such as the Rowlatt Bills to bring a rising India into submission.

The crux of the call, Gandhi said, was directed inwardly; it was aimed at self-purification and penance. The call was necessitated by India's complicity in her own subjugation. "The English", in Gandhi's ideological assumption, as he had put down in *Hind Swaraj*, "have not taken India; we have given it to them. They are not in India because of their strength, but because we keep them." In *Hind Swaraj*, Gandhi states the role played by the educated and wealthy in abetting the continuance of British rule in India. Of the educated he says: "It is we, the English-knowing men, that have enslaved India." And of the moneyed men: "I fear we will have to admit that moneyed men support British rule; their interest is bound up with its stability."[1] Even earlier, in 1908, Gandhi wrote, "British rule in India is an evil but we need not believe that any very great advantage would accrue to the Indians if the British were to leave India. The reason why they rule over us is to be found in ourselves; that reason is our disunity, our immorality and our ignorance."[2] Gandhi's thoughts might have been inspired by Leo Tolstoy or he might have come independently to the same conclusion. In a "Letter to a Hindoo", Tolstoy had written: "What does it mean that thirty thousand people, not athletes but rather weak and ill-looking, have enslaved 200 millions of vigorous, clever, strong, freedom-loving people? Do not the figures make it clear that not the English but the Indians have enslaved themselves?"[3]

Gandhi's non-cooperation call received support and energy from the contemporary politics at play. But its roots went back to the time when the British had begun their colonisation of India, stating "trade and not territory" as their goal. Though it seemed a long time ago, yet it was brought close to the present by the debris of its impact visible in the destruction of Indian industry, in the immiseration of the Indian people, and in the faminisation of the Indian economy. If there was anything that most succinctly defined British rule, it was its role in the destruction of hand-spinning. The same was a "black memory" which drove Gandhi's politics and made him harshly criticise British rule. He saw the pernicious impact as caused by a Satanic

1 Cf. Anthony J. Parel, 39, 104, 108.
2 "Savodaya-IX", *Indian Opinion*, 18 July 1908, *CWMG* 8: 371–75.
3 "Preface to Leo Tolstoy's 'Letter to a Hindoo'", 18 November 1909, *CWMG* 10: 5.

Empire that, in the Indian metaphor, was *Ravan Raj*, a phrase repeatedly evoked by Gandhi in his campaign of non-cooperation.

The depth of the injury caused by the East India Company and the magnitude of suffering that India then went through loomed large over Gandhi's consciousness and politics. By whatever means—fair or foul—the Company crippled the Indian weaving industry, forcefully imported foreign cloth, accumulated wealth, waged wars, acquired control of ports, monopolised trade, and finally established their rule over India. The country was enslaved to satisfy the greed of foreign cloth manufacturers. By a "deliberately planned destruction of the spinning and weaving industries of India",[4] the indigenous cloth industry "was made to die".[5] Indian craftsmen were "obliged to cut off their own thumbs in order to avoid imprisonment".[6]

While Indian manufacturers paid with their thumbs, starvation, and lives, indigenous consumers were tempted by imported cloth. "Why was India Lost?" Gandhi asked. "Who was tempted at the sight of their silver? Who bought their goods? History testifies that we did all this".[7] In an article, "The Secret of Swaraj", Gandhi wrote, "Foreign cloth constitutes the largest drain voluntarily permitted by us".[8] Indians, therefore,

[4] "Notes: Why Burn?", *YI*, 28 July 1921, *CWMG* 20: 432. "Discussion on Boycott at AICC Meeting, Bombay", on or after 28 July 1921, *CWMG* 20: 443.

[5] "Speech at Rotary Club", Calcutta, *The Englishman*, 19 August 1925, *CWMG* 28: 84.

[6] "Who Cut The Thumbs?" *YI*, *CWMG* 19: 487. In an interview to Katherine Mayo on 17 March 1926, Gandhi repeated the charge: "The East India Company came to buy, and remained to sell. It compelled us to cut off our thumbs. They stood over us and made us behave against our wills till thousands of us cut off our thumbs. Practically at the point of the bayonet they forced us to work. For suppose I am tired of work—tired as we were tired till we cut off our thumbs to avoid being driven further—is not that the pressure of the bayonet?" (*CWMG* 30: 119).

[7] "Why was India Lost?", *Hind Swaraj* (Parel, 40).

[8] "The Secret of Swaraj", *YI*, 19 January 1921, *CWMG* 19: 239.

needed to do penance on two counts; the first for the oppression the ancestral producers had to endure and the second for the sin of succumbing to the Satanic influences of foreign manufacturers. If the former meant destruction of foreign cloth, the latter required taking up spinning as a national duty and khadi as the state dress.[9] In such a scheme, incineration of foreign cloth was as much a sacrament as the spinning of khadi yarn. The twin acts of adoption of charkha and replacement of foreign apparel by khadi was the central thesis of the non-cooperation movement.

During the four years after 1915, Gandhi through his speeches, writings, and the observance of silence once a week, was attempting to impress one point on his Indian audience: "Foreign cloth constitutes our slavery. You should throw it off...Regard foreign cloth as no better than beef or liquor."[10] His political language was replete with references to foreign cloth as "sin", "filth...dirt...plague", "pollution", "a badge of our slavery", which had to be discarded, burnt, and against which an aversion had to be cultivated.[11]

A year later, in 1921, Gandhi gave an inspired twist to his campaign. At the height of the campaign, Gandhi called for the actual destruction of foreign cloth as a token of one's self-respect. Foreign cloth, Gandhi averred, was contaminated by the blood of our forefathers. Now, one's national existence could only be redeemed, Gandhi expounded, by burning all stock of such cloth. On 31 July 1921, he himself lit the bonfire made from a huge collection of foreign cloth in the premises of a sympathetic Bombay textile mill. "I regard this day as sacred for Bombay", Gandhi said on the occasion.[12] "We are purifying ourselves by discarding foreign cloth which is the badge of our slavery". As

[9] "Speech at Public Meeting", Bombay, 1 August 1921, *CWMG* 20: 458.
[10] "Speech at Public Meeting", Bombay, 2 July 1921, *CWMG* 20: 317.
[11] "Why a Bonfire?", *Navajivan*, 17 July 1921, *CWMG* 20: 381.
[12] "Speech on Swadeshi", Bombay, 31 July 1921, *CWMG* 20: 434.

the flames leapt up to the skyline of Bombay on that fateful day, a sea of humanity wearing coarse white khadi witnessed the electrifying spectacle. For Gandhi the exhilarating moment was a "soul-stirring sight", and he called it a *yajna*. "Untouchability of foreign cloth is as much a virtue with all of us as untouchability of the suppressed classes must be a sin with every devout Hindu." In using language imbued with such moral overtones, Gandhi was using the traditional metaphor to fight a dual battle against social obscurantism and economic exploitation that the onset of British rule had made inevitable.[13]

In his speech at the public bonfire, Gandhi, who was yet to assume the minimal khadi clothing that became his iconic trademark, hoped that the fire would not die out but that a similar fire would be lit "every week...in every town and every street of India".[14] This must be continued "till every article of foreign clothing" had been reduced to "ashes". The "sacrificial fire" was the pinnacle of and preceded by one of the most aggressive and determined campaigns in the history of modern India. But, this campaign increasingly brought upon itself accusations of fomenting hatred and violence against fellow human beings and their work. Gandhi was accused of fostering narrow nationalism against India's cherished *Vasudhaiv Katumbakam* (Guest-is-God). The volley of accusations came from friends and foes alike. While friends were pained, foes felt vindicated at Gandhi's violence, manifested in the act of his burning the pile of cloth.

"Cleansing of filth is not violence" was Gandhi's point-blank reply.[15] "It is a mockery to ask India not to hate when in the same breath India's most sacred feelings are contemptuously

[13] "Speech at Public Meeting", Bombay, 1 August 1921, *CWMG* 20: 458.

[14] "My Notes: Bombay Surpasses Itself", *Navajivan*, 7 August 1921, *CWMG* 20: 472.

[15] "Discussion on Boycott at AICC Meeting", *Navajivan*, 11 August 1921, *CWMG* 20: 446.

brushed aside", Gandhi wrote in response to some criticism.[16] He shrugged off all opposition, even from as close a friend as Andrews, who advocated giving the discarded foreign cloth to the poor. Gandhi was unconvinced. "The central point in burning", he responded to Andrews, "is to create an utter disgust with ourselves that we have thoughtlessly decked ourselves at the expense of the poor."[17] About the burning itself Gandhi said "it was a noble act nobly performed".[18] With this one act, Gandhi said, people were "silently and unconsciously transferring their hatred of sinners to sin itself". Burning was a life-saving "surgical operation". If there was any anger or ill-will, the fire gave it a disciplined outlet. Fire was a symbolic transformation of impotent rage into conscious self-pity. Giving to the poor discarded foreign cloth was like giving "discarded costly toilet brushes to them". "Why should the poor adorn themselves with what we have discarded?" Such an "inartistic and incongruous" charity was an insult to their sense of patriotism and the state of poverty. The sin lay neither in foreign fineries nor even the foreign conquest, but in the folly of Indians' taking the conquerors' bait in the past.[19]

The past therefore was an important reference point for Gandhi just as it is now for proponents of Hindutva. In the contemporary contention for hegemony, it is necessary for the present to hark back to the past to stand witness to it. Gandhi used facts from the past, aptly supported by historical research by Naoroji and Romesh Chandra Dutt, to support his argument that British machinations rather than their machinery decimated India's once-flourishing craft-based cloth industry and consequently

16 "Notes: On the Wrong Track", *YI*, 8 December 1920, *CWMG* 19: 81.

17 "Letter to C.F. Andrews", 13 August 1921, *CWMG* 20: 499.

18 "Burning in Bombay", *YI*, 11 August 1921, *CWMG* 20: 486.

19 "Speech on Swadeshi," Bombay, *The Bombay Chronicle*, 1 August 1921, *CWMG* 20: 455.

impoverished her.[20] In drawing from the past, Gandhi felt as legitimated as are the Hindutva exponents. Hindutva politics ostensibly revolve around alleged historical abuses of medieval Islamic rulers. Their temple-demolishing spree, the Hindutva cadres state, was an affront to Hindutva. In their view, the only way a past wrong can be redeemed is by avenging it in the present. Gandhi too was of the same opinion. But, while Gandhi used atonement to avenge the wrong in succumbing to temptation and turmoil,[21] the politics of the Hindutva desire revenge through ethnic cleansing or subordination. Gandhi not only fixed responsibility for the destruction but also attempted to reinstate the indigenous economy. The responsibility for destruction was attributed equally to the British perpetrators and Indians, who had caved in to pressure and temptation. Thus avenging the wrong perpetrated in the past lay not in hating the British rulers but in reclaiming an empowered self by stripping off all weaknesses. The ideology of Hindutva directs its destructive energy against "Babar's progenies", the Muslims. By thus anointing the Muslims of today, it holds not just the Mughal rulers but the whole Islamic population of India responsible for India's medieval "ignominy". In this indiscriminate demarcation of enemy, there is no inward-looking but an infantile blame-displacement.

Gandhi drew a distinction between bad actions and bad people. Gandhi's politics, as he reiterated, was "directed not against men but against measures". It was not directed against the governors, but against the system they administered. The roots of his politics lay not in hatred but in justice, if not completely in love. "And so I hope this great movement... has made it clear... that whilst we, may attack measures and systems, we

[20] "History does not tell us that khadi went out of use because foreign cloth was better and cheaper." "Triumph of Spring", *Navajivan*, 25 May 1924, *CWMG* 24: 128.

[21] "Notes: Difficulties in the Way", *YI*, 13 July 1921, *CWMG* 19: 356.

may not, must not, attack men".[22] If he did use harsh language, Gandhi said, they were condemnations free of any evil intention. Even on 31 July 1921, when passions ran high at the sight of that massive bonfire, there were English men and women on the platform witnessing the spectacle along with Gandhi.

The Mahatma strove to establish swaraj in India by appealing to moral forces, which to attain he relied on selflessness and sacrifice. "We should try to end British rule not by visiting them with punishment but by acquiring strength through self-purification", he said in a speech to a group of students.[23] It is this fine distinction that needs to be understood by free India even as it sets itself on the agenda of correcting the past. While Gandhi's destruction of foreign cloth was meant to strengthen India as a nation, the Hindutva's campaign for the destruction of the Babri mosque brought only civil chaos and bloody reprisal.

Sartorial Anxiety and Enigma of Identity

On 9 January 1915, a forty-six-year-old Gandhi disembarked at the Bombay docks. After twenty-one years of stay and struggle in South Africa, "the saint"[24] was returning to his homeland. He wore a "Kathiawari suit of clothes consisting of a shirt, a *dhoti*,

[22] "The Simla Visit", *YI*, 25 May 1921, *CWMG* 20:134.

[23] "Speech to Students of Gujarat Mahavidyalaya", 13 January 1921, *CWMG* 19: 225.

[24] The parting comment by General Smuts, "The saint has left our shore", was not the only comment that acknowledged in Gandhi traits of saintliness. In India, as Kripalani writes, he was seen more as a religious reformer than as a political leader (J.B. Kripalani 1970, 56). Nanda writes, "The fact is that the image of Gandhi in his home land was that of a high-souled reformer rather than of a political leader" (B.R. Nanda 1990, 29). Margaret Chatterjee quotes C.F. Andrews writing to Rabindranath Tagore of his impression at the first meeting with Gandhi in January 1915 as being "a saint of action rather than contemplation" (Margaret Chatterjee 1983, 1).

a cloak and a white scarf, all made of Indian mill-cloth".[25] He had long been preparing for this day. In 1914, a month before his departure from South Africa, Gandhi had instructed his twenty-five-year-old nephew and co-worker, Maganlal, about the dress code while arriving on Indian shores. "I want every child to land in India", Gandhi instructed, "with Indian-style clothes on." He even said what dresses were to be worn. "The very young should have a *lungi*, a shirt and a cap. The grown ups like you should wear a *safa* and a long coat. .... I see no need for the boys to have shoes... .The boys...should start wearing *dhotis* on the steamer.... It would be good if everyone learnt to eat with one hand only (the right one) and that too sitting cross-legged on the floor."[26]

Sartorially, Gandhi was a man transformed indeed. In about a quarter of a century of struggle in South Africa that established him as a front-ranking activist for people of Indian origin, he had shed his Western fads and reclaimed his Indian roots. His sartorial profile had begun to change in South Africa itself, "in keeping with that of the indentured labourers", his constituency. Formerly he had Westernised tastes. In 1888, as reflected in a well-known autobiographical snippet, Gandhi had sailed wearing fashionable Bombay suits but had still fallen short of London's fashion standards. Even in 1903, when he went to South Africa along with his wife and children, he was particularly conscious of what he and his family wore. At the time, much to her discomfiture, Kasturba wore a Parsi style long *sari* in imitation of India's most modernised community, although there were very few of them in South Africa. His sons wore shoes and stockings. They ate or were made to eat only with forks and spoons.

Thus, the change in his style of dressing seemed dramatic. Throughout his career in India, his manner of dressing would

[25] "An Autobiography", part V, chapter 3, *CWMG* 39: 299.
[26] "Letter to Maganlal Gandhi", 8 March 1914, *CWMG* 12: 379.

attract pungent sarcasm from his opponents. In Champaran, while on "a humanitarian mission" in 1917, Gandhi was pilloried by officials and the English press critical of his work for his dressing, and more so as he was yet to achieve the mahatmahood and political pre-eminence that would be his in the next two years. He was investigating the oppressive system engendered by the English planters against which the poor farmers protested for redress to no avail. The methodical manner of his investigation and the deft dealing with high Empire officials helped Gandhi to successfully outmanoeuver the planters' lobby and bring about their indictment. Thus, the planters and their sympathisers searched for issues to malign Gandhi. They choose to ridicule his style of dressing. Their charge was that Gandhi's dress, "temporarily and specially adopted", was designed to produce an effect upon the credulous farmers. Gandhi was quick with a rejoinder on an issue that clearly marked him apart from the contemporary anglicised politicians. Writing in *The Pioneer*, "the leading organ of Anglo-Indian opinion in the country", he called his dress a national dress which suited India's climate and which "for its simplicity, art and cheapness, is not to be beaten on the face of the earth and which answers hygienic requirements."[27] Copying the English style of putting one's "legs into the bifurcated garment", we signified "our degradation, humiliation and our weakness". And then, Gandhi invited the English to leave their "false pride and equally false notions of prestige" and adopt Indian dressing when in India. That, however, was not the last word on his sartorial transformation. The final change was to come in 1921 at the height of the khadi movement when he appeared for the first time in public covered only by his now patented loincloth.[28] The annual expenditure on his clothes, he noted in 1924, was not more than three rupees.

27 "Reply Regarding Dress to *The Pioneer*", 30 June 1917, *CWMG* 13: 450.

28 Gandhi explains that the change came out of conviction and was gradual in coming. It was at Madura, in September 1921, that he *(contd.)*

Gandhi had transformed his identity too. From being a successful lawyer he had turned to "agriculture and weaving".[29] As his involvement with the politics of rights grew, much of Gandhi's legal engagements in South Africa went to Ricth and Polak, his comrades-in-arms in the struggle for expatriate Indian identity and dignity. He had himself built the Phoenix Settlement as the citadel of his experiments, calling it a unique institution in the world "in its ideals or its way of life". "If there is any [other], the civilized world has not heard of it."[30] After Phoenix, he and Kallenbach developed the Tolstoy Farm. In 1911, at the Tolstoy Farm, Gandhi proposed to give more attention to weaving. He even sent a colleague to get acquainted with handloom weaving in a factory. It is another matter that the timing of Gandhi's avowal to become a "farmer and weaver" coincided with the irreparable estrangement from his eldest son, Harilal. In South Africa, Gandhi was increasingly getting disenchanted with the gloss of modern civilisation.

In 1909, Gandhi went on deputation to England. He wrote to his second son, Manilal, who had been pining for an opportunity to be educated in London, "The more I observe things here", the more I feel that there is no reason to believe that this place is particularly suited for any type of better education."[31] The mother metropolis with all its opulence had disheartened him. It was on this return voyage that Gandhi penned his ideological masthead, *Hind Swaraj*, in which many

(contd.)

brought such a "radical alteration" in his dress (*CWMG* 21: 181). Emma Tarlo says, "No Indian leader took the problem of what to wear more seriously than Mohandas Karamchand Gandhi and probably no other leader changed his clothes so dramatically." See, for a chronology of Gandhi's changing dress, 62–93.

29 "Letter to Dr Pranjivan Mehta", 8 May 1911, *CWMG* 11: 66.

30 "Letter to Maganlal Gandhi", 10 December 1914, *CWMG* 12: 560.

31 "Letter to Manilal Gandhi", 10 August 1909, *CWMG* 9: 352.

analysts see a severe condemnation of modern Western civilisation.[32] Again in 1914, during the small interregnum spent in war-torn England between his departure from South Africa and arrival in India, England seemed "like poison" to him. "My soul is in India", he wrote in a letter to his colleague and cousin, Chaganlal.[33] The words showed the transformation Gandhi had undergone since his own determined departure in 1888 for an education at the London Bar. Twenty-seven years later, in 1915, Gandhi disembarked in Bombay a visibly changed man—both outwardly and inwardly.

Yet, the arrival in India was "suffocating". Bombay, where he had landed, looked more like "the scum of London".[34] His reception meetings were well attended, though people who were not very sympathetic to his agenda and activities chaired those meetings. The very first meetings soon after his arrival were chaired by Pherozeshah Mehta, Tilak, Jinnah, and by the members of the Servants of India Society.[35] He was also unsure of the future that awaited him in India. "I have been so often prevented from reaching India", a pensive but exuberant Gandhi had written weeks before, aboard the S.S. Arabia, to a Phoenix colleague, "that it seems hardly real that I am sitting in a ship bound for India."[36] "And having reached [India] what shall I do with myself", Gandhi had wondered. Gandhi's arrival in 1915 was preceded by two noteworthy achievements which were to facilitate his future engagements. First, in South Africa, he had led a protracted struggle which was, as he had written to his ideological

[32] Rudolf Heredia calls *Hind Swaraj* "a foundational text for any understanding of the man and mission" (Heredia 1999, 1497–1502).

[33] "Letter to Chaganlal Gandhi", 19 September 1914, *CWMG* 12: 533.

[34] "Letter to Maganlal Gandhi", 11 January 1915, *CWMG* 13: 4.

[35] Pherozeshah Mehta (*CWMG* 13: 5), Tilak (*CWMG* 13: 7), Jinnah (*CWMG* 13: 9) and by members of the Servants of India Society (*CWMG* 13: 8).

[36] "Letter to A. H. West", 23 December 1914, *CWMG* 12: 465.

teacher Tolstoy, the "greatest of modern times" inasmuch in its goal as in the methods adopted to reach the goal.[37] Second, *Hind Swaraj*, published in 1909, stood embargoed by the Government of India as it was thought to be "seditious" and subversive to British rule. He had returned to India with the ambition, as he stated in a letter to Lord Ampthill, of taking his "humble share in the national regeneration".[38]

He arrived in Bombay proclaiming passionate loyalty to the Empire. His notion of loyalty however had a subtlety that would keep the Empire befuddled till clarity dawned four years later in 1919, when he rebelled to "mend or end the Empire". Gandhi's notion of loyalty, he wrote in the 1910 preface of the English translation of *Hind Swaraj*, was based not in the present quality of governance dispensed by the Empire;[39] it was based "in a future acceptance by Government of that standard of morality in practice which it at present vaguely and hypocritically believes in, in theory". He further added that he was not particularly enamoured by the stability of the Empire compared with the ancient civilisation of India, which, in his opinion, "represents the best that the world has ever seen".

Soon after his arrival in India, Gandhi began his ashram enterprise simultaneously with his tour of the country. For various favourable reasons, he chose to settle down in Ahmedabad.[40] The establishment of the Satyagraha Ashram in May 1915 was

[37] Gandhi asked Tolstoy's help to popularise his movement. He had enclosed a biography of his written by Doke ("Letter to Leo Tolstoy", 10 November 1909, *CWMG* 9: 528). To Gokhale he wrote calling it "the greatest struggle of modern time" ("Letter to G. K. Gokhale", 11 November 1909, *CWMG* 9: 531).

[38] "Gandhi's Letter to Lord Ampthill", 30 October 1909, in Parel, 133.

[39] "Preface to 'Indian Home Rule'", *CWMG* 9: 189.

[40] It was an ancient centre of handloom weaving and thus an appropriate location for his proposed scheme to revive hand-spinning and weaving (Tendulkar 1951, 163–75).

a continuation of his experiments at the Phoenix Settlement and the Tolstoy Farm in South Africa, with weaving and agriculture being its designed activities. While his co-workers, comprising some fifty inmates, struggled to settle down, Gandhi took to travelling. Bound by Gokhale's "compact of silence" for a year,[41] he took to travelling by train with a vengeance. He travelled third class, but shot off missives complaining about the plight of passengers. "The latrines were in a dangerously filthy state", and still he would not allow the hapless Kasturba the benefit of comparatively clean second-class bathrooms. After one such long train journey, *The Hindu* reported his condition thus: "Mr. Gandhi looked thin and emaciated, a loose shirt soiled by four days of continuous travel covered his body and a pair of trousers similar in appearance covered his legs."[42] He had expected to join the Servants of India Society in Poona at the behest of his "friend, philosopher and guide", Gokhale, whose death in February 1915, however, left Gandhi "without shelter". Immediately after Gokhale's death, the society regrouped and rejected Gandhi's overtures. His application for admission into the society was dictated either by his reverence for Gokhale or his own insecurity upon arriving in India, for Gandhi had nurtured an ambition contrary to the ideals of the society. Very early, in 1909, immediately after he had authored *Hind Swaraj*, Gandhi had vented his opinion of the society in a letter to Maganlal. "It is simply an indifferent imitation of the West", he had then written. "Phoenix is comparatively better than the pomp and show of Poona."[43]

During this period, Gandhi, with wisdom born from his travels, was in a belligerent mood: "I am at war with my leaders",

41 "Letter to Gokhale", 27 February 1914, *CWMG* 12: 360.

42 "Speech on Arrival at Madras", *The Hindu*, 17 April 1915, *CWMG* 13: 47.

43 "Letter to Maganlal Gandhi", 27 January 1910, *CWMG* 10: 137–40.

he noted in a speech.[44] He spoke as if to educate, without fear or favour. In a country dominated by giants in parliamentary debates, from Ranade to Mehta to Gokhale, his speeches, at various public gatherings, showed empathy and not eloquence. He preached politics to people far away from the podium—the forte of the Moderates. There was much to be desired from the Indian political class. Their speeches were alien—both in content and language—and lacked mass appeal. Lost in the labyrinth of verbiage, resolutions passed at conferences went into limbo even before the ink dried. Wealthy princes displayed concern for the poverty around, in stark contrast to their lifestyles. Gandhi spoke famously about these prevailing inconsistencies at the Banaras Hindu University in February 1916, and, while students applauded, princes led by Annie Besant walked out.

Politically, in 1915, India was beginning to show signs of renewed vigour. An attempt was being made to put aside the stupefying spell of Surat, which had splintered the nationalist platform and dampened the national upsurge since 1907. Tilak had been released, and with the Surat sentiment on the wane, he naturally became the focus of the revitalised Indian polity. His re-entry into Congress was facilitated not just by the demise of his most vociferous critic, Pherozeshah Mehta, but also by the aggressive campaigning done on his behalf by Annie Besant. She, in recognition of her contribution, was chosen to preside over the annual Congress session of 1916 at Lucknow. Later, she and Tilak founded their respective Home Rule Leagues to expedite India's march to self-rule (Besant's followers in the league such as Omar Sobhani and Shankarlal Banker later became close adherents of Gandhi, and organisers of the khadi movement).

While in Lucknow the politically established leaders were involved in hammering out a Hindu-Muslim Pact, Gandhi was in the background, garnering support for Indians settled in

[44] "Speech at Reception at Mayavaram", 1 May 1915, *CWMG* 13: 69.

South Africa. He cajoled the leaders on the dais to allow him to put before the august Congress a resolution on the system of indentured labour. He demanded an end to the system, as it was an "evil which cannot be mended but only be ended". Most of the leaders present hardly took notice of his plea. One man, an illiterate villager named Brijkishore Shukla, however, saw in him a spark which made him pester Gandhi to accompany him to Champaran. "Drawn more or less accidentally" to the arena of indigo, Gandhi viewed the issue not in terms of a political campaign and easily found success here.

Soon, however, he found himself embroiled in a labour strike at Ahmedabad. He exhorted the mill-owners to bind their workforce with the "silken thread of love". The first serious conflict with British authorities, however, was yet to take place and that happened at Kheda. "Authority", Gandhi said while fighting for farmers' rights "is blind and unjust". The gains at Kheda were insubstantial. These skirmishes only fuelled his appetite for a "genuine search of knowledge".[45]

His itinerary invariably included a visit to the indigenous cloth-making centres. He appeared to be an educationist, researching and pointing out problems and also presenting solutions through appropriate actions and thought. Gandhi's speeches were laden with swadeshi messages. The constant refrain in his speeches was that swaraj and swadeshi had to go together.[46] At Karachi, he spoke of his strong belief that in the absence of "swadeshism, there can be no self-government".[47] In his speeches, he enquired about the local handloom weaving practices and the condition of weavers in the area. At Mayavaram, near Madras, he was told that the handloom weavers were chiefly engaged in

45 "Letter to Maganlal Gandhi", 16 April 1917, *CWMG* 13: 366

46 "Speech at Reception in Hyderabad", *The Hindu*, 29 February 1916, *CWMG* 13: 251.

47 "Speech In Reply to Address", Karachi, February 1916, *CWMG* 13: 254.

making saris for women. "Is Swadeshi to be confined only to women?" he chided the crowd.[48] At Nellore, in a speech to students, he bemoaned the fact that the educated lacked any appreciation for swadeshi enterprises. He found that cloth woven on fly shuttles and put on sale at meeting places had remained largely unsold. In such a divergent environment, there was no chance for indigenous enterprises to flourish.[49] In March 1916, at Gurukul, Hardwar, he exhorted his student audience to take on hand-weaving because more than 85 per cent of India comprised the peasantry.[50] Making India produce its own cloth formed an inevitable component of his primary aim, though in real terms what it meant and how it could be achieved became clear in the course of the next three years. In 1909, when Gandhi for the first time wrote that "handloom" was a panacea for India's poverty, he had no idea yet how to bring this about. But his knowledge was to grow rapidly after his arrival in India.

Much of what Gandhi had seen during his nationwide tour had shaped his opinions and they found their place in the constitution of the ashram, first drafted in May 1915. It was through the ashram that the ideal of swadeshi was laid out. Gandhi began by earnestly including in the constitution the "sacred law of Swadeshi" and "hand-weaving" to realise "the dignity of labour".[51] The constitution laid down "the virtual disappearance of spinning wheels and handlooms" as one of the chief causes of poverty.[52] Gandhi's ashram intended to begin the

48 "Speech at Reception at Mayavaram", *The Hindu*, 1 May 1915, *CWMG* 13: 71.

49 "Speech at Students Meeting", Nellore, *New India*, 6 May 1915, *CWMG* 13: 75.

50 "Speech at Gurukul Anniversary", 20 March 1916, *CWMG* 13: 264.

51 "Speech On 'Ashram Vows' at YMCA Madras", 16 February 1916, *CWMG* 13: 234.

52 "Draft Constitution for the Ashram", before 20 May 1915, *CWMG* 13: 95.

process of repair and recovery. In the constitution, Gandhi included some vows which were a prerequisite for being a resident at the ashram.[53] For a man whose life was dictated by "disciplinary resolutions"[54] such a course was a natural corollary.[55]

53 Vows, a product of his deep and abiding religiosity, unbounded by scriptural dogma, had been an important aspect of his growing up. "A vow is nothing but a fixed resolution to do or abstain from doing a particular thing", Gandhi explained from his sickbed in Bombay to Esther Faering on 25 January 1919 ("Letter to Esther Faering", 25 January 1919, *CWMG* 15:76). Esther Faering wrote, seeking a deeper meaning, "Do we take a vow in order to help and strengthen our character? Does God require us to take any kind of vows? Can a vow not become fatal?...(I)f God is a father, and if God is perfect love, does it not then cause suffering to Him when His children take burden upon them, which they are not asked to carry?" (footnote 4 in "Letter To Esther Faering"). Gandhi replied, bringing out the dichotomy between the body and soul. "Body is matter, soul is spirit, and there is eternal conflict between the matter and spirit. Triumph of matter over the spirit means destruction of the latter" (Ibid., 77). The body is merely an instrument for uplifting the soul. Since the soul is imperishable and lives in a body which is perishable and transitory, for the body to yield to the soul it needs to be controlled through the mechanism of vows.

54 *An Autobiography*, part 5, chapter 8, *CWMG* 39: 310.

55 Gandhi's penchant for vows came under close scrutiny in 1918 when he fell prey to an incapacitating illness bringing him close to death's door. Kedha's lukewarm response to his call for recruitment to assist the British war effort contributed to Gandhi's nervous breakdown and the first major debilitating illness. For six months he remained confined to bed; his body wracked and his morale low. Friends advised him to include milk in his diet. Gandhi refused because in 1912 he had vowed not to take milk (*CWMG*), as he had heard stories of maltreatment of cows and cruel practices to extract as much milk from the animal. In a letter to a friend, Gandhi wrote, "From a religious point of view what I said about milk still stands. But from the point of view of health and under Indian conditions, giving up of milk seems an impossibility. It is many years since I gave up milk and I am under a vow never to take it in this life. But I can not advise others to give up milk so long as I have not a substitute having the qualities of milk" ("Letter to a Friend", 9 August

(contd.)

Among the cluster of vows (truth, non-violence, celibacy, palate-control, non-stealing, non-possession) was included a subsidiary vow of swadeshi. The vow of swadeshi was made under the belief that foreign manufactures were a violation of truth. The inmates were required to shun artificial beautifying of the body and adopt simplicity. They were also to abjure foreign fineries. These resolutions were meant to strengthen the vow of brahmacharya. The vow of swadeshi thus had subtle moral bearing.[56]

Founding the Fabric

Gandhi admitted that the ashram was in a position to observe swadeshi with respect to only cloth. The ashram's foray into cloth making began with weaving. One of its objectives was to

(contd.)

1919, *CWMG* 15:12). Further, since 1906, he was practising *brahmacharya* and had found by experience that milk acted as a stimulant. Gandhi therefore, was most obstinate to any suggestion to break his vow. He, however, did bring his scientific temperament to use and requested Dr P. C. Ray, the swadeshi chemist from Calcutta, to suggest a vegetable substitute for milk ("Letter to P.C. Ray", 27 August 1918, *CWMG* 15: 32 also *CWMG* 15: 43). During the illness, it became a source of deep consternation and agony for his friends and family members. In the end, however, the desire to live and work, and also implored by Kasturba, he began to take goat's milk. Gandhi justified this by asserting that while undertaking the vow against milk he meant only cow's milk. This did not satisfy many who requested him to give up the vow and not violate it gradually ("Letter to Narhari Parikh" 21 January 1919, *CWMG* 15: 73; also "Letter to Narhari Parikh", 27 January 1919, *CWMG* 15: 78). Gandhi did concede painfully that though the letter of the vow remains, by taking goat's milk he diluted the spirit (*Autobiography*).

56 "Letter to Ranchhodlal Patwari", 10 June 1915, *CWMG* 13: 104. In his New Year message of 1909, Gandhi wrote: "Swadeshi does not mean merely the use of what is produced in one's own country. Swadeshi means reliance on our own strength." ("New Year", *Indian Opinion*, 2 January 1909, *CWMG* 9: 118).

make residents learn hand-weaving which would then help them to study the secrets and defects of the art and explore the means to save it. Gandhi envisaged a three-dimensional plan. The first was to initiate research on traditional looms to introduce corrective reforms, if any. Gandhi in fact discouraged any alteration of traditional machines. He had written to a friend that he should first experiment on the traditional machines before introducing any innovation. "I would advise alteration in Indian looms, only after they have been patiently handled and such alteration is found necessary."[57] The second was to make weaving as respectable a profession as any other middle-class vocation. Last, it was to facilitate the reclamation of the abandoned profession of weaving. In the next ten years to come, Gandhi hoped, the ashram would become a hub of industrial resurgence. In the ashram school curriculum, instruction in "handloom weaving" was included. The ashram would use the minimum machinery and depend mostly on human labour.

The ashram was to weave its own cloth to provide necessary inspiration for a resurgence of the craft in the country. The inmates resolved to discard their mill-woven cloth in favour of handwoven cloth. They were keen to assemble the elements of cloth making by hand. But Gandhi was constrained by the limited experience and expertise of the inmates. In June 1915, he wrote to his friends to send "the loom and the man who will teach how to operate it".[58] Lacking the expertise proved a challenge but in meeting it, they were exposed to the trials and tribulations of the weaver community. The weavers were perpetually indebted and were at the mercy of traders owing to their dependency on the supply of yarn. Most of the handloom weaving of fine cloth at the time was done using foreign yarn. Indian mills spun yarn of a lower count (coarser) but mostly to feed their weaving plants or for export. Handlooms using Indian

[57] "Letter to Ratilal M. Sheth", 27 February 1915, *CWMG* 13: 30.
[58] "Letter to Ranchhodlal Patwari", 10 June 1915, *CWMG* 13: 101.

mill yarn were non-existent. Fine cloth, handwoven from Indian yarn, therefore, was difficult to procure either from dealers or from weavers themselves. After much persuasion, some weavers agreed to weave Indian mill yarn on the condition that the entire cloth produced would be bought by the ashram.

By early 1917, the ashram boasted that almost every inmate knew the rudiments of weaving. It had seven looms operating within the precincts with five running outside the ashram but under its supervision. It had made a capital investment of Rs 3,000 and had sold cloth worth Rs 500. Seventeen persons were making a living out of the weaving work. The ashram made yarn available to these weavers, arranged to collect the woven cloth, and paid the market rate in cash.

In July 1917, Gandhi bought a fifty-five-acre plot on the banks of the Sabarmati on the outskirts of Ahmedabad for his ashram. The inmates now moved to this new site from their earlier place at Kochrab. Weaving and agriculture were the main occupations of the inmates. Gandhi, however, was primarily worried about the weaving programme. He had even hoped that all deficiencies of the ashram, such as the inevitable ego clashes or bickering among its inmates, would be remedied once the ashram's "atmosphere is loud with weaving".[59] Maganlal, the manager, was told to employ paid labour in the ashram for any work but weaving and was advised to "develop still further weaving, carding and spinning and make these processes more scientific".[60] The inmates were freed from their work in the community kitchen and other miscellaneous chores so that they could concentrate on learning to run the loom. Maganlal himself was sent to the Madras Presidency to learn weaving.

Champaran in Bihar, which in 1917 had become a temporary "domicile" for Gandhi, showed him with greater intensity the

[59] "Letter to Maganlal Gandhi", last week of January 1919, *CWMG* 15: 82.
[60] "Letter to Maganlal Gandhi", after 18 August 1921, *CWMG* 24:113.

damage done to India by the collapse of the cloth industry. "Here people shiver in the cold for want of clothes", he wrote to his ashram workers. "Every moment", he wrote, "I realize the value of cloth."[61] Gandhi narrated an incident that had a profound effect on him. On seeing a woman clothed in rags, he asked his wife to investigate the cause. The woman took Kasturba aside and said, "The sari I am wearing is the only one I have. How am I to wash it?"[62] Gandhi communicated this to Maganlal in order to create a sense of urgency in the ashram-weaving enterprise. He reasoned: "If the handloom, which they formerly worked in the pit, had been flourishing today and if we had been spinning all the yarn we require, we would not, with all this cotton available, have to face this terrible rise in the prices of cloth."[63] His letters were a constant source of guidance for the young but battle-hardened Maganlal.

In February 1918, a visitor noted, that the ashram was not self-propelling and appeared lifeless without Gandhi.[64] Gandhi's absence would grow longer as he got intensely involved at first in localised satyagrahas and later as he got sucked into national activities. This would disturb Maganlal, who wrote a scathing letter in 1918 telling Gandhi that his involvement in activities all over India was ruining his true calling. But Gandhi's mind was always focused on the ashram's weaving activities irrespective of his physical presence. The enterprise was gradually expanding and required greater financial support to carry on. In July, from Motihari, the district town of Champaran, Gandhi wrote a letter marked "For Private Circulation Only". It outlined the ashram's

[61] "Letter to Maganlal Gandhi", 20 January 1918, *CWMG* 14: 161.

[62] Gandhi had written to a friend describing the condition of the masses: "I have come in the closest touch with them in Kaira and Champaran. They have nothing" ("Letter to Prof. Jevons", 11 August 1918, *CWMG* 15: 15).

[63] "Letter to Maganlal Gandhi", 20 January 1918, *CWMG* 14:161.

[64] "Letter to Prabhudas Gandhi", 2 February 1918, *CWMG* 14:180.

expanding activities including hand-weaving which now required-greater resources. He hoped that the hand-weaving enterprise at the ashram would soon become self-supporting. In a clinching statement Gandhi noted that many who had hitherto been using "shoddy mill-made stuff, whether foreign or home-made" had begun using "durable Ashram-made cloth". As the letter was primarily meant for his rich textile-mill-owner friends, he, however, did not wish to ride roughshod over their benevolence. "It is admitted on all hands that, even if the textile mills stay, there is sufficient scope in the country for hand-weaving", he wrote calming perhaps their rising apprehensions.[65]

But, hand-spinning as yet was not on the agenda of the ashram. Gandhi's own clothes were "hand-woven and hand-sewn". In fact, as his autobiography testifies, he had neither seen a wheel nor had a notion of it.[66] His facts about the weaving culture in the country too lacked clarity. Commenting on the system of education, Gandhi desired that the students should be taught farming and weaving, because "nearly 95 per cent of the country's population is engaged in agriculture, while *90 per cent* of these used to be engaged in *weaving*". Never before in the country's history was such a vast population engaged in the occupation of weaving, either for themselves or for the market, a fact Gandhi would soon recognise and cause him to change his emphasis from weaving to spinning. Weaving as a vocation was defined by caste and was largely specialised. Spinning was a casteless vocation. Later, Gandhi came to regard spinning as a hereditary occupation common to all castes and to both sexes.

[65] "Circular Letter for Funds for Ashram", 1 July 1917, *CWMG* 13: 455.

[66] In 1909, for the first time, in *Hind Swaraj*, Gandhi wrote of "ancient and sacred hand-looms". He writes in *Autobiography*, "I do not remember to have seen handloom or a spinning wheel when in 1909 I described it in *Hind Swaraj* as a panacea for the growing pauperism of India" (*CWMG* 39: 389).

This broadening understanding created the need for producing self-spun yarn. Gangabehn Majmudar was "that remarkable lady" who scouted the Gujarat countryside and found the spinning wheel at Vijapur in the Baroda state. The discovery inaugurated a process that made the ashram as well as Gandhi acquainted with the whole range of hand-spinning. At Vijapur, women agreed to spin upon being assured of a regular supply of cotton slivers and a steady purchase of the spun yarn. Majmudar began a production centre there but there were many barriers. Procuring slivers was the first hurdle. Gandhi sought help from his friends in the textile sector. Omar Sobhani, a Bombay mill-owner, provided the slivers. Since they were mill slivers doubts were naturally raised: "if one could use mill slivers, why not use mill yarn as well?" This probe for solutions made Gandhi and his team get to the bottom of the spinning activity. They came to know that it was from the carding of raw cotton that slivers were made. The knowledge led to the discovery of carders, who taught the entrepreneurs to draw slivers out of carded cotton. Thus a simultaneous process went on at both the ashram and at Vijapur. Soon the ashram was devoting its best time to carding, spinning, and weaving.[67] In due course, collective spinning became one of the most visible features of community life in the ashram. And, in this way Gandhi's khadi was born.

While Gandhi and his ashram inmates were wrestling with the wheel, the Government of India, in early 1919, thought it prudent to foist what came to be called the Rowlatt Bill. It was a most recklessly conceived legislation and showed "the aggravated symptoms of the deep-seated disease", as expressed by Gandhi to V. S. Srinivasa Sastri in February 1919. It also presented an

[67] Gandhi required more money to expand his work. In this regard Gandhi said to his old benefactor: "Work on cloth is expanding rapidly. After the Ahmedabad strike, I have come into contact with a number of weavers. About three hundred women have started working the *rentia*" ("Letter to Dr. Pranjivan Mehta", 2 July 1918, *CWMG* 14: 467).

opportunity, for when the Bills became public, Gandhi, who was in Bombay, recuperating from a serious illness that he had suffered from for the last six months, called for satyagraha. The main element of the satyagraha against the Rowlatt Bill was adoption of the swadeshi pledge.[68] The swadeshi pledge confined itself to only the issue of clothing. With pragmatic foresight it did not include the vast array of goods that India imported from abroad. Even in its limited scope, the observance of the swadeshi pledge was not without difficulties. The pledge required adherents to shun cloth manufactured from anything foreign, be it machinery, raw cotton, or yarn. Given the contemporary indigenous manufacturing base, Gandhi's swadeshi pledge was nothing more than a show of courageous defiance. That a scarcity of swadeshi clothes could have constrained the success of his campaign did not occur to Gandhi. He asked people to take to wearing minimal clothing as the "general climate of India is such that we require very little clothing".[69] India needed just two elements of "self-denial and honesty". He wanted people to fortify their swadeshi pledge with religious conviction. "When the religious sense is awakened, people's thoughts undergo a revolution in a single moment", he said. But in the absence of a favourable manufacturing environment, the pledge was more on paper than a practical proposition.

The swadeshi pledge comprised three options to cater to varying degrees of people's preparedness and convenience. One could wear cloth woven on handlooms out of yarn spun in Indian mills or cloth woven and spun in Indian mills, or cloth woven in Indian mills/handlooms from imported foreign yarn. A correct observance of the pledge required people to don only handwoven cloth made out of handspun yarn, but that was clearly impossible. In the circumstances, swadeshi primarily came to be identified with cloth that was woven on handlooms out

[68] "The Swadeshi Pledge-I & II", 8 April 1919, *CWMG* 15: 195–201.
[69] "The Swadeshi Vow-I", 8 April 1919, *CWMG* 15: 196.

of yarn spun in Indian mills. The ashram's role was crucial for even the minimal success that the swadeshi campaign was to achieve. With its limited manpower and expertise, the ashram had not yet begun its spinning enterprise, though it was on the threshold of such a breakthrough. Gandhi called for a "Herculean effort" and asked all the ashram inmates to begin spinning and weaving earnestly. He curtailed other activities in the ashram to focus on spinning and weaving alone.

The campaign around the Rowlatt satyagraha gave a spurt to the production and sales of khadi. In a letter to a South African friend, Gandhi reports the progress of his nebulous swadeshi campaign. "I have begun an active Swadeshi campaign", Gandhi wrote, "and within the short period of six weeks, it has spread very rapidly".[70] Gandhi's spirited advocacy of swadeshi inspired many enterprising people to open "stores" selling swadeshi cloth. In Vittalbhai Jerajani, he had the first enthusiastic supporter, who dedicated himself to organising sales of khadi in Bombay by opening swadeshi stores. After the launch of the satyagraha in April 1919, setting up of swadeshi stores at different places gained momentum.[71] Swadeshi stores were seen as a tool of

[70] "Letter to a Lady Friend in South Africa", 18 June 1919, *CWMG* 15: 384.

[71] In November 1918, Gujarat Swadeshi Store was opened at Ahmedabad. "Being bed-ridden", Gandhi wrote in his message for its inauguration, "I am unable to be present, but my spirit is there, of course." ("Letter to Jamanadas Gandhi", 21 December 1917, *CWMG* 14:114). At Nadiad, a company called "Swadeshi Bhandar, Limited" was established. It was declared to be an enterprise to propagate khadi with service and not profit as its motive. ("Letter to Jamanadas Gandhi", 21 December 1917, *CWMG 14: 114*). In June 1920, while declaring the bhandar open, Gandhi expressed the hope that the shop would not buy its inventories from Bombay but from villages around Nadiad. This would represent the application of the principle of neighbourliness that is a catalyst for local production and consumption ("Speech on Swadeshi", Bombay, 4 *(contd.)*

propaganda. Invitations poured in asking Gandhi to open stores and that encouraged people to take to swadeshi cloth.

Soon, however, the satyagraha was suspended in the wake of violence that broke out in several parts of the country. The satyagraha was short-lived, as was the spurt in khadi sales. The energy infused into it, too, dissipated and demand for khadi generally declined. Even Jerajani's Swadeshi Store in Bombay reported a slackening demand.[72] The stock of khadi produced at the Sabarmati ashram piled up. The prospect of the end of this nascent enterprise loomed large. Besides in-house production, the ashram had also tied up with many spinning and weaving centres that were spawned in the wake of the swadeshi campaign. They sustained however meagerly many destitute families. Such centres now faced the specter of closure.

In some way, the scenario that emerged was a measure of the campaign's success in inducing people to spin and weave. The glut meant that consumption was not keeping pace with rising production. It was a question of managing the market, promoting sales, and projecting khadi as a commodity of conscious choice. The greatest handicap of the public image of khadi was its perceived unfinished quality, lack of variety, colour, and decorative value. It crumpled on wearing, shrank on washing, was heavy, demanded maintenance, and "looked like a sieve". This pale looking colourless fabric held little attraction for the young and

---

(contd.)

June 1920, *YI, CWMG* 17: 479). The mathematics of business was methodologically worked out although it was mixed with a suitable dose of moral-play and request for fair play from the merchants. Most of the stores used ashram-produced clothes for sales. Swadeshi stores were asked to cut five per cent of their profit. The ashram however forsook its profit margin in order to keep the prices low and to this end its labour was given free.

72 Gandhi wrote a letter to Chaganlal Gandhi, "I have heard that, in the old Swadeshi Store, no one looks at our Khadi" ("Letter to Chaganlal Gandhi', 7 June 1919, *CWMG* 15: 350).

the old of the ashram. It was too heavy, coarse, and thick to be worn as a sari. Gandhi was unable to convince the women of the ashram to adopt khadi in full. Even Kasturba found it difficult to perform domestic chores in a heavy khadi sari. He wrote to Maganlal in March 1920 that he saw "no compelling reason why the women should have no garment of khadi on their bodies".[73] If that was the state of its acceptance in the ashram, how would Gandhi invite national patronage? Gandhi implored women inmates of the ashram to wear at least "loose blouses made of Khadi". Another handicap the ashram suffered in the beginning was its inability to produce a sari with colour. A white sari without a coloured border was a sign of widowhood, and no married Hindu woman conscious of her social status would agree to wear such a sari. He tried to redefine the colourless khadi with his own interpretations. The whiteness represented purity, the coarseness that of simplicity. He asked his wife to set an example and requested her not to object to wearing a white sari without a border. "True learning and greatness lie in this", he said idolising her sacrifice.[74] He also disapproved of the idea of her wearing something lighter while cooking. If asked to choose between food and khadi, Gandhi said, he would choose the latter.[75]

Simultaneously, Gandhi took to an aggressive brand-building exercise for khadi. Overcoming prejudices against khadi was as important as streamlining its production. He wrote an article in his newspaper outlining the defects of khadi and yet brandishing its utility.[76] The generally held prejudices against khadi were seen as qualities. "In my eyes Khadi is artistic enough. Khadi has the property of absorbing moisture. Khadi's roughness was particularly suited for being used as a towel, as cleansing the

[73] "Letter to Maganlal Gandhi", 17 March 1920, *CWMG* 17: 94.
[74] "Letter to Kasturba Gandhi", 23 April 1918, *CWMG* 14: 367.
[75] "Speech at Borivili Meeting", 30 June 1912, *CWMG* 20: 306.
[76] "Uses of Khadi", 25 April 1920, *CWMG* 17: 338.

body with it after a bath stimulates the skin. Khadi is a more useful and superior cloth. It is more beautiful than calico because it has a soul in it. There is some craftsmanship at any rate in the making of Khadi. Just as no two leaves of a tree are exactly alike, no two lengths of hand-spun, hand-woven Khadi can be so." He readily admitted that "all Khadi is not of equally good quality". He exhorted religious fervour and patriotic vigour from the patronising consumers. Thus, wearing khadi as a national duty occasioned sacrifice of art and aesthetics, tastes and fashion, choices and colours. Gandhi's general admonition was coupled with practical tips to potential converts. Khadi, if perceived as unsuited for garments, could still be used for coverings and curtains, loose shirts and undergarments, carpets and canopies. This clever but sensitively written article brought immediate response as bulk orders poured in from across the country clearing the stock of khadi in a very short span. Gandhi's article evoked orders for khadi from as far as "Baluchistan, the Nilgiris, and even Aden".[77]

For a long time Gandhi was the sole brand ambassador for khadi. He was its ideologue and brand manager, its public relations officer, its "model" to show it off, and its venture capitalist; he was everything that a fledgling business concern required. With time, however, he began to attract a number of like-minded people to his cause. "I try especially to seek out sisters", Gandhi wrote while boasting of his conquests. "...In Ahmedabad I have found such a sister. At Bombay, Madras, and elsewhere, too, I have found someone or other. In Punjab, I found Sarladevi."[78] Anasuyabehn, Gandhi's colleague during the strike of mill-hands in Ahmedabad and sister of mill owner, Ambalal Sarabhai, was the first to dedicate herself to the cause

[77] "For Users of Khadi", *Navajivan*, 16 May 1920, *CWMG* 17: 419 and "Swadeshi day by day", *YI*, 19 May 1920, *CWMG* 17: 428.

[78] "Speech at Ahmedabad", 27 February 1920, *CWMG* 17: 53.

of spinning. In mid-1918, Gandhi presented her with a spinning wheel.[79] By September 1919, he had succeeded in recruiting the socialites of Bombay such as Lady Tata, Lady Petit, Mrs. Jaiji Petit to his spinning cause. Gandhi's advocacy of charkha through society ladies was full of ironical twists. In one of his letters to Lady Tata, Gandhi offered to send her a charkha if she could send her car to pick it up.

Gandhi had a penchant for seeking out highly placed women and men to be his khadi ambassadors. He firmly believed in the *Bhagwad Gita*'s dictum that *what the eminent man does, others do. The standard he sets up, the rest of the world follows*. Accordingly, he made a conscious drive to recruit the high and mighty of the state and of civil society to the service of his cause. He wanted Viceroy Lord Hardinge to inaugurate the fashion of khadi wearing just as Lord Curzon in his time had done with tea. The viceroy however remained unmoved. In April 1919, in the midst of the satyagraha against the Rowlatt Bills, Gandhi wrote to the new viceroy, Chelmsford, reiterating his plea. Maffey, the viceroy's secretary, was told, "What a great thing it would be if the Viceroy would take the vow [of swadeshi]." "Even if the Viceroy cannot see his way to take the vow, but if he approves of the scheme, I would like you to let me have a separate letter for publication".[80] Gandhi had also written a similar plea to other high dignitaries including the editor of the *Times of India*. To every one of them he had also enclosed a form for the swadeshi pledge.

In August 1919, Gandhi wrote an impassioned letter to the governor of the Bombay Presidency when his repeated request for an audience failed to interest the "preoccupied official".[81] In his letter, Gandhi was cautious enough to specifically mention the "religious and economic aspects" of the swadeshi movement

[79] "Letter to Maganlal Gandhi", between April-May 1918, *CWMG* 14: 384.
[80] "Letter to J. L. Maffey", 5 May 1919, *CWMG* 15: 275.
[81] "Letter to PS to Governor", Bombay, 25 August 1919, *CWMG* 16: 60.

although, he admitted, the movement was fraught with "political consequences of the lofty, moral type" as well. After placing his arguments in favour of swadeshi, Gandhi requested the governor to "secure Lady George Lloyd's patronage for my spinning classes". He also desired active support and encouragement from district officials. Gandhi desired to have a letter of support from the governor himself for publication. The governor did not reply—predictably so as earlier in May 1919, he had written to Montagu, the secretary of state, about Gandhi being "really pretty wicked, as cunning as a fox and at heart entirely anti-British."[82] These were during Gandhi's loyalist days.

Gandhi recruited highly placed Indians too. He invited nationally renowned men to his ashram and took them on a guided tour, showing the weaving work that was being done. In March 1919, Mahatma Munshiram visited the ashram. Maganlal was asked to "drench him with love" and give the "Ashram cloth as a gift". In April 1919, Gandhi wrote to Tagore asking for a message—"a message of hope and inspiration for those who have to go through the fire"—and intimating that "the forces arrayed against me are, as you know, enormous." In 1920, Madan Mohan Malviya not only introduced looms in the precincts of the Banaras Hindu University but also endeavoured to convert the royal families of India among whom he carried substantial influence. Shankarlal Banker was one of the first men dedicated to the cause of khadi that Gandhi attracted. There were other notable figures who were also swept off their feet by Gandhi's persuasive power. Among these, three individuals—Sarladevi Choudhrani, Maganlal Gandhi, and P. C. Ray—are the subjects of our following discussion.

Sarladevi Choudhrani was Rabindranath Tagore's niece. She was married to Rambhuj Dutt Choudhri, a man from Punjab.

[82] Cf. B.R. Nanda, *In Gandhi's Footsteps: The Life and Times of Jamnalal Bajaj*, 42.

In the immediate aftermath of the Jallianwala Bagh massacre, she went on public tours with Gandhi. They shared a common interest in khadi. During the anti-partition swadeshi movement in Bengal in 1905, she was one of its front leaders. In 1920, Gandhi toured widely and conducted public meetings jointly with her in the cause of khadi. "Thanks to Sarladevi, she has shown that it is possible to make even saris out of khaddar", he wrote giving publicity and prominence to her khadi work.[83] He also ensured that she read his writings and heard his speeches to the country. "Do please read the article on khaddar", he wrote her in a letter.[84] His newspapers regularly reported on her travel, speeches, and changing wardrobe. His reports of Sarladevi's public meetings brought in heightened drama. Sarladevi's khadi sari had greater eloquence and élan than her speeches. On seeing a khadi-clad Sarladevi, hitherto silk-laden, speaking on the virtues of khadi, women resolved to discard their foreign fineries in favour of coarse khadi. Sarladevi reported her success in bringing wives of jailed victims of the Martial Law and widows of the Jallianwala Bagh massacre to adopt spinning. She opened a school to teach spinning to women.

During the khadi campaign and joint tours, they seemed to have developed a special bond. "I have just got up with two dreams, one about you and other about the Khilafat...", Gandhi wrote on 30 April 1920. And for good measure he added, "I expect you to join the party and enliven it with your music and your laughter". Then again, two days later, on 2 May, Gandhi complained: "You still continue to haunt me-even in my sleep." He was upset that her letters to him were not arriving. "I was certain of a letter from you yesterday. But none came. Today too there is a blank. I wonder, however, I know you have not failed me. It is the wretched post." In August 1920, Gandhi wrote to

[83] "The uses of Khaddar", *YI*, 28 April 1920. *CWMG* 17: 353.
[84] "Letter to Sarladevi Chowdhrani", 29 April 1920. *CWMG* 17: 357.

Kallenbach, a friend from his South African days, of a woman who had come to occupy in his life a position of "spiritual wife", an intriguing designation.[85] Kallenbach, a German architect, was a fellow experimenter with Mohandas "Bhai" Gandhi in South Africa. Gandhi had written to him after a gap of about four years. It was natural for Gandhi to confide in him. "I have come in closest touch with a lady who often travels with me", Gandhi informed him. While he himself called the relationship "indefinable", one of his colleagues saw it akin to an "intellectual wedding". He wrote seemingly infatuated, "I want you to see her" and, mentions "Mrs. Gandhi" as having "aged considerably" with all her "faults and virtues".

Gandhi often admitted differences in temperament between him and his wife. "Ba does not understand me", Gandhi wrote to Mahadev in 1921.[86] Earlier, in January 1920, Gandhi had written to Esther Faering, "Ba has not an even temper. And she can be petty."[87] In the same month, Gandhi again wrote to Esther, who was then staying in the Sabarmati ashram, "the evil in Ba, for instance, must not be resisted. She can no more go against her nature than a leopard can change his spots."[88] It was difficult for him to find a woman he could identify with and hence this fascination for the modern yet traditional "Shakti" in Sarladevi.

But soon, within ten days of the letter to Kallenbach, Gandhi was admonishing Sarladevi—"you remain a school girl"[89]—for her "decidedly despondent and skeptical and suspicious"[90] letters that distressed him. It contained signs of a cleavage that had begun to haze their "intellectual wedding" and divorce seemed

[85] "Letter to H. Kallenbach", 10 August 1920, *CWMG* 18: 129.
[86] "Letter to Mahadev Desai", 17 August 1921, *CWMG* 20: 516.
[87] "Letter to Esther Faering", 16 January 1920, *CWMG* 16: 486.
[88] "Letter to Esther Faering", 25 January 1920, *CWMG* 16: 506.
[89] "Letter to Sarladevi Choudhrani", 24 August 1920, *CWMG* 18: 193.
[90] "Letter to Sarladevi Choudhrani", 23 August 1920, *CWMG* 18: 191.

imminent. "My Dearest S" wanted "rewards" from her "Law-Giver" and not "sermons" for her "great surrender". Gandhi was non-committal and wrote that surrender is its own reward. He also defended those ashram inmates who were criticised by Sarladevi by saying that they were "superior" people, "jealous of their ideal which is my character". That almost ended the fragile relationship that had began hesitantly in 1901 when Gandhi had met Sarladevi for the first time. It was the last of the passionate exchanges that took place between them. Later, letters took a somewhat accusing tone.

She protested his not understanding her "complex nature"; he grumbled that she was not being thoughtful enough. By December 1920, Gandhi wrote: "I had two letters from you, one a scrap, the other a longish letter which shows that you do not understand my language or my thoughts."[91] He asked her to cultivate "patience and trust"; she wrote of his delibrately leaving her out. The tension in the relationship was palpable when Gandhi wrote that she was clinging to her defects even when he pointed them out in a friendly manner. It was an equal relationship and yet he reserved the right to "teach". "Among lovers and friends there is neither sinner nor saint. We are all equal, but there are wise and unwise men and women among equals. And who knows who is wiser? You must let me delude myself into the belief that I am wiser than you and therefore fit to teach you and train you."[92] The "Law-Giver" Gandhi signed off the letter stating "With dearest love I [*still*] subscribe myself."[93] It was the last "big letter" he wrote to his "spiritual wife". The letters they exchanged were now reduced to a trickle. Though Sarladevi from time to time kept abreast with Gandhi's trials and turmoil, its immediate fallout was her open criticism of

91 "Letter to Sarladevi Choudhrani", 11 December 1920, *CWMG* 19: 93.

92 "Letter to Sarladevi Choudhrani", 4 December 1920, *CWMG* 19: 69.

93 "Letter to Sarladevi Choudhrani", 17 December 1920, *CWMG* 19: 138.

Gandhi's non-cooperation programme for its inherent "negativity". She saw the movement as a fountainhead of hate-politics. It was an opinion that her celebrated uncle, Rabindranath Tagore, too shared. He called the non-cooperation movement a "spiritual suicide". Whereas Gandhi engaged Tagore in a public debate, to Sarladevi, he wrote a private letter, almost the last one. "Hatred is essentially the vice of cowards... I am gathering together all the forces of hate and directing them in a proper channel".[94] It was a short-lived relationship, at most a platonic one, that had developed through the cause of khadi. But when the relationship was in danger of spilling over the boundaries of the cause, it collapsed.

Gandhi's relationship with Maganlal survived against all odds. This relationship evolved into an important partnership for the development of khadi. Maganlal's work in the ashram was the backbone of Gandhi's khadi enterprise. If Gandhi was the brand-manager, Maganlal was the behind-the-scenes organisation man, innovating and forging the network of spinners, weavers, and buyers. Gandhi envisioned that after Maganlal had mastered the art of his work he would by himself, independent of Gandhi, take up the cause of handloom weavers.[95] Maganlal possessed a natural talent for mechanics. He mastered the art of weaving quickly and then began training other inmates of the ashram. As the manager of Satyagraha Ashram, Maganlal handled the improvements and inventions in the charkha. All experiments, big or small, were done under the guidance of Maganlal. He scrutinised advertisements that boasted of new charkhas, but, in his opinion, there was nothing to beat the original charkha in simplicity, ease, or output. He advised the Congress committees on how to guide spinners.

[94] "Letter to Sarladevi Choudhrani", 17 December 1920, *CWMG* 19: 137.

[95] "Letter to Maganlal Gandhi", 1 June 1917, *CWMG* 13: 432.

Among the co-workers of Gandhi, Maganlal is the least known. Yet, as Gandhi wrote to Maganlal on his twenty-seventh birthday in July 1917, "You are all that I have and all I desire".[96] Maganlal's relationship with Gandhi was filial and professional, deep and long, spoken and silent. Maganlal was the man responsible for achievements on the ground with regard to khadi. What Gandhi thought, Maganlal executed. In 1903, Maganlal had accompanied Gandhi to South Africa in search of a living. Within a year Maganlal, however, left his nascent retail business in response to Gandhi's call for self-imposed poverty and joined the Phoenix Settlement. Since then, Maganlal engaged himself in Gandhi's experiments and grew from being a nephew to a co-worker to being the "best comrade". Maganlal, who had never before handled a tool or machine took to printing, composing, and engineering with equal ease in Phoenix. Without any formal academic degrees he learnt while on the job so much so that later in India, he was the real man behind the organisation of the ashram's spinning and weaving enterprise. He assembled machines, innovated technologies, cultivated science, and authored books to pass on his accumulated experience. It was he who first coined the term "sadagraha" to denote Gandhi's philosophy of struggle, which hitherto was somewhat inappropriately being called passive resistance. Gandhi later improved sadagraha into satyagraha. Maganlal was more an executor and manager than a political worker. He choose the "path of silent, selfless constructive service" rather than political action. Even during the struggle in South Africa, he was confined to Phoenix, faithfully printing out *Indian Opinion* every fortnight. In 1924, when Gandhi published his account of *Satyagraha in South Africa*, he dedicated this work to Maganlal.

Gandhi's affinity with Maganlal was one of the many discordant notes that simmered in the Gandhi household.

[96] "Letter to Maganlal Gandhi", 24 July 1917, *CWMG* 13: 475.

Harilal's abrupt and angry rejection of his father's home is to some extent attributed to Gandhi's alleged love for his nephew. Harilal was a self-defeating derelict; a son whom the disciplinarian and conscientious Gandhi could never understand; a son who somehow knew that in his self-destruction alone lay his revenge. Kasturba, with a mother's instinct was uneasy about Maganlal usurping her son's place. When Harilal moved out, Maganlal too, aware of Kasturba's sentiments, contemplated parting company with Gandhi. But Gandhi dissuaded him as they were "engaged in a mighty task". Even in 1918, Gandhi had been trying to soothe Kasturba's feelings. He pleaded with his wife to be like a mother to Maganlal, because it was for his work that Maganlal had left his parents. Kasturba was consoled. "At present it is Maganlal, if anyone, who has so trained himself that he can carry on my work after me. It is for you to show concern for his suffering, to be solicitous of his meals, to save him from all manner of worries", Gandhi wrote to his wife in April 1918.[97] Till the end, however, Kasturba longed for the well-being of her eldest son and had empathised with his tragic rebellion.

While he was in India, the full development and implementation of Gandhi's ideas through his ashram fell on Maganlal. Gandhi called Maganlal the "soul of the ashram". In roughly fifteen years of work in India, he became a close confidant of Gandhi's and he was one of the few workers who could talk to Gandhi to his face. In 1915, Maganlal, among others, rebelled against Gandhi's effort to recruit a Dhed "untouchable" family for the ashram. It was a temporary rift and the prodigal son soon returned and took to constructing and managing the Satyagraha Ashram. He immersed himself in the task of organising the ashram at Ahmedabad. He was "the watchdog of the Ashram in all its aspects—material, moral and

[97] "Letter to Kasturba Gandhi", 23 April 1918, *CWMG* 14: 367; also, "Letter to Maganlal Gandhi", 7 December 1919, *CWMG* 16: 334.

spiritual." While Gandhi travelled all over India Maganlal toiled to realise Gandhi's concept in practice. As a "born mechanic", Maganlal took to assembling all the processes that eventually led to the weaving of khadi. When the All India Spinners' Association was born, he was made the director of its Technical Department. Richard Gregg, Maganlal's co-author of the book *Takli Teacher*, was told by Gandhi that Maganlal had "assimilated the inwardness of the spinning movement".[98]

In the beginning of 1919, Maganlal faced a rebellion of sorts from the inmates of the ashram with regard to his alleged dictatorial management of the ashram. Gandhi stepped in to quell it and bring order to the ashram. His remedy was characteristically unequivocal. He asked those critical of Maganlal's management to leave the ashram. He declared Maganlal to be indispensable and that without him the ashram would have never been founded.[99] "One of my creations here in the Ashram is Maganlal. If I have found from experience five million shortcomings in Maganlal, I have found ten million virtues in him...Maganlal has offered all his work as sacrifice, not for my sake but for the sake of an ideal. It is not for me he is staying; he is wedded to an ideal." It was a blunt, straight but restorative speech. "You must take it as proved that I am bad to the extent that Maganlal is bad.... You may persuade me to give up either the Ashram or Maganlal", Gandhi spoke in an address to the ashram inmates in February 1919.[100] But, when in 1919–20, by his own admission, the Mahatma "slipped" for a charismatic woman, it was Maganlal's turn to advise caution to the daring experimenter.[101] In March 1930, the Mahatma left the Satyagraha

[98] "Letter to R. B. Gregg", 27 May 1927, *CWMG* 33: 376.

[99] "Letter to Fulchand Shah", 9 August 1918, *CWMG* 15: 10.

[100] "Address to Ashram Inmates", 17 February 1919, *CWMG* 15: 91.

[101] In 1933, in a letter to a Christian priest, Gandhi admitted to having "all but fallen…not very many years ago" but was saved by those who *(contd.)*

Ashram on his trek to Dandi with the promise to return with freedom. Gandhi never came back. His departure from the ashram was dictated also by Maganlal's untimely death in 1929.[102] It had left an irreparable void. The ashram after Maganlal got distanced from "its ideal of truth". And soon it became obvious that it was a moribund institution. In 1932, while he was imprisoned in Yeravada Central jail, Gandhi wrote a "history of the Satyagraha Ashram", a requiem for his pet project and later suggested closing it.

Maganlal died of typhoid at Patna on 23 April 1928. Although Gandhi himself felt "widowed" on the death of his "heir", he cabled family members to abjure from grief. In a tribute written immediately after Maganlal's death, Gandhi wrote, "he was my hands, my feet and my eyes." And then added, "the world knows so little of how much my so-called greatness depends upon the incessant toil and drudgery of silent, devoted, able and pure workers, men as well as women. And among them all, Maganlal was to me the greatest, the best and the purest."[103] Magnalal was Gandhi's "first disciple", striving constantly to achieve a "unity of action and thought". To the last, Maganlal remained fully submerged in the Gandhian ideal. Jawaharlal Nehru, mourning the death of Maganlal, wrote in a letter to Gandhi, "to you and the khadi movement his passing away must be a great loss".[104] "His life", Gandhi wrote in a tribute titled "My Best Comrade Gone", "is an inspiration for me, a standing demonstration of the efficacy and the supremacy of the

---

(contd.)

surrounded him ("Letter to Bill Lash", 5 February 1933, *CWMG* 53: 229; also, Martin Green, 1993, *Gandhi: Voice of a New Age Revolution*, 273–85).

[102] Thomas Weber, 2004, *Gandhi as Disciple and Mentor*.

[103] "My Best Comrade Gone", *YI*, 26 April 1928, *CWMG* 36: 261–63.

[104] "Letter to Mahatma Gandhi", 14 April 1928, *Selected Works of J. Nehru*, 3 (1972): 105.

moral law." "I believe," Gandhi wrote in August 1932 from his prison, "that in his short life Maganlal did as much work as another man might do in a hundred or several hundred years."[105]

The AISA decided to establish a Khadi Museum dedicated to Maganlal Gandhi. Such a museum was built in Wardha. The idea of a museum was inspired by Maganlal, who himself ran a very small museum at the Sabarmati ashram. Now his idea became a tribute to his memory and work. The museum was designed to house books dealing with cotton culture of the past and the present, specimens of the finest to the coarsest khadi produced, specimens of spinning wheels, hand-gins, carding-bows and handlooms from the earliest ones to the most modern ones. In the museum itself a plot of land was allocated to carry on experiments in growing cotton suitable for hand-spinning rather than for the world market. At Sabarmati, Maganlal had successfully carried out many experiments in growing different varieties of cotton, which had become very popular with hand-spinners.

Like Sarladevi and Maganlal, Dr P. C. Ray (1861–1944), in Bengal, was the "Apostle of Charkha", whose Khadi Pratishthan explored the possibilities of the wheel and khaddar as a permanent supplementary industry for the Bengal agriculturists. The renowned "chemist, educationist, and entrepreneur"[106] whose valuable contribution during the Bengal partition movement had made him a household name, took to khadi spinning and campaigning for it. Ray's adoption of khadi and his work in his organisation provided an ideological breakthrough in the province. Gandhi gave a prominent place to Ray's speeches and works in his journals and defended him against attacks from people such as M. N. Roy and others. In 1922, Gandhi wrote

[105] "A Letter", 7 August 1932, *CWMG* 50: 347.

[106] Deepak Kumar, 2000, "Reconstructing India: Disunity in the Science and Technology for Development Discourse, 1900-1947", in *Osiris*, 241–57.

in *Navajivan*, based on the authority of a "famous chemist like Dr P. C. Ray", that Dr Ray had observed that it was through the spinning wheel and not through his laboratory researches in chemistry that famine could be vanquished in Bengal. Ray was so impressed with the khadi movement that he underlined the futility of the first swadeshi movement in bringing mill clothes from Bombay to meet Bengal's needs. Ray became the biggest messenger of charkha in Bengal. Ray tried to instil the fashion of wearing coarse khadi by wearing only the coarse variety. Although in poor health, he undertook extensive tours of rural Bengal to provide relief for the victims of famine and floods. Ray regularly reported the living examples of khadi enterprises. He designed a spinning wheel called the Khulna spinning wheel and distributed it among the poverty-stricken people in the villages of Khulna. He started to store cotton to provide it to the local spinners. Gandhi found some work of the Khadi Pratishthan so exemplary that it surpassed even that of his ashram.

Dr Ray founded many organisations for the khadi movement in Bengal. The Khaddar Board, the Khadi Pratishthan, and the Deshi Rang Fund were few of those organisations. He ran many centres for spinning and weaving. They were mostly located in the rural tracts of Chittagong. Here, he and his close associate, Satish Chandra Dasgupta, also formerly a chemist, ran a school for ginning, carding, spinning, dyeing, and weaving. In the school, volunteers, workers, and inspectors were trained. Atrai was the base where they stocked cotton and distributed it in the surrounding villages for ginning, carding, spinning, and weaving. Atrai had an old silk industry, which was practically killed by the East India Company. Ray's effort revived this industry. The work was most methodically organised. Satish Chandra Dasgupta helped in standardising the gin, the carding-bow, and the charkha. He wrote three instruction booklets in Bengali for the workers. He introduced a complete system of records. There were altogether eighteen different kinds of printed account books to keep a complete record of cotton purchased, issued, and stocked; of cotton purchased, issued, and carded; of cotton spun and of yarn woven. There were ledgers containing records of carders, spinners, and weavers. There were the weekly reports, and classified records of gins, carding-bows, charkhas, and looms. The Pratishthan's weekly investment into charkhas and looms was to the tune of three thousand rupees. The Pratishthan patented a model of charkha that not only worked efficiently but also sold cheaply. It cost just above two rupees a piece. From being an embryonic small experiment, the Pratishthan developed into a big organisation. It opened branches in many parts of Bengal. Its object was to manufacture and sell pure khaddar and popularise the wheel and khaddar through publications, lantern-lectures, etc. In order to give it a more stable character, it was converted into a public trust.

The Pratishthan had a trained contingent of workers, who regularly visited villages with cotton, spare parts, scales, and account sheets. They gave cotton, collected yarn, paid money, and maintained the spinners' account cards. They repaired charkhas and instructed them on how to improve yield. The weavers also came to the centre for procuring yarn, delivering woven khadi, and getting paid. Both Ray and Dasgupta invested their own savings in the khadi work. Dasgupta prepared slides for the khadi campaign which he showed with the help of a lantern. He also wrote an illustrative book on the charkha.

3 Mobilising a Movement

Discipline and Disobedience

The satyagraha against the Rowlatt Bill in early 1919 brought the nascent khadi activity from the confines of the ashram to the public realm. The short-lived satyagraha provided a much-needed launching pad for the swadeshi campaign. Gandhi, however, was keen to detach the swadeshi movement from that of swaraj, which was more sensitive to political vicissitudes. In a very subtle way, however, Gandhi made it clear that the path to swaraj lay through swadeshi. If swaraj was the end, swadeshi was the means. Neither was superior to the other, but the fact that the former was dependent on the latter made the choice of means a matter of prime relevance. The means adopted determined the content of the ends achieved. Swaraj, therefore, was embedded in swadeshi. In other words, swadeshi led to swaraj. Issues like the Rowlatt Bills, Gandhi said, were "a mere trifle", while the swadeshi campaign was more permanent. In the political arena, however, a contention for hegemony between means and end ensued; swadeshi as a means vs. swaraj as an end was a specific Gandhian concept.[1]

After the embargo on his Punjab visit, imposed in the wake of the Rowlatt satyagraha, was revoked in October 1919, Gandhi undertook a whirlwind tour of the afflicted state. The spinning wheel and its product, khadi, were the central concerns of his thought and speech. He found the people receptive to his ideas, which gave him precarious hopes for reviving khadi, as people here had not yet forgotten the art of spinning. Moreover, self-spinning in Punjab was a matter of pride among the people. He did not like being presented with flower garlands at his public meetings. He appealed for garlands made of yarn. He got a big response to this as can be seen in his *Punjab Letter*, a sort of travel diary that he wrote for *Navajivan*. "In every place, the women made offerings to me of yarn spun with their own hands". Gandhi reported many such "scenes on the way". "...But at a station named Dhinga...(t)he women stood behind the men and, from there, they threw ball after ball of handspun yarn and we in the train and the men who stood in between caught them as they came. ...I understood...that the women of Punjab have understood my message."[2] The message was of swadeshi that protected India's wealth and women's honour.

Gandhi denounced the use of foreign articles to decorate diases or places for rallies or meetings. He pointed out the incongruity of "decorations, presents, and medals" made of foreign cloth and material for a person who advocated khadi and swadeshi. He did not shirk from admonishing an adoring audience that had come wearing foreign cloth. He chided, cajoled, and coaxed the assembled crowd to adopt spinning and wear khadi. At the same time, he eulogised any use of khadi that he witnessed. The practice of presenting a welcome address printed

1 "Speech at a Public Meeting", Surat, 26 May 1919, *CWMG* 15: 328.

2 "Scenes on the Way", 15 February 1920, *CWMG* 17: 31.

on khadi cloth came to be widely adopted. Muslims in Jallandhar used khadi for the bier. He appealed to Hindus and Muslims to use khadi for their holy occasions. "I often feel like insisting that I would bow my head only when the officiating priests made our Thakoreji swadeshi by dressing him in khadi", Gandhi wrote.[3] "Khaddar was the best and holiest of cloths"; idols of worship must be dressed in khadi.[4] He was unhappy that the Puri temple idols were draped in foreign cloth. "There was nothing better, nothing purer and nothing more beautiful than khadi made of yarn spun by Indians."[5] Gandhi also went to the extent of proposing changes in marriage customs. Marriages could be solemnised by the exchange of yarn garlands. Thus, he set up new traditions by altering existing ones.

The charkha was the panacea for all ills. At Barisal in Bengal, he told a group of prostitutes who had come to visit him to redeem their fallen status by spinning on the charkha. To widows, Gandhi suggested spinning as a "remarriage of the purest kind". "It is my conviction", Gandhi wrote to the widow of his nephew, "that any man or woman who produces cloth for the people will have earned the highest *punya*".[6] Spinning was a sacred vocation. When communal riots broke out in Malabar, he offered hand-spinning as the "greatest and the most efficacious antidote". "If I could only get the whole of India to become busy with [hand-spinning], it would stop all violence in the movement." He came down heavily on almsgivers. "Let those who wish to feed the poor, find spinning-wheels for them."[7] The charkha was to spin rebellion too. In late 1921, Gandhi openly claimed that if

[3] "Notes: My Last Visit to the Punjab", *Navajivan*, 20 March 1921, *CWMG* 19: 455.

[4] "My Orissa Tour: Foreign Apparel", *Navajivan*, 10 April 1921, *CWMG* 19: 550.

[5] "Speech at Mass Meeting", Bombay, 29 May 1921, *CWMG* 20: 153.

[6] "Letter to Nirmala", 6 May 1919, *CWMG* 15: 281.

[7] "Notes: The Only Activity", *YI*, 6 October 1921, *CWMG* 21: 239.

he had not yet called soldiers to leave their cantonment, it was due to the nationalists' limitation in offering them alternative gainful employment. "I promise, that as soon as the Indians begin to feel that weaving gives anybody any day an honourable livelihood, I shall not hesitate, at the peril of being shot, to ask the Indian *sepoy* individually to leave his service and become a weaver."[8] He warned the public that prosecution for "tampering with the loyalty of the army" was but the precursor of prosecutions for tampering with the loyalty of the people to foreign cloth.

The chain of events inaugurated quite inadvertently by the promulgation of the Rowlatt Bills culminated in the launching of the movement for swaraj, although then it did not seem so. On 13 April 1919, the Jallianwala Bagh massacre, the great catharsis of the Indian national movement, took place. The massacre took a toll of at least 370 people, whose collective crime was that they were part of an innocent protest gathering. It hurt and aroused the patriotic sentiments but opposition lay within the bounds of constitutionalism. Gandhi at the annual Congress in December 1919 supported the Montagu-Chelmsford reform package and welcomed the Royal Proclamation. Gandhi's loyalty to British rule was still strong. But soon he was on the warpath to mend or end the Empire. General Dyer's brutality, especially after the declaration of an insensitive and misleading verdict by the Hunter Commission, came to symbolise a "Satanic" empire, whose obliteration became a goal that was made into a fine art. The aim fixed, the method took time to be formulated, though the signs became starkly evident. Rhetoric now took a sharp turn towards political viciousness. Though grudgingly, a political Gandhi was definitely born. As if to cement his new approach, he agreed to be president of the All India Home Rule League in April 1920, "to affect its policy and not be affected

[8] "Tampering with Loyalty", *YI*, 29 September 1921, *CWMG* 21: 221.

by it".[9] He changed its name to Swaraj Sabha with swadeshi as its creed. While Gandhi was assuaging the pain of Punjab, he also got involved with the Khilafat agitation. He agressively related the administrative brutality in Punjab with the cause of the eclipsed Khilafat. While retaining the uniqueness of both situations, he forged the two major communities of India through their common opposition to the British. He was called to Delhi with regard to the Indian response to the impending removal of one caliphate. He advised Muslims to withhold cooperation but to abjure boycott. He asked them to pitch for non-cooperation.

Gandhi was opposed to the creed of boycott. The difference between non-cooperation and boycott, he asserted, was that of "an elephant from an ass". He proposed swadeshi in cloth and boycott of only foreign fabrics as a part of the agitation. This left many Muslim leaders dissatisfied. Muslims took to swadeshi only in a reflected sense. At that point in their political development, a part of the Muslim intelligentsia saw British rule as adversely affecting Islamic identity in the world. Since the Khilafat issue was far removed from the Indian reality—deprivation of rights, poverty, and political subjugation—large sections of the Muslim masses remained alienated from the pan-Islamic cause. Despite this, propelled by political propaganda, the Khilafat did become a factor in identity formation among Muslims. Hence, Muslim response towards the Turkish turmoil was one of civilisational confrontation and an assertion of the pan-Islamic identity. Their historical resentment against Christian rulers, despite Gandhi's espousal to the contrary, predisposed them to choose boycott of British goods as a political strategy. "Boycott is a sign of anger; to refuse co-operation, on the other hand, is a sign of firmness", Gandhi reasoned.[10] "Boycott indicates our weakness; non-cooperation proves our strength."

[9] "Letter to V.S. Srinivasa Sastri", 18 March 1920, *CWMG* 17: 97.
[10] "Punjab Letter: Khilafat Meeting", 1 December 1919, *CWMG* 16: 318.

If the strategy of boycott was inevitable, Gandhi preferred boycott of not just the goods of the Empire but all foreign goods. He further advocated continuance of boycott beyond the limited goal of redressing immediate wrongs. He was against the inclusion of boycott in the non-cooperation resolution. His reasoning was dictated both by moral and practical considerations. Boycott was contrary to the "spirit of self-sacrifice", was "ineffectual" and "thoroughly unpractical". "Boycott of British goods to be effective must be taken up by the whole country at once or not at all. It is like a siege."[11] Boycott was vindictive, too, and therefore alien to the philosophy of non-cooperation, which was conceived as a movement for self-purification by undergoing suffering and offering sacrifices. The effectiveness of boycott lay in its being swift, certain, and adequate, but it was impractical, as it demanded sacrifices from the rich who were timid, cautious, stingy, and without forbearance. Boycott was constrained by India's unpreparedness to observe it wholly and at the same time by the whole country. Lastly, Gandhi could have added, accepting boycott stood low in the moral struggle that he was engaged in with the raj. The difficulty in making boycott effective soon dawned on the Muslims. Apart from sporadic incidents, as in Damnagar where some 300 Muslims on Id day had resolved to boycott the use of foreign goods, the movement generally failed to elicit response. It was then that the chastened community leaders veered towards swadeshi and insisted on its inclusion in the non-cooperation programme.[12]

[11] "Boycott of Goods V. Non-co-operation Programme", *YI*, 25 August 1920, *CWMG* 18: 198.

[12] Even in 1928, in *The Poverty of India and its Cure*, Nehru was advocating a creed contrary to Gandhi's understanding of boycott. His focus was on boycotting British cloth. He wrote: "British cloth can be ousted either by Indian mill-made cloth or by khadi or by both. There is no objection to wearing Indian mill-made cloth but it should be remembered that there are many mills in India which are being run with British capital, and the profits of which go to Britain. There is no difference

(contd.)

Despite Gandhi's disapproval, the Calcutta Congress in September 1920 did include a clause on the boycott of foreign goods in the non-cooperation resolution that Gandhi himself introduced. He called the inclusion "an anomaly" for which, he said he was not "originally responsible".[13] His main contention was that there was an "inwardness" in the non-cooperation movement of which the essence was "discipline and self-sacrifice"[14]. Inclusion of the Boycott Clause, an "unfortunate interpolation" in this enterprise of self-suffering and self-sacrifice, marred the "musical harmony of the programme". He regarded swadeshi to be the most powerful weapon against bureaucracy. Declaring swadeshi to be an "eternal rule of conduct", Gandhi called for its adherence beyond the immediate political exigency. Such an autonomy was necessitated by the need to protect a nascent, constructive activity of khadi from the government's angry reprisals. Swadeshi, he declared, was "the biggest, the safest, and the surest part" of the non-cooperation agenda in its constructive form.[15]

"Place Khadi in My Hands and I shall Place Swaraj in Yours"

Thus began one of the most celebrated struggles in the history of nations. After the launch of the non-cooperation movement

(contd.)

between the cloth made in these mills and the foreign cloth. Secondly if we want to boycott all British cloth immediately, that cannot be done by replacing it with Indian mill cloth." Nehru, though speaking the same language as Gandhi diverged in that he advocated boycott of only British cloth and not all foreign-made cloth (*Selected Works of Jawaharlal Nehru*, 3: 367).

13 "Item is a Practical Impossibility", "Speech replying on Non-cooperation Resolution", *CWMG* 18: 251; "The Congress", *YI*, 15 September 1920. *CWMG* 18: 262.

14 "The Inwardness of Non-cooperation", *YI*, 8 September 1920, *CWMG* 18: 235.

15 "The Mists", *YI*, 20 April 1921, *CWMG* 20: 15.

in August 1920,[16] Gandhi's countrywide tours became more intensive and long. His task now was to facilitate a national awakening to be expressed in constructive action. Each of his political moves was to enable Congress to proximate a mass organisation and make it an instrument of effective action. In December 1920, at Nagpur, he got the Congress to accept the creed of winning swaraj by "all legitimate and peaceful means". Here he also gave the country a powerful dream of "Swaraj in one year". Gandhi was on the move practically all the time. In September 1921, he looked back and wrote: "Hardly anyone could have toured India as I have done in the last 13 months."[17] During his tours he addressed vast audiences and wrote voluminously. In Bihar, where he was in August 1921, he found that the masses brimmed with faith in the khadi programme. Spinning and weaving of khadi was going on apace and thousands had started wearing exclusively khadi. This was due to the Congress workers in Bihar, who were "men of such simple and pure lives" with deep "faith in non-violent non-cooperation".[18] Assam's capacity for khadi production and consumption was greater than that of Punjab's. Here all the women, as those in Andhra, carded their own cotton. "If the women here take up spinning and weaving, they will do so out of love for the country and not for love of money", Gandhi wrote of the Assamese women.[19] Bengal disheartened him but it showed signs of a possible reversal of the situation. Gandhi concluded that "in point of Swadeshi, of all the provinces, Bengal stands at the

16 It is said that Gandhi instituted a dialogic form of politics in place of an antagonistic one (Hardiman 2003).

17 "My Notes: End of the Tour", *Navajivan*, 9 October 1921, *CWMG* 21: 268.

18 "My Notes: Bihar Tour", *Navajivan*, 21 August 1921, *CWMG* 21: 3.

19 "Every woman of Assam is a born weaver. No Assamese girl who does not weave can expect to become a wife. And she weaves fairy tales in cloth" ("Note: Lovely Assam", *YI*, 1 September 1921, *CWMG* 21: 29).

bottom."[20] Khadi was thinly spread in this thickly populated province. Yet at P. C. Ray's National School in Barisal, he saw "very fine and even yarn". The khadi programme in Madras, however, proved that Gandhi's impression about Bengal's performance was mistaken. "The use of swadeshi seems to have spread even less in the Madras Presidency than in Bengal", Gandhi conveyed to Mahadev Desai, "and, among the women one may say that it is practically nil".[21] His overall conclusion from his tours was that the masses accepted his belief in the spinning wheel. If, however, khadi was to spread progressively, "efficient and enthusiastic" workers were needed to harness the momentous enthusiasm of the people.

If swaraj hung on a slender thread, if charkha held the key to India's economic freedom, if spinning provided subsidiary occupation to famished multitudes, it was necessary that all the sections of India's population were involved in spinning and its related activities. Only by involving various sections of the population in the process of hand-spinning would India's required target of yarn production be met. As part of the campaign strategy Gandhi wrote pamphlets appealing to different segments of society, such as mill-owners, cloth merchants, weavers, women[22], students, etc. From each of them he asked for solidarity.

He requested mill-owners "to introduce ...a little of the national spirit" in their business. "I do not say you should be

[20] "Notes: Bengal", *YI*, 22 September 1921, *CWMG* 21: 162.

[21] "My Notes: People of Madras", *Navajivan*, 2 October 1921, *CWMG* 21: 232.

[22] "The women have parted with cash and fine jewellery. You have wandered from house to house to make collections. Some of you have even assisted in picketing. Some of you who were used to fine dresses of variegated colours and had a number of changes during the day have now adopted the white and spotless but heavy Khadi sari reminding one of a woman's innate purity. Boycott is impossible *unless you will surrender the whole of your foreign clothing*" ("To the Women of India", *YI*, 11 August 1921, *CWMG* 20: 495).

philanthropic. But I do plead for the conduct of your business on national rather than purely selfish lines."[23] He pointed out their unpalatable role during the 1905 swadeshi movement when they had caused prices to rise and palmed off foreign cloth under the name of swadeshi. His appeal to cloth-merchants was to "subordinate your individual gain to the country's".[24] He held them responsible for India's "deep and distressing poverty". He urged them to stop the import of foreign cloth. Once they stopped import, there would be an abundance of opportunity for the production and distribution of khadi, they were told. "It is an enterprise worthy of your patriotism." Patriotism against profit was the new ethics that he tried to inculcate in the business community.

Gandhi targeted women through his massive propaganda exercise.[25] In some tangible way, the khadi movement's biggest beneficiaries were women. It is argued that it was a libertarian

[23] "An Appeal to Mill-Owners", 6 July 1921, *CWMG* 20: 331.

[24] "Open Letter to Cloth-Merchants", 7 July 1921, *CWMG* 20: 335.

[25] Even in South Africa, Gandhi's settlements provided "spiritual and physical freedom" to women, which were then unavailable to them in India ("Letter to Maganlal Gandhi", 31 August 1910, *CWMG* 10: 311). Yet, sometimes Gandhi's attitude betrayed his insolence to his wife. In 1918, Kasturba was invited by Hindu Stri Mandal to preside over the annual function of the Mandal and the Dadabhai Naoroji birthday celebrations. In response, Gandhi, on behalf of his wife, wrote back declining the invitation. He replied: "Though we two are independent and have equal rights, we have decided our spheres of work for the sake of convenience. Moreover, at the time of our marriage, my wife was altogether illiterate. I gave her some education with great effort, but, for several reasons, I have not been able to do so to my satisfaction. It is not possible, therefore, for her to accept your proposal. I don't think my wife can read out her speech from the chair. She will certainly not be able to prepare her own speech. She is not at all conversant with your activities and hence cannot say anything extempore either" ("Letter to Rasikmani", 12 August 1918, *CWMG* 15: 17).

movement for Indian women.[26] The revival of spinning brought into being interaction between needy Indian women and the men who organised the khadi network, provided raw cotton and charkhas, and acted as facilitators. Spinning also brought women together when they took to collective spinning at the centres, mostly called Gandhi *bhavans*. It brought them out of their domestic realms into the politicised arena. It provided them much-needed economic support. It played a role in their lives while enhancing interpersonal exchanges in a society that valued seclusion of women. In ordinary circumstances not many women would have taken to spinning enthusiastically. The movement brought women out of the confines of their homes and provided them a new opportunity for social interaction. A new space for interpersonal exchange was created for the women hitherto limited to home, hearth, and harvest. Thousands of women daily went to khadi centres to collect cotton, deliver self-spun yarn, and get remuneration. Women organised spinning clubs and spinning competitions. In a silent way the khadi movement gave a new spatial autonomy to women.

Gandhi's attitude towards women was similar to his imagery of India. Her civilisation was the best in the world but because she was betrayed by her own people, India found herself in a sad morass. Similarly, it was the men who put Indian women into seclusion because of their negligence of them. Gandhi drew women into the public arena like no one had done before. The focus on women was to encourage them to have a covenant with spinning. This was symbolic of their contribution to the national awakening and participation. He was aware of the ills that afflicted Indian women, but his prescriptions were singularly ingenious. Unlike the early reformers, he did not lay emphasis on widow remarriages of which of course he never disapproved either. Instead

[26] Sujata Patel, "Construction and Reconstruction of Women in Gandhi", in *EPW*, 20 February 1988.

he urged them to spin and thus saw women, as Madhu Kishwar says, "not as objects of reform and humanitarianism, but as self-conscious arbiters of their own destiny".[27] In addressing public meetings attended by women his subject invariably was the spinning wheel. "*Brahma* saw that if India was to remain free her women should be persuaded to look upon it as their sacred duty to produce some yarn [every day]. That is why it happened that he did not create a distinct community whose function would be to spin but made that obligatory on all women."[28] Gandhi urged all women to spin. It was also a religious sacrament to spin regularly. Men were asked to procure cotton and provide slivers—the carded cotton—to their womenfolk. It was a gender relationship that was interdependent. "So long as women in India do not take equal part with men in the affairs of the world and in religious and political matters, we shall not see India's star rising", Gandhi said to a gathering of women.[29] He wanted women to have an equal share in winning swaraj. "Probably in this peaceful struggle woman can outdistance man by many a mile", he wrote in the article "Women's Part".[30]

The spinning wheel was presented as a mechanism by which gender discrimination could be rectified. Spinning was widely held to be a womanly vocation. As one man wrote to Gandhi, "Let your great programme of Charkha and khaddar be confined to women for the present."[31] Such arguments, Gandhi averred, were misplaced. No gender had any exclusive monopoly over any specific vocation, he said. The khadi movement needed both genders in equal partnership. "Women are...not designed

[27] Madhu Kishwar, "Gandhi on Women", *EPW*, 20, no. 40 (5 October 1985): 1691.

[28] "Speech at Weavers Conference", Nagpur, 25 December 1920, *CWMG* 19: 147.

[29] "Speech at Women's meeting", Bombay, 8 May 1919, *CWMG* 15: 290.

[30] "Women's Part", *YI*, 15 December 1921, *CWMG* 22: 21.

[31] "Not Man's Work", *YI*, 11 June 1925, *CWMG* 27: 220.

to organize on a large scale. She is not inventive. Man, being restless and often destructive, is inventive...All the greatest inventions have been made by men", Gandhi argued.[32] So, while women spun the yarn, men wove the organisation of commerce. The majority of the khadi workers were male and it was they who were making all the necessary technical improvements to the wheel. Further, it was through men only that political messages could be given to women who for a large part were politically immune and led their lives in seclusion. Spinning therefore was for both men and women. If the spinning wheel was an instrument of economic freedom and social integration for women, spinning was a "sacrificial rite" for men.

Women were targeted both as producers as well as consumers. If they had a substantial say in the purchase of family clothes, they also had idle hours which could be harnessed for spinning. In his public speeches, he used examples to influence his women audiences. In a meeting in the Bombay Presidency, he spoke of the Punjabi women, who, irrespective of their caste, spun their own yarn and had the village weavers make cloth for them. He made use of allegorical references from the holy books in order to make them eschew their taste for fine clothes. In the days of Ravana, "Sita Devi had to wear for fourteen years the rough garment made from the bark of the tree". Today's women, living in this modern Ravana raj, too, must, discard their foreign garments and adopt coarse khadi. "Simplicity is the best adornment", he said at a meeting in Allahabad.[33] At Bhuvasan, he asked the women, "how good would it be if you wore a sari out of hand-spun yarn? It is through you that I seek *Ramarajya*." Women were to disregard the quality of cloth produced from handspun yarn and use such cloth functionally for the purpose

32 "Notes: Not by Deputy", *YI*, 25 September 1924, *CWMG* 25: 153.

33 "Speech at Public Meeting", Allahabad, 29 November 1920, *CWMG* 19: 45.

of covering their bodies. "Take up the sari that the charkha can give you."[34] He appealed to their sense of piety and asked them to spin and as "of all charities the charity of cloth was the best".[35]

Gandhi's next target was students who he thought would restore the spinning vocation to its "respectable status". They could make spinning and wearing of khadi fashionable. They would help to convert more of the floating consumers to wearing khadi. Gandhi focused on the young with a view to make education self-sustainable and to help the rapid spread of the spinning activity. The campaign to recruit students to the khadi and spinning programme received a massive boost with the declaration of non-cooperation that called students to withdraw from attending government-owned and -affiliated educational institutions. Gandhi asked students to spin for an hour daily. He aimed to produce "spinning addicts" among students. Every national educational centre was to convert itself into a principally carding and spinning institute. Gujarat Vidyapith recommended that the schools affiliated to it introduce spinning in the regular curriculum to help produce the required yarn. Various municipalities under the nationalist leadership introduced spinning in the curriculums of schools affiliated to them, but with varying success. The Surat municipality was requested by Gandhi to forgo a government grant and introduce an education system that was funded by spinning. The municipality of Lahore prescribed khaddar dress for all the municipal employees. Gandhi wanted the Salem municipality in south India to make spinning compulsory in municipal schools. He envisaged a curriculum in which the spinning wheel and loom would form a permanent part. At the Nagpur Congress in December 1920, Gandhi gave

[34] "Speech at Rajahmundry", 3 April 1921, *CWMG* 19: 509.

[35] "Speech at Women's Meeting", Patna, *The Serachlight*, 8 December 1920, *CWMG* 19: 68.

a call for swaraj-in-a-year. In the year 1921, Gandhi advised the suspension of all activities except spinning, as that was an emergency duty. So during the emergency of the national struggle, a national school became a school for spinning. Once swaraj was established, they could revert to academics Gandhi argued.

In Gandhi's analysis, India was a "slave-owning state". "I have never yet known a slave-owner teaching his slave the price of freedom, the price of liberty. Wherever slaves have enfranchised themselves, they have done so in spite of the slave-owner."[36] Spinning was to free pupils from their servitude to the colonial state. Further, educational infrastructure hitherto was financed by taxation from liquor sales; under Gandhi's swaraj scheme, the resources for education would come from neither liquor nor land but from the spinning wheel. The education system was to make pupils self-reliant from their early years.

Gandhi had high hopes in the experiment of introducing the charkha in national schools. It was the most efficient method of introducing education in the villages of India. It required no extra financing and no immoral sources of taxation. The chief difficulty in executing the scheme, besides making the idea nationally acceptable, was with regard to the availability of spinning wheels. They had to be manufactured in large numbers to meet increased demand. Having the village carpenter was not enough as an organisational network was non-existent. It was for this reason that Gandhi at the very beginning of his call to students was uncertain of what engagements they should have after having withdrawn them from their education. Gandhi later thought he had erred. "I should have boldly said the whole truth and suggested hand-spinning and hand-weaving as an integral part of the proposition regarding boycott of the

[36] "Speech to Student", Dacca, 15 December 1920, *CWMG* 19: 125.

educational institutions."[37] He also found an easy solution in takli, the iron spindle for hand-held spinning activity. It took practically no storage space and demanded no repair and was cheap and readily available.

Gandhi called himself a "farmer-weaver". Weaving was a specialised vocation, a sophisticated art. Unlike spinning, it was a complete means of livelihood. Because weaving attracted higher wages, it was one occupation that Gandhi suggested to many. To the striking railway workers at Chittagong he suggested weaving as an alternative occupation. Weavers were the greatest victims of the mercantile imperialism of the East India Company. Millions had been left in a state of shock as their hereditary skills were no match for the machination and machinery of the British. Those who had survived the initial rapaciousness now wove only foreign yarn as the use of handspun yarn for weaving had become almost extinct. Further, handspun yarn was uneven, feeble, and snapped repeatedly on the loom. Most of the weavers themselves used foreign garments for personal wear. While all sections of society were called to participate in the yarn production process, there were specific efforts to entice away weavers from weaving imported yarn. The public appeals of the Congress and the Khilafat Conference especially targeted the weaver communities who were the direct victims of British industrialism but now were co-opted by it. They pleaded with the weavers to use exclusively handspun yarn for weaving. They held special meetings for the weavers. Gandhi even suggested a special drive for their enrolment into the Congress. Converting the weavers and other complementary craftsmen such as carders, carpenters, blacksmiths, etc., to the cause was important for the movement. But success was not substantial as Gandhi wrote exasperatedly,

[37] "The best national education for India is undoubtedly an intelligent handling of the spinning wheel" ("A Confession of Errors", *YI*, 18 August 1921, *CWMG* 20: 529).

"I have resolutely set my face against doing anything for weavers who weave mill-spun yarn, for they cut their own throat by weaving mill-spun yarn, and they know it."[38]

In an economy that itself produced few consumer commodities, swadeshi was more to do with traders and merchants. The earlier wave of the swadeshi movement during the anti-partition agitation had ebbed largely because of avaricious merchants. A pragmatic Gandhi this time appealed to the merchants exhorting them to "follow truth in their business". "Just as the *kshatriya*'s duty is not killing [but protecting], so also the business man's duty is not amassing wealth".[39] Here is an example of, as Parekh says, Gandhi taking liberties with the interpretation of tradition to suit his intention.[40]

Interaction with merchants was a common public exercise in Gandhi's tours. "Throughout my travels in the different parts of India I have taken good care to see the merchant community", Gandhi said in September 1921 at the meeting of the Madras Piece-Goods Merchants Association.[41] The meeting was convened to discuss the boycott of foreign cloth. "You will be glad to learn from me that in all these places they have been in full sympathy with this great Swadeshi movement." Gandhi also attempted to entice potential converts by presenting a rosy picture of the profit gained from trading in khadi in place of what they now got as commissions. "You get perhaps Rs 5 out of every hundred rupees worth of cloth. But Rs 95 entirely goes out to your principals. Now, imagine that you are the manufacturers of the cloth that we need in India itself. Then the whole of the hundred rupees would remain in India." Gandhi exhorted the merchants

38 "Letter to Achyut Patwardhan", 30 January 1935, *CWMG* 60: 139.

39 "Speech at Karachi", 29 February 1916, *CWMG* 13: 256.

40 Bhikhu Parekh, 1999, *Colonialism, Tradition and Reform: An Analysis of Gandhi's Political Discourse.*

41 "Speech at Piece-Goods Merchants Meeting", Madras, 16 September 1921, *CWMG* 12: 127.

to sacrifice the trade in foreign cloth and organise the khadi trade. Jamnalal Bajaj negotiated with the Calcutta merchants for the implementation of the boycott programme.

If khadi was to succeed, arousing patriotic fervor in merchants was a necessity. Gandhi's aim was to enlist their support. He appealed to their hearts: "I lay my hand on my heart and say that when the merchant class understands the spirit of patriotism, then only can we get Swaraj quickly."[42] His speeches contained moral overtones as he advised merchants to shun "unfair means" in trading practices. He was sure the public would not "tolerate divorce between profession and practice". That was the nearest he came to issuing a diktat. But he also knew the futility of a mere appeal to patriotism to those whose chief aim was profit. Merchants were the mainstay for financing the Congress machinery. They had helped the Congress, for example, to meet a target of one crore rupees by 30 June 1921. In 1919, in Bombay, at Gandhi's suggestion, a committee of leading men was appointed to raise a volunteer body to assist in the preservation of order at the cloth market and the surrounding locality.

Merchants largely remained indifferent to the "growing popular dislike" for foreign cloth. Their import of foreign cloth did not stop. Instead, the textile mills took advantage of swadeshi propaganda and sold their manufacture as khadi to gullible customers. Cloths stamped with the "Swadeshi Cloth Mark" invaded the market and were sold as khadi. Gandhi countered this invasion of spurious cloth by issuing leaflets informing people on the true intent and texture of khadi. "Volunteers should very politely put this leaflet into the hands of all persons who are not clad in Khadi. Description of Khadi should be written out on large wooden boards and big leaders, not hired men, should

[42] "Speech at Reception by Merchants", Broach, after 19 October 1917, *CWMG* 14: 6.

parade the streets wearing these."[43] Gandhi himself offered to roam one hour every day in the Ahmedabad market with a board suspended round his neck. He advised the swadeshi shops to appoint inspectors who were experts in distinguishing between foreign cloth and swadeshi and between handspun and machine-spun cloth.

Gandhi attempted to reorient the consumption patterns of the rich and the educated by advocating use of mill cloth for the less privileged, as mass-manufactured foreign fabrics were available at cheap prices. Such a reorientation was designed to give the demand for khadi a spurt and to draw people's attention to the lives and work of artisans whose craftsmanship and inventive faculties had been stunted owing to a lack of patronage. But Gandhi soon found that it was difficult to make the rich adopt khadi. Spinning too was unattractive for them. Gandhi called the educated to spin, if for nothing, but "quiet reflection". The lukewarm response of the educated to his call made him declare that they had lost the art of labouring for their bread.

The Congress at Nagpur in December 1920 adopted a new constitution with a changed creed of "the attainment of Swarajya by the people of India by all legitimate and peaceful means".[44] It underwent massive organisational restructuring to bridge the gap between "precept and practice". It instituted an All-India Tilak Memorial Swaraj Fund with a target of one crore rupees to be met by 30 June 1921. The target was to bring more people into the net by garnering small contributions instead of having a few persons donate large amounts. There were other targets to be met as well; they were (i) enrolment of one crore primary members in the Congress, and (ii) distribution of

43 "My Notes: Mill-Made Khadi", *Navajivan*, 1 June 1924, *CWMG* 24: 168.

44 "Congress Constitution Adopted at Nagpur Session", December 1920, *CWMG* 19: 190.

20,00,000 charkhas. The fund-collection drive was focused on appealing to the piety of women. Gandhi's meetings reverberated with calls to surrender "superfluous ornaments", adopt temperance, give up smoking, and donate generously.[45] More than two-thirds of the collected funds was to be spent on spinning, weaving, and educational activities. Despite the avowed aim of collecting money from the maximum number of people, ultimately it was Bombay, the commercial hub, on which the Congress came to depend. In the fading hours of 30 June, the Congress scrambled to meet its targeted amount, which it did with Gandhi himself supervising the drive during the last fourteen days.

The achievement of the target enthused Gandhi, and in quick succession, remarkable for its high-voltage propaganda and confident assertions, Gandhi set target after target upon a bracing country. The new target that he proclaimed immediately after the achievement of the three-point Bezwada programme was that of a complete boycott of foreign cloth to be achieved by 30 September 1921.

Bombay was made the centre of two boycott campaigns as it controlled India's cloth market. It was the gateway to foreign import. From here the symbolic battle of complete boycott of foreign cloth was to be led. Therefore, heavy responsibility was placed on its commercial class. The merchants were to cease their cloth imports; mill-owners were to reorient their outlook; consumers had to strip themselves of their foreign fineries. "If Khadi was non-available, people must minimize their clothing needs."[46] They were to consign their wardrobe of foreign clothes to the fire. But companion to this mandate was a liberal spending

[45] "The National Tilak Swaraj Fund", *Navajivan*, 20 March 1921, *CWMG* 19: 460.

[46] "How to Boycott Foreign Goods", *The Bombay Chronicle*, 4 July 1921, *CWMG* 20: 321.

on khadi. "Bombay the Beautiful has a golden opportunity. She must add to her beauty, or be prepared to lose what she has", Gandhi exhorted.[47]

On 31 July 1921, Bombay showed evidence of its beauty. Gandhi lit a huge bonfire of foreign cloth, which was witnessed by a great gathering. Once the fire was lit in Bombay, it soon became a practice in demonstration, and at various places people began to set fire to their caps of foreign fabric. The movement spread with "telepathic communication". Gandhi's clarion call focused on atonement for the past and revival of the old professions of spinning and weaving. He advocated either the incineration of existing stock of foreign cloth or its dispatch to other nations. There was no question of giving them to the poor. At Gauhati, where Gandhi had been in August, the practice of burning of foreign cloth was continued. The heaps contained "a great number of fine dhotis, fine saris and caps and a good quantity of lace". As the fire was lit, "hundreds of fine shirts and other garments of foreign cloth flew up in the air and fell back into the fire."[48]

Critics overwhelmed Gandhi. "The picture of you lighting that great pile, including beautiful fabrics", C. F. Andrews wrote, "shocked me intensely."[49] It was something "violent, distorted, unnatural". There was a subtle appeal to "racial feeling" that exemplified "selfish nationalism". The act, Andrews wrote, would go against the poor, as the price of cloth shall escalate beyond their reach. Andrews suggested distribution of the discarded foreign clothes among the poor. Gandhi was not convinced. Had the emphasis been on all foreign goods, it would have been rightly termed as "racial, parochial and wicked". The emphasis

47 "Bombay the Beautiful", *YI*, 6 July 1921, *CWMG* 20: 330.

48 "Experiences in Assam-I", *Navajivan*, 4 September 1921, *CWMG* 21: 56.

49 "Ethics of Destruction", *YI*, 1 September 1921, *CWMG* 21: 41.

was on foreign cloth alone. The distinction made a world of difference. Tainted with shame and self-degradation, foreign cloth was a painful reminder of India's capitulation to temptation and persecution. It therefore, was fit to be destroyed.

On 22 September 1921 at Madura in south India, Gandhi effected a "radical alteration" in his dress.[50] It was initially motivated by the seeming incapacity of the people to buy khadi. The change in the dress—stripping to "only a loincloth and a *chaddar* whenever found necessary for the protection of the body"—was the final act that would transform Gandhi's persona and would give him a uniquely branded personality. The idea that he could advise the country to adopt simple and minimal clothing in the time of transition only when he practised the same was the inspiration beneath the change. It was not only remarkable for its political honesty but it also showcased his empathy with his poor compatriots. "I wish to be in tune with the life of the poorest of the poor among Indians", he said.[51] But boycott of foreign cloth unlike the goal of collecting a crore of rupees was not an easy task. The target remained elusive. The swaraj-in-a-year too remained a mirage.

Through this maze of propaganda duels, Gandhi prepared for mass civil disobedience at Bardoli and camped there with uncertain determination. While Bardoli was being prepared for civil disobedience, its inhabitants were asked to wear khadi and spin on the charkha. "a preparation for civil disobedience means intensifying constructive and productive activities such as popularizing Khadi and the spinning wheel."[52] A prerequisite for the launching of civil disobedience was the adoption of khadi by the people of the place where it was to be launched. "Civil disobedience without Swadeshi is death without hope of

50 "Message on Loin Cloth", Madura, 22 Sep 1921, *CWMG* 21: 181.

51 "My Loin Cloth", *Navajivan*, 27 July 1924, *CWMG* 24: 456.

52 "My Notes: About National Schools", *Navajivan*, 12 February 1922, *CWMG* 22: 391.

creation. It is like tearing down a field without any prospect of sowing a new crop."[53] Civil disobedience was an added incentive to the khadi movement.

The non-payment of tax as part of civil disobedience held out a "material bait", a privilege which Gandhi wanted to be balanced with a disciplined response. He demanded strict adherence to non-violence and an unswerving acceptance of the moral and economic value of khadi. Bardoli was set on a fast track for civil disobedience and yet it fell short of Gandhi's exacting standards. Addressing a strong khadi-clad crowd, Gandhi admonished: "You are not yet in a position to produce all the Khadi you require for yourselves. You still do not have as many handlooms as you require for weaving the Khadi you need."[54] He was in a way forced into the Bardoli civil disobedience campaign, but was relieved from this course following the incident at Chauri-Chaura where an enraged mob burnt a police station resulting in the death of some policemen. Gandhi unilaterally declared the suspension of the still unfolding programmes, making the AICC sign on the dotted line to the astonishment of both colleagues and opponents. In March 1922, Gandhi's arrest brought an end to one of the most activist phases of the national movement. His parting message was a reflection of his commitment. In a letter written from Sabarmati Jail on the same day, he told Indulal Yagnik, "Place Khadi in my hands and I shall place Swaraj in yours".[55]

Repressions and Resistances

Throughout the period of the non-cooperation movement a spate of government-sponsored bans came to confront those who wore

53 "Notes: 'Already Free'", *YI*, 12 January 1922, *CWMG* 22: 160.

54 "Speech at Bardoli Taluka Conference", 29 January 1922, *CWMG* 22: 288.

55 "Interview to Indulal Yagnik", 11 March 1922, *CWMG* 23: 86.

khadi caps, irrespective of whether it was worn out of patriotism or convenience. Khadi caps became a site of conflict between loyalty to the Empire and patriotism to the country. There were government decrees that made the wearing of khadi caps a crime. At many places, the innocuous khadi cap, popularly called Gandhi *topi*, became an issue of contention. As *Young India* reported in January 1922, a European youth shot dead a Muslim Indian for the offence of wearing a khadi cap. The chief justice of the Bombay High Court issued a ban on pleaders wearing the "Gandhi Cap" while appearing before the judge.[56] Any breach of the order was deemed contempt of court. Some of the government departments took stringent measures to suspend or remove employees who used khadi topis. In March 1921, at Jubbalpore, one railway department prohibited its employees from wearing white topis. The government of the Central Provinces decreed against the wearing of khadi topis. The collector of Allahabad forbade the government employees from donning, in Gandhi's words, "beautiful, light, inoffensive caps". Young men had their khadi vests and caps torn from them and had to witness their being burnt. One man had his cap spat into and was then forced to wear it. These instances illustrated that, increasingly, wearing khadi was becoming a penal crime.

As the non-cooperation movement unfolded, in its bare simplicity it required the people to adopt spinning and to court imprisonment. And once in prison, they were to spin there, too. Many imprisoned activists took to protest when denied the spinning wheel. Through a network of political workers spread all over the country acting as correspondents, the editor Gandhi marshalled facts and figures to show a crumbling government resorting to repression through arrests and bans. In Calcutta, a batch of women selling khadi to commuters was arrested on a charge of obstructing the highway. Among the arrested were the

56 "Notes: Ban on Khadi Cap", *YI*, 15 December 1921, *CWMG* 22: 15.

wife and sister of Chittaranjan Das. But this arrest presented a model of action for other women in different parts of the country, who took to hawking khadi on the roads and other public spaces. Gandhi himself encouraged such actions by saying that "it is a most harmless challenge to the police to arrest them if they dare".[57] "If a spinning wheel can by any possibility be turned into a seditious article, its possession will be another honourable method of seeking imprisonment."[58] In Amritsar, as in numerous other places, people holding processions in support of the khadi movement were asked by the authorities to disperse, and when they refused, they were beaten mercilessly. In Andhra Pradesh, a person called Venkatappaya was jailed. His only crime was his efforts to popularise khadi. In the wake of the Moplah outbreak, the khadi movement in Malabar received a crippling setback. The declaration of martial law provided an opportunity to the government to suppress the khadi movement. Government soldiers tore away khadi clothes worn by the people. Khadi caps, spinning wheels, etc., were among the things burnt by force. The result was that khadi caps and spinning wheels, which used to be displayed in the shops of Calicut, disappeared.

In 1921, rattled by a sustained movement against foreign cloth, various governments took countermeasures. Provincial governments resorted to official dictates to repress surging interest in spinning. In Bihar, a magistrate sent hawkers to sell foreign cloth. In Dharwar the local government issued an official circular in which it was said:

> All officers subordinate to the Collector and District Magistrate are desired to take steps to make people realize, that inasmuch as India produces less than her population requires, a boycott of foreign cloth and its destruction or export must inevitably lead to a serious rise in prices, which may lead to a serious disorder and looting, and that these

[57] "Notes: Selling Khadi", *YI*, 22 December 1921, *CWMG* 22: 71.
[58] "Notes: What Are They?", *YI*, 18 May 1921, *CWMG* 20: 105.

consequences will be the result, not of any action on the part of Government but of Mr. Gandhi's campaign.[59]

The communiqué also suggested other means and ways to combat the swadeshi movement. One of the ideas it conveyed was to initiate meetings by dealers opposed to swadeshi. There were indirect pressures on dealers to refrain from countenancing the boycott agenda. Some nationalist members put a resolution in the Madras Council recommending improved spinning wheels to stimulate spinning and weaving by hand. The resolution was debated and then summarily defeated. Those who opposed this argued that khadi was not only economically unviable but it lacked the qualities of a wearable fabric. It was not just that handspun yarn was weak; the whole idea of hand-spinning was technologically deficient. It was said that any expenditure of public money over the failed enterprise of hand-spinning was a criminal waste.[60]

Taking up cudgels against khadi was limited not just to the legislatures; it also took the form of aggressive pamphleteering. The Bihar government's publicity department issued pamphlets giving reasons on the futility of the swadeshi movement.[61] It said that given India's insufficient textile production and limited industrial capacity, boycott would fuel cloth scarcity and civil chaos.

The Government of India went a step ahead and financed the publication of a bulletin on the Indian piece-goods trade prepared by one A. C. Coubrough.[62] It played safe, however, by distancing itself from the contents. The introductory note read: "Statement made and the views expressed in the bulletin are those of the

59 "Notes: How to Kill Swadeshi?", *YI*, 1 September 1921, *CWMG* 21: 33.

60 "Notes: Charkha in Madras Council", *YI*, 22 December 1921, *CWMG* 22: 83.

61 "Notes: Ten precious Reasons", *YI*, 3 November 1921, *CWMG* 21: 385.

62 "Indian Economics", *YI*, 8 December 1921, *CWMG* 21: 545.

author himself." But it did not escape the notice of the nationalists that the government financially supported its publication. The views in the bulletin went against the founding tenets of the khadi movement. It argued that the movement would fuel a prohibitive tariff and therefore would enrich Indian capitalists at the cost of the consumers. There was no competition between imported and indigenous fabric as they both catered to distinct tastes (there were contradictory claims by the central and the Bihar governments). The destruction of the spinning wheel was the inevitable outcome of advancing technology which mercilessly makes obsolete that which fails to keep pace. Farmers were ruined because of negligence of the once flourishing cotton culture in the country. Gandhi was wasting his efforts. Instead, he could advantageously advocate among agriculturists the cultivation of improved cotton. The report concluded patronisingly when it said:

> If instead of filling homes with useless charkhas he were to start a propaganda for the more intensive cultivation of cotton and particularly for the production of longer-staple cotton, his influence would be felt not only at the present day but for many generations to come.[63]

Gandhi saw the insults inherent in such government decrees as more humiliating for the nation than the physical oppression. In his strong indictment, Gandhi wrote: "Under the rule of Ravana, keeping a picture of Vishnu in one's house was an offence. It should not be surprising if in this *Ravanarajya* wearing a white cap, or not using foreign cloth, or plying the spinning wheel came to be considered as offences."[64] In the repressive gestures of the government lay fears that people were working towards economic freedom. Gandhi said the government "by book or by crook" was trying to put such people into jail. It

[63] "Indian Economics", *YI*, 22 December 1921, *CWMG* 22:83.

[64] "Notes: Ban on White Cap", *Navajivan*, 27 March 1921, *CWMG* 19: 482.

was, therefore, the duty of Indians to go to jail wearing pure white khadi. Gandhi admonished Malabaris for allowing their khadi cloths to be torn and burnt. It was cowardly, he said. "We ought to be ready always to lay down our lives for Khadi."[65] It was a religious duty. He did not want Indians to possess charkhas to worship them but to take the same work from them, which, as Maulana Mohammed Ali said in one of his speeches, the British government took from machine guns.

Conclusion

The khadi movement's citadel was the self. It included as much a sartorial as an ideological transformation. The non-cooperation movement emerged out of the khadi movement. "Swadeshi is your duty. Wear Khaddar. Non-Cooperation consists in doing all this", Gandhi said at Banaras.[66] The immediate aim of the non-cooperation movement was not "protest but purification".[67] It was through self-purification that purification of the other party was achieved. Non-cooperation was a programme of a simultaneous dismantling of institutions buttressing foreign rule and replacing them with indigenous ones. If boycott of institutions affiliated to British rule was its destructive part, khadi was its constructive agenda. It was a political movement demanding swaraj. But swaraj was not to be a project sponsored by a select few. It was to be an enterprise in which millions were to participate. In this enterprise an awakened self rather than a naked sword was required. "Do not draw the sword. Sheathe it. The sword will only cut our own throats", Gandhi cautioned at a public meeting.[68] If the sword were to win swaraj, the majority

65 "My Notes: Moplah Riots", *Navajivan*, 25 September 1921, *CWMG* 21: 204.
66 "Speech at Public Meeting", Banaras, 26 November 1920, *CWMG* 19: 33.
67 "Discussion aboard the Gurkha", 16 December 1920, *CWMG* 19: 130.
68 "Speech at Public Meeting", Banaras, 26 November 1920, *CWMG* 19: 33.

of Indians would remain perpetually "dumb, driven cattle".[69] Spinning was the alternative to the sword. It was the weapon of non-violence.

A violent route to the capture of the governing apparatus entailed permanent subservience of the non-participating majority to the violent minority. A violent path would only further perpetuate slavery and misery. Those who advocated violence desired centralisation of power in them. "They do not even know that their activities are bound to have this result....By our experiment in non-violence, we show even to the poor that, if they choose, they can display the same strength of their soul as an emperor can through his."[70] The enfranchisement of millions of Indians was possible only through a non-violent struggle. When it was argued that it was beyond the power of Indians to dethrone the British, Gandhi differed. "I believe", Gandhi iterated, "that every man or woman has in him or her necessary strength for winning Swaraj."[71] The power of conviction unleashed by Gandhi would take many a hue that in a year or so would surprise a good many sceptics.

The non-cooperation movement aimed at severing people's affiliation to government-supported institutions. One key aspect of the movement was to boycott the Legislative Councils. The Congress's old guards were generally opposed to such a move. They argued that the elected members would use their representative character to obstruct the council work. Their arguments fell flat as the movement's goal was not for the obstruction but complete paralysis of the government. The privileged political class opposed the non-cooperation movement as it demanded sacrifices, which had a measure of suffering inherent in them. "No nation", Gandhi said in a speech delivered

69 "Notes: Advice", *YI*, 1 December 1920, *CWMG* 19: 56.

70 "My Disappointment", *Navajivan*, 5 March 1922, *CWMG* 23: 9.

71 "Speech on Creed Resolution at Plenary Session of Congress", 28 December 1920, *CWMG* 19: 165.

at Chowpatty, Bombay, on 6 April 1919, "has risen without sacrifice."[72] Sacrifice is satyagraha. But sufferings and sacrifices were asked from the economically privileged, who had professions and enjoyed governmental patronage. It was this class of people also, which was the target of the khadi movement—strip off fineries, adopt the coarse. Thus, in the name of freedom and national reconstruction and in the name of swaraj, it was the upper crust that was implored to sacrifice their comfort, privilege, and professions, their titles and council memberships. The lowest bottom, inhabiting the margins of starvation and leading a life of eternal scarcity, contrary to the post-independence developmental experience, were not asked to make the sacrifice. Amin contends that in keeping the subalterns as mere spectators, Gandhi acted as a comprador.[73] By keeping subalterns confined to the project of spinning, Gandhi emaciated their revolutionary potential. But here Amin misses a vital point: Gandhi's demand of sacrifices from the affording class is symbolic of extremely progressive thinking.[74] It was Gandhi's way of breaking the complicity of the rich and educated classes in their exploitation of the poor and arousing them to their national responsibility. It was the affording middle class that was to perform penance. It was the moneyed men whose survival was linked to the Empire's security. It was they who had to withdraw their support to British imperialism. It is another matter that despite creating a rebellious and fearless environment around the country by his call, as the assessment made by various evaluators would later suggest, the movement attracted very few of those who were

72 "Speech at Chowpatty", Bombay, 6 April 1919, *CWMG* 15: 186.

73 Shaid Amin; "Gandhi as Mahatma: Gorakhpur District, Eastern UP, 1921–2" (1998).

74 Arundhati Roy has been one of the more recent writers to discuss, at a popular level, the plight of India's displaced. Others who have been writing for long are Smitu Kothari, *Whose Nation? The Displaced as Victims of Development*, 1996, in *EPW* (15 June): 1476–85.

actually targeted by the call. The non-cooperation movement died, as Gandhi had predicted, at the time of its launch, owing to the "poverty of response".[75]

Gandhi had perhaps anticipated Amin's charge but his reasons for the khadi movement were different. In hindsight, in the context of the post-independence plethora of development-induced displacement of marginalised people, legitimised in the name of "national interest", Gandhi's stand admits of a hierarchy based on ability to sacrifice. Ashis Nandy, writing on Tagore's novel *Ghare-Baire* says: "a nationalism which steam-rollers society into making a uniform stand against colonialism, ignoring the unequal sacrifices imposed thereby on the poorer and the weaker, will tear apart the social fabric of the country, even if it helps to formally de-colonize the country."[76] As the dependency of the politically aware class on colonialism is more than that of the poorer sections whose direct benefit accruing from colonialism is almost negligible, Gandhi asked for a proportionate sacrifice from the class that became rich and powerful during the colonial period.

Speaking in August 1920, Gandhi warned of the consequences if "classes" failed to abide by the first step towards the withdrawal of cooperation. "...If they fail in this primary duty, they will certainly fail in non-cooperation unless the masses themselves reject the classes and take up non-co-operation in their own hands...leaving aside the leaders...I want no revolution. I want ordered progress."[77] This "ordered progress" was only possible when the politicised section of the population, the literates, the middle class, take to suffering and sacrifices. It was they who had hitherto represented the mute millions to the government; it was they who had put forth sectional demands,

[75] "The Doctrine of the Sword," *YI*, 8 August 1920, *CWMG* 18: 134.

[76] Ashis Nandy, *The Illegitimacy of Nationalism*, 19.

[77] "Speech on Non-cooperation", Madras, 12 August 1920, *CWMG* 18: 152.

clothed as national aspirations, to the government. Gandhi therefore directed his appeal to this section of the population for the success of the first phase of the non-cooperation movement.[78]

But, Gandhi was soon to realise the folly of his assumptions. The reality of this "politicized class" confronted him during his nationwide tireless tour to garner support for the non-cooperation movement. To his shock, Gandhi found that the people were not the least enthused to abjure schools, law courts, or councils—the "three infatuations" he called them. He faced vociferous opposition to his idea of council-boycott, mainly from the aspiring politicians who wanted to enter the newly expanded council.[79]

It was an ironical situation. As his popularity—propelled by a combination of mystique, moral stature, and charisma—peaked among the "masses", his programme of non-cooperation contained little possibility of action for them. While his political base made a quantum leap among the illiterate and rustic rural masses, he demanded political action from only the literates, the minuscule but powerful middle class. The first phase of the non-cooperation, as Gandhi tirelessly reiterated, was directed to the "politicized class". To the newly emerging middle class, their very political awareness was a ladder for upward mobility and professional success. Given the restricted representation that was allowed at the time, reaching the rarefied environment of the Legislative Council was a realisation of ultimate social achievement. What he termed the "three infatuations" were the three most developed channels of upward mobility available in a restricted colonial environment. Gandhi was to painfully realise that his political colleagues lacked faith in the non-cooperation programme, or

78 "Boycott of Goods V. Non-cooperation Programme", *YI*, 25 August 1920, *CWMG* 18: 198.

79 Gandhi's imprisonment in 1922 debarred him from contesting elections for the council. His name had been struck off from Inner Temple rolls, disqualifying his eligibility for law practice (*CWMG* 27: 2).

had no capacity for sacrifice or suffering, or even sincerity of purpose. The non-cooperation movement despite getting mass sanctions, was tossed around and failed to achieve its objective. But the bold language that Gandhi used and the mass adulation he received created a climate in the country that bore rebellious portents. The masses with their perception understood Gandhi's message in their unique way.[80]

Gandhi was severely against political violence and brooked no concessions. Though no selfish consideration motivated him, he was aware that the first casualty to any such conflict would have been his own national leadership. Gandhi was cautious, as prior to the Congress's laborious approval, the strongest opposition to the non-cooperation programme came from those who expected violence breaking out in its wake. His earlier satyagraha against the Rowlatt Bills had ended up in a burst of violence and Gandhi had admitted his "Himalayan miscalculation". He firmly believed in the efficacy of non-violent non-cooperation and therefore he needed to assuage the concerns of the established politicians. He was also aware with a deep intrinsic knowledge that in a situation where violence gained freedom, the power instead of going to the masses would be concentrated in the barrel of the gun and its bearer. In that eventuality, it would unsettle the agenda of power to the people, perhaps forever. The non-violent non-cooperation movement was therefore an attempt to awaken the masses to a sense of their power.[81] In the project

[80] Shaid Amin, "Gandhi as Mahatma: Gorakhpur District, Eastern UP, 1921–2", in *Subaltern Studies III.*

[81] Such an understanding was inherent among the nationalist leadership as shown by Subhas Chandra Bose's presidential address at the Maharashtra Provincial Conference, Poona, on 3 May 1928. He said: "Mass consciousness has been roused in India, thanks to the extensive and intensive propaganda undertaken during the non-cooperation movement; and the mass movement can not possibly be checked now.

(contd.)

to achieve power for the people, he was ready to underplay his own role. "I see nothing but harm to the people and to me in my being looked upon as a giant. Instead of their believing that they got anything through my strength, it is much better that they should believe every achievement to be the result of their own *tapascharya* (penance) and self-purification."

But, ironically, the content of his appeal focused more on the abstract notions of identity, self-respect, honour, dignity, justice, etc. These were inspired by the insult of the Rowlatt Bills, the wounded honour of Punjab, and the betrayal of the Khilafat—subjects of concern more for the "politicized class" than for the masses who were more or less perceived to be "dumb, driven cattle".[82] The crux of political demagoguery during the non-cooperation movement lay in the hurt sentiment of national identity which catered more to the "politicized class". For the masses there was the regenerative agenda under the generic term of constructive work, which included spinning and weaving. It was only during later movements that Gandhi would openly incorporate the issues that really mattered at the grassroots and to the masses.

(contd.)

The only question is along what lines this mass consciousness should manifest itself. If the Congress neglects the masses it is inevitable that a sectional—and, I may say so, anti-national movement will come into existence and class war among our people will appear even before we have achieved our political emancipation. It would be disastrous in the highest degree if we were to launch class war while we are all bed-fellows in slavery, in order that we may afford amusement to the common enemy" (Sisir K. Bose and Sugata Bose 1997, 85).

82 "Non-co-operation is an attempt to awaken the masses to a sense of their dignity and power. This can only be by enabling them to realize that they need not fear brute force if they would but know the soul within" ("Advice", *YI*, 1 December 1920, *CWMG* 19: 56).

4 Ideology of Innocence

"A Proclamation of Ideological Independence"[1]

It was in *Hind Swaraj* that Gandhi first mentions the "ancient and sacred hand-looms".[2] The idea is presented at the beginning of his critique of the machinery that he held partly responsible for India's impoverishment. Although incorrectly understood at the time, Gandhi presents the idea on the culmination of two dominant but inter-connected themes that weave through the

[1] Dennis Dalton, 1993, *Mahatma Gandhi: Non violent Power in Action,* 16.

[2] M.K. Gandhi, *Hind Swaraj*, chapter 19. The edition of *Hind Swaraj* referred to here is from Anthony Parel, *Gandhi: Hind Swaraj and Other Writings.* Written in Gujarati in ten days, between 13 and 22 November 1909, on board the ship *Kildonan Castle* while returning to South Africa from Britain after an abortive lobbying mission, Gandhi's literary style in *HS* is something which he had perfected in SA where he, as an editor of *Indian Opinion* and as leader of the people, constantly felt the need to make his compatriots understand the motive of his actions. The form he adopted was of a dialogue. Earlier, in February 1908, he

(contd.)

text. The first asserts that the theoretical and institutional operatives—the philosophical, political, social, and economic—required to run a civilisation cannot be determined by factors shorn of what Ruskin terms "social affection".[3] According to the second theme, if the civilisation does turn into a "slavish" system, then only through the observance of the ideals of satyagraha or soul force—"it involves sacrifice of self"—as against the application of "brute force" can one re-establish the mores of morality in the civilisation gone astray. It is the morality of existence as well as of the struggle to exist that link the two themes. The core of *Hind Swaraj* wrestles with "the condition of India", as that is the name given to five of its chapters. Gandhi grapples with the issue of India's bondage, the ideology and strategy of the liberation struggle, and the content of freedom. It is in this context of India, its past civilisation and present "degeneration", its pristine "interior", and enslaved "educated" that *Hind Swaraj* advocates the morality of swadeshi.

Hind Swaraj is the document where Gandhi enunciates ethical principles of a desirable civilisation. "Read *Hind Swaraj*",

---

(contd.)

worked out a compromise formula with General Smuts of Transvaal, SA, on the law of compulsory registration by taking fingerprints. It eluded the comprehension of many of his compatriots. It was then for the first time he adopted the dialogue format to explain many of the contentious issues in his compromise (*CWMG* 8: 76–86). He would also write letters under his name to the self-edited *Indian Opinion* to answer many of the issues that would be raised by the correspondents. All to be better understood—a need that was acutely felt by the emerging leader who also had the benefit of editing a newspaper.

[3] John Ruskin's *Unto This Last* was paraphrased by Gandhi and published as a series of articles under the title of "Sarvodaya" in *Indian Opinion* in 1908 (*CWMG* 7: 240). Gandhi in his *Autobiography* describes Ruskin as "one of the three moderns…who made a deep impress on me". *Unto This Last* "brought about an instantaneous and practical transformation ... I arose with the dawn, ready to reduce these principles to practice" (*Autobiography*).

Mahadevan exhorted his readers, in the preface of *Dvija: a Prophet Unheard*, "if you love the human family and this earth which is our home."[4] In 1939, Gandhi asked the readers to see the booklet as "an attempt to see beauty in voluntary simplicity, poverty and slowness."[5] Critiqued by some as "a text for its times, not for all time",[6] *Hind Swaraj* has been called "a very basic document for the study of Gandhi's thought".[7] *Hind Swaraj*, "the seed from which the tree of Gandhian thought has grown",[8] encapsulates Gandhi's self-experience and learning gained through an intensely engaged life of twenty years in South Africa. But at the same time, one may, in sympathy with Gokhale's celebrated reaction, christen the thoughts expressed there as the youthful exuberance of an idealist considering the hardline attitude of Gandhi towards the technological development of the human race.[9] Gandhi was forty years old, just at the crossroads of his middle age, when he wrote *Hind Swaraj*.

Hind Swaraj, in brief, severely condemns modern civilisation as represented by the professions of medicine and law and

[4] T. K. Mahadevan, 1977, preface to *Dvija: A Prophet Unheard*.

[5] "The Unbridgeable Gulf", *Harijan*, 14 October 1939, *CWMG* 70: 242.

[6] Rajmohan Gandhi, 1995, *The Good Boatman: A Portrait of Gandhi*.

[7] Margaret Chatterjee, 1983, *Gandhi's Religious Thought*, 889.

[8] Anthony Parel, 1997, *Gandhi: Hind Swaraj and Other Writings*.

[9] Despite their mutual respect for each other, Gandhi's calling Gokhale to be his political guru and Gokhale's forewarning the country about Gandhi as its future man, the two differed on the vital questions relating to modern technology, Western education, and industrialisation. The first reaction of Gokhale's after he read *Hind Swaraj* was a mocking rejoinder in which he stated that the author would change his view in times to come. In order to avoid any backlash to his movement, Gandhi found it necessary to reiterate in a letter to Gokhale, "I do hope that my action in publishing *Hind Swaraj* in Gujarati and now the translation in English does not in any way affect the struggle that is going on in the Transvaal. The opinions expressed by me in the booklet are personal to me" ("Letter to G. K. Gokhale", 2 May 1910, *CWMG* 10: 239).

institutions such as the modern parliament and industrial society. Gandhi's condemnation of the "parasitical professions" of modern industrial society is on the plane of morality. Ancient India did not invent machinery as the society then was "all within bounds" held by its "moral fiber". But modern age has unhinged the professions and institutions, self and society from the self-cultivated restraints required by traditional morality. For example, the railways "today accentuate the evil nature of man" as "good travels at a snail's pace" whereas "evil has wings" seen in terms of the mobility the railways provide as a "distributing agency". The lawyers "profession teaches immorality; it is exposed to the temptations from which few are saved." The profession of medicine is "certainly not taken up for the purpose of serving humanity".[10]

During Gandhi's time in South Africa, he was much concerned about how he could lead the expatriate Indians' struggle to earn a dignified living in a foreign country. What ought to be the best method in this struggle to wrest initiative from the oppressing system? His search led him to an analysis of movements such as the suffragette movement, the struggle of English women to gain political rights[11], the Irish Sinn Fein—"exactly our Swadeshi

[10] In 1928, Gandhi suggests a reform in the professions of law and medicine. "I am strongly of the opinion that lawyers and doctors should not be able to charge any fees but that they should be paid a certain fixed sum by the State and the public should receive their services free" (*CWMG* 36: 84). *Hind Swaraj* had a controversial re-birth during the confrontational months of the non-cooperation movement. His Empire opponents tried to use the booklet as a wedge to divide the precariously built national unity (*CWMG* 19: 79). Gandhi minced no words in a rejoinder (*CWMG* 19: 78, 103, 169, 178). "What is that modern civilization? It is the worship of the material, it is the worship of the brute in us—it is unadulterated materialism, and *modern* civilization is nothing if it does not think at every step of the triumph of *material* civilization" (*CWMG* 19: 266).

[11] Gandhi's enthusiasm for women warriors fighting for their rights waned when, in 1909, he realised that their movement was "giving way to

(contd.)

movement",[12] the Hungarian effort to dislodge Austrian rule, and Thoreau's resistance against the American civil government in the form of not paying his taxes to protest against the "sin of slavery". A common strand found in all these varied struggles was the morality of suffering as well as sacrifices by the protagonists. The element of suffering and sacrifice was the "sword of ethics", as exemplified by Socrates, who was a "soldier of truth".[13] These were also the bedrock of satyagraha, Gandhi's own weapon in the moral battle for truth. Sacrifice, Self-denial, and Simplicity were also the cherished values behind the khadi campaign.

Gandhi's practice of paraphrasing important theoretical-inspirational literature for *Indian Opinion* readers gives an insight into his ideological development. As an editor, running a self-edited newspaper, he learnt the value of being a journalist and the need for effective and sustained communication. His well-directed and purposeful biographies of personalities from across the globe betrayed his own ambition as well as set a high moral standard for his readers.[14] In retelling the story of Egypt's famous

---

(contd.)

impatience". A movement from which he had drawn many inspiring lessons for his South African comrades, Gandhi noted, "For a certainty, they will suffer a set-back now" ("London", *Indian Opinion*, 23 October 1909, *CWMG* 9: 433).

12 "Benefits of Passive Resistance", *Indian Opinion*, 7 September 1907, *CWMG* 7: 213.

13 Gandhi introduced a series of articles in *Indian Opinion* titled "Story of a Soldier of Truth" in 1908 on the trial and rejoinder speech of Socrates in the city of Athens. Socrates was condemned to death by the elders for the alleged crime of treachery in his teachings. Gandhi wrote that "we must learn to live and die like Socrates" (*CWMG* 8: 173).

14 Gandhi profiled men of character who had traversed all odds and had become an inspiration for human society. Persons such as Maxim Gorky, Mazzini, Elizabeth Fry, Curzon, Lincoln, Tolstoy, Vidyasagar, Washington, Henry Lawrence, Horatio Nelson, Thomas Munro were a few of the people he wrote about. Their life stories were worth emulating. The

(contd.)

leader Mustafa Kamal Pasha or of Socrates, Gandhi eulogised their passion for patriotism and truth.[15] His concern for the moral and physical health of his readers was reflected when he paraphrased *Ethical Religion* by William Salter and wrote a series on naturopathy culled from various sources.[16] In 1908, Gandhi wrote a nine-part series titled "Sarvodaya" based on Ruskin's *Unto This Last* in the journal's Gujarati section.[17]

In presenting the series on "Sarvodaya", Gandhi questioned the assumption that trade and its concomitant practices was removed from human sensitivity or, in Ruskin's phrase, the *social affection*. "Why the assumption that a trader is always moved by self-interest?" was his main concern. "Why is it that trade is always associated with unscrupulousness?" he asked. If a soldier can sacrifice his life for his country, why can't a trader be expected to sacrifice his profit in the time of famine or a national crisis? Gandhi's paraphrasing of *Unto This Last* began with a critique of the principle that deemed pursuit of "the greatest good of the greatest number" as the correct path. Gandhi opposed this on moral grounds. Such a principle disregarded the rights of the minority while privileging those of the majority. It also did not believe in the inviolability of moral laws in pursuit of such an object. Therefore, in economic laws there is no consideration for the factor of social affection. The generally held assumption that the "science of economics" is independent of moral laws, Gandhi argued, was a fallacy. Unlike physical sciences, economics is a

---

(contd.)

recurrent themes in the stories of all the greats were their loyalty to parents and country, their dedication to work, and their high moral characters. Those character traits fascinated Gandhi and later shone most brilliantly on Gandhi himself (*CWMG* 15).

15 "Egypt's famous Leader - I", *Indian Opinion*, 28 March 1908, *CWMG* 8: 166.

16 "General Knowledge about Health", *CWMG* 11 & 12.

17 *Indian Opinion* published a series of articles on Ruskin's book. ("Sarvodaya", *CWMG* 8).

human-centric discipline and its governing axioms are different from those of physical laws. Arguing for the circulation of wealth among the people, he said, "The circulation of wealth among a people resembles the circulation of blood in the body".[18] Its concentration in a few individuals signals the sickness of society as a whole. It was an idea that inspired Gandhi, as one of the basics on which the khadi movement was built was its ability to distribute wealth among the largest possible people. Textile mills, in contrast, concentrated wealth on a few mill-owners.

The economics of khadi was not dictated by the principle of high profit and low wages. There is nothing more disgraceful, Gandhi wrote in *Sarvodaya,* than the principle of "buy in the cheapest market and sell in the dearest". The organising principle of the khadi economics was contrary to those enunciated by Adam Smith who considered the human element a disturbing factor in economic phenomenon. "Political economists assert that social affections are to be looked upon as accidental and disturbing elements in human nature; but avarice and the desire for progress are constant elements", Gandhi wrote.[19] He argued, "...it is this 'human element' on which the entire economics of Khadi rests". Generally accepted business practices, such as the "debasing of quality, adulteration, pandering to the baser tastes of humanity" had no place in the khadi organisation. The spinner is "not a machine" and therefore standards of production and quality control connot be uniformly fixed. Each piece of fabric is bound to have a unique texture and pattern. Khadi is a superior cloth as "it has a soul in it". The "art in Khadi appeal first to the heart and then to the eye". Ruskin, too, criticised the construction of a science of economics on the Newtonian model from which social affection had been wholly abstracted. Ruskin argued that the greatest art or science was that which

[18] "Savodaya-VI", *Indian Opinion*, 20 June 1908, *CWMG* 8: 303.
[19] "Interview to Khadi workers", 24 August 1934, *CWMG* 58: 353.

aroused "the greatest number of the greatest ideas".[20] Gandhi did not believe in the "heartless doctrine" of the greatest good of the greatest number.[21] He concluded that generally held economic principles, if followed, would make individuals and nations unhappy. [22]

He argued for the unquestioned validity of morality in all spheres of life, be it politics, religion, social institutions, human relationships or economic exigencies. Morality, Gandhi notes in his *Autobiography*, "is the basis of things" just as truth is the substance of all morality.[23] A good action is moral if performed with "good intentions".[24] But even an intentionally good action performed under duress or dread is amoral. In other words, an act to be moral should not only produce good results and be acted with good intentions, but it must be executed by the dictates of conscience, irrespective of the consequences.

As stated earlier, *Hind Swaraj* is a crystallisation of Gandhi's many-faceted ideological developments in South Africa. It was furthered in shaping Gandhi's conviction on non-violence. The application of the principle of non-violence in economics can be

20 "Sarvodaya-I", *Indian Opinion*, 16 May 1908, *CWMG* 8: 241.

21 "Letter to Jal A. D. Naoroji", 4 June 1932, *CWMG* 50: 15.

22 "That nation is wealthy which is moral...It is wrong normally for one nation to rule over another....Both those who manufacture gun-powder and those who fall victims to it suffer in consequence" ("Savodaya-IX", *Indian Opinion*, 18 July 1908, *CWMG* 8: 371–75). In an article written in London, Gandhi criticised the practice of adulterating food for profit. "The conclusion to be drawn is that the producers have their eyes only on profit and never care what harm they do to people. In this civilization, therefore, immorality presents itself as morality" ("Civilization or Barbarism?" *Indian Opinion*, *CWMG* 9: 424).

23 *Autobiography*, part I, chapter 10, *CWMG* 39: 33.

24 Gandhi summarised into Gujarati *Ethical Religion* by William MacIntyre Salter, the founder of the Society for Ethical Culture, Chicago, and published it in a series of eight articles in the Gujarati column of *Indian Opinion* in 1907.

found in the prevention of hoarding. Hoarding amounts to stealing from the socio-economic pool and thereby spreads inequality. Gandhi argued for renunciation of and contentment with a minimum of things. Unnecessary consumption brings violence against fellow beings. On the other hand, austerities, actuated by the ideal of non-violence and self-control, produce compassion. A compassionate person will never hope for profit from another's misery. "The science which tells us that America's need is our opportunity is a science not for men but for monsters."[25] It is not science that sees opportunity in somebody else's distress. Thus, it was with these principles, exemplified in him, that he approached the Indian people, whether they were mill-owners, merchants, middle class, or the bureaucracy. It was on these principles that the swadeshi movement, which was the ideological cover for the khadi movement, was founded. While building the khadi network, Gandhi repeatedly asked the cloth-merchants and mill-owners to observe morality in trading and manufacturing as they had invaded the niche market created by the national campaign with spurious khadi. The cloth merchants were selling mill textiles embossed with the stamps of Gandhi's face as swadeshi. In a cautionary article, *How to Guard Against Being Cheated?*, Gandhi wrote, "when the entire system of government is based on fraud, what else can we expect from people?"[26]

Gandhi's South African experience substantially contributed to the development of the swadeshi ideology. Here Gandhi witnessed the beginning of the protectionist embargo on free transcontinental movement of the people. Migration of people in search of economic benefit was regulated and restrained by

25 "My Notes: Hoarding of Cotton", *Navajivan*, 9 October 1921, *CWMG* 21: 270.

26 "Notes: How to Kill Swadeshi?", *YI*, 1 September 1921, *CWMG* 21: 33; also, "My Notes: How to Guard Against Being Cheated?", *Navajivan*, 7 September 1921, *CWMG* 21: 52.

policies of national interest and by the pernicious ideologies of race and apartheid. The only migration allowed, as a policy or surreptitiously, was for people who came as either slaves or indentured labourers. While migration was selectively embargoed, the principles of free trade with unhindered mobility of capital were forcibly imposed. Such policies and practices destroyed the native economy as their markets were swamped by cheap, industrially produced goods from the metropolis. In the precise phrase of Naoroji, it led to the "Drain of Wealth".

In response, Gandhi discouraged the out-migration of Indians. Even while in South Africa, he had written: "the condition of Indians in South Africa is pitiable. We go out to distant lands to make money…(but it) does not profit us as much as it ought to."[27] Earlier, however, Gandhi had taken along many of his young relatives to South Africa. He noted in his *Autobiography*, "I believed then that enterprising youths who could not find an opening in the country should emigrate to other lands".[28] But the plight of indentured labourers made him revise his opinion on immigration, and he was later responsible for its statutory abolition. His criticism of the system was on the plane of morality, patriotism, and economics.[29] Gandhi's struggle in South Africa was directed as much against the globalisation of capital as against the rich countries' threat to restrict the movement of labour to the boundaries of the nation-state. In it also lay an inspiration for swadeshi. In his view, the restoration of the charkha automatically solved the difficult problem of enforced emigration.[30]

[27] "Sarvodaya-I", *Indian Opinion*, *CWMG* 8: 240.

[28] *Autobiography*, *CWMG* 39: 202.

[29] "Emigration cannot solve the problem of Indian poverty" (*CWMG* 17: 9). Then again to V. S. Srinivasa Sastri Gandhi wrote: "I feel that we cannot countenance any emigration at the present moment. The environment in Fiji and British Guiana is reeking with the odour of indentured labour" (*CWMG* 17: 11).

[30] "Notes: Tamil Sister Again", *YI*, 25 August 1921, *CWMG* 21: 11.

Much before Gandhi, in the 1870s, swadeshi as a term, was in vogue in the writings of Gopal Hari Deshmukh a Maharashtrian reformer known by his pen name of Lokhitwadi. Then, during the anti-partition agitation in Bengal, it made its appearance as a political slogan. The real credit, however, for making swadeshi a part of the political agenda goes to Gandhi. He, by his writings and speeches, invested it with religious, political, and economic meanings. He exhorted "every man, woman and, child", "from the Viceroy down to the sweeper", to realise that it is through swadeshi that India would get swaraj. His swaraj traversed through swadeshi and was propelled with the power of satyagraha. It was swadeshi, the means, on which Gandhi rested every fibre of swaraj, which was the end.

Gandhi's swadeshi, like his other two ideological contributions of swaraj and satyagraha, has a specific Gandhian semiotic. Green, in his New Age biography of Gandhi deduces, "The Bengal agitation was something for Gandhi to learn from, when he began his own agitation in India a decade later."[31] Green goes on to say that Gandhi followed many a lead offered by the anti-partition movement, "for instance in dramatizing the issue of foreign imports, which he and the Bengalis fought with the cry of 'swadeshi,' homemade." However, the point that Green's allusion misses is that Gandhi's swadeshi was ideologically distinct from its earlier avatars. In 1905, the anti-partition agitation had given a spurt to the boycott of British goods and had encouraged Indian industrial productions.[32] In *Hind Swaraj*, Gandhi wishes that "If Bengal had proclaimed a boycott of *all* machine-made goods, it would have been much better".[33] Gandhi's concept of

[31] Martin Burgess Green, 1993, *Gandhi: Voice of a New Age Revolution*, 210.

[32] "Swadeshi movement of 1905–8 had no knowledge or organization behind it. It made the boycott of British cloth a shibboleth, and relied on the broken reeds of the mills of Bombay and Ahmedabad" ("Interview with a Friend", 15 May 1925, *YI*, 2 July 1925, *CWMG* 27: 103–05).

[33] Chapter 19, *Hind Swaraj* (Parel 1997).

swadeshi gradually evolved to primarily mean encouragement to struggling village industries.

In a remarkably cogent speech delivered to Christian missionaries in Madras, Gandhi gave meaning to his conception of swadeshi. It was the first major laying down of his thoughts on the subject. "Swadeshi", the written speech read, "is that spirit in us which restricts us to the use and service of our immediate surroundings to the exclusion of the more remote."[34] The principle applied to all segments of life—be it religion, economics, politics, or social institutions. Thus defined, the onus for its ceaseless application lay on the morality of the self rather than the external machinery of governance. And for the self to be awake to its application and also to the corrosive elements that accumulate with time, "an ever-increasing vigilance and searching self-examination" is required.

By constant redefinition and adjustments, the substance and practicality of swadeshi was determined. Gandhi's first emphatic step was to identify swadeshi with swadeshi in clothing to the exclusion of other commodities. Why did Gandhi confine swadeshi to clothing alone? The answer lay in Gandhi's analysis of the earlier swadeshi movement during the Bengal partition agitation of 1905. Then, swadeshi had spread itself too thin. "It is plain enough", Gandhi said in Ahmedabad while on a campaign tour, "that we cannot have everything swadeshi all at once"[35] for it would be impractical. India's manufacturing base then was too narrow to provide for everything that India needed. But there were other reasons, too, that restricted swadeshi to clothing alone.

Gandhi's analysis of Indian poverty led him to assert that the chief cause of poverty was due to a departure from the principles

34 "Speech on Swadeshi at Missionary Conference", Madras, *CWMG* 13: 219.

35 "Speech on Swadeshi", Bombay, 17 June 1919, *CWMG* 15: 376.

of swadeshi. In 1814, two crore rupees worth of hand-made cloth was exported from Calcutta alone. A hundred years later, in 1914, India imported sixty-six crore rupees worth of piece-goods. In a letter to Andrews, Gandhi asserted that only a reintroduction of the spinning wheel could ameliorate the sad existence of the poor. While spinning was a non-caste occupation and every home spun its own yarn, weaving was a caste occupation and every village had one or more weaver families devoted to meet this need. A revival of hand-spinning and weaving could distribute wealth from an occupation next in importance only to agriculture. Gandhi conceived swadeshi, as early as 1917 "as a religious principle to be followed by all".[36] He framed swadeshi vows to fortify religious resolve and asked the people to adopt swadeshi with "religious devotion". Framing of vows was the product of Gandhi's unique understanding of the Indian civilisation.[37] In Gandhi's conception, vows were imperative as man was constantly under strong temptation. The swadeshi vow was designed to impart "stability and firmness to one's

[36] "Speech at Gujarat Political Conference-I", 3 November 1917, *CWMG* 14: 48–66.

[37] He believed that India, contrary to the material West, was a country swathed in religious fervour. "India alone is the land of karma and the rest is the land of *bhoga*" ("Speech at Gujarat Political Conference-I', 3 November 1917, *CWMG* 14: 48). Properly channelled, religious fervour could bring about a positive and constructive turnaround of the Indian condition. "Be that as it may, this is the maxim of life which I have accepted, namely, that no work done by any man, no matter how great he is, will really prosper unless he has religious backing" ("Speech on 'Ashram Vows' at YMCA, Madras", 16 February 1916, *CWMG* 13: 226). In his conception, religion and politics led a symbiotic existence. "The latter divorced from religion is like a corpse only fit to be buried". Religion that he constantly referred to was not that which fomented sectarianism and neither did it spring from scriptural readings. "It is always within us, with some consciously so; with others, quite unconsciously" (Ibid).

character",[38] as "anything less than inflexible determination cannot be called a vow".[39]

By making people wear khadi, Gandhi desired a revolution in decentralised spinning. While the poor could use mill-made cloth, the affording middle class was to use khadi alone. To offset any immediate fear of a scarcity of cloth, Gandhi exhorted people to wear minimal clothing as an example in "self-denial and honesty"—men to be satisfied with just loincloths and women just enough to satisfy the requirements of modesty. When Bihar procured its cloth from Bombay, it was met with disapproval from Gandhi. It was swadeshi only when Indians began to use cloth produced in their own locality. "In days gone by we used to do like this and were not helpless." India must not baulk at using locally produced cloth irrespective of its quality. It was swadeshi dharma. "Coarse cloth is pure and sacred." Swadeshi means "you look after your needs". "My patriotism tells me that I must first make my own home independent, then my town and then my province." The spinning wheel appeared to Gandhi to be the only foundation on which village life could be rebuilt. It was the centre round which village reorganisation was aimed at.

Gandhi, with an arsenal of arguments, launched a massive khadi campaign. His propaganda was passionate. He travelled tirelessly, and though the content of his speeches remained the same, the language was moulded according to his audience. The educated and urbane were given a first-hand account of poverty. "Throughout my wanderings in India", Gandhi said at a political conference, "I have rarely seen a face exuding strength and joy".[40] In 1916, Gandhi visited Puri, the temple town of Orissa. Five years later he wrote of his visit: "I was prepared to see skeletons

38 "The Efficacy of Vows", *YI*, 22 August 1929, *CWMG* 41: 272.

39 "The Swadeshi Vow-I", 8 April 1919, *The Bombay Chronicle*, *CWMG* 15: 195.

40 "Speech at Gujarat Political Conference-I", Godhra, 3 November 1917, *CWMG* 14: 54.

in Orissa but not to the extent I did." Sometimes he quoted established names, such as Harold Mann on the four months of idleness prevalent in villages.[41] He quoted Hunter who had stated in 1880 that three crore Indians got only one meal a day comprising no more than plain bread and salt.[42]

Gandhi's most potent arguments came from the womb of history: a history written by Dadabhai Naoroji and R. C. Dutt. With their incisive analysis, both of them had made a whole generation of Indians take notice of the economic cost of imperialism. Gandhi acknowledged their contribution in shaping his thoughts in *Hind Swaraj*. In 1936, R. Palme Dutt wrote: "For two centuries, the history of Europe has been built up to a greater extent than is always recognized, on the basis of the domination of India."[43] This building of Europe was accompanied by a simultaneous under-development and destruction of the Indian economy. In 1915, India presented a spectacle of squalid poverty and mass misery. The population of India in 1901, as estimated by Daves, was thirty crore.[44] The distribution of wealth was brutally uneven.[45] The per capita national income for the

[41] Dr Harold Mann of the Poona Agricultural College, author of *Land and Labour in a Deccan Village*, had surveyed the conditions in a village near Poona and he had observed that a considerable part of the population was without work for a large part of the year and had to depend on daily labour, e.g., carrying milk to Poona, working in the Ammunition Factory, etc., and for the most part it was the males only who found work.

[42] Sir William Hunter (1840–1900) was a member of the British Committee of the Indian National Congress, London. A historian and an authority on Indian affairs, he served in India and was sympathetic to Indian aspirations. He was the author of *Indian Empire* ("Speech at Gujarati Bandhu Sabha", Poona, 8 August 1919, *CWMG* 16: 19).

[43] R. Palme Dutt, 1992, *India Today*, 8.

[44] Dharma Kumar, 1984, *The Cambridge Economic History of India, 1757–1970*.

[45] Statistics showed that 33.3 per cent of the wealth of the country was in the hands of one per cent of the population, the next 33. 3 per cent

(contd.)

year 1868, as noted by Naoroji in 1876, was 20 rupees.[46] In living conditions these figures mean what economists Shah and Khambata conclude that, "The average Indian income is just enough either to feed two men in every three of the population, or give them all two in place of every three meals they need [sic], on condition that they all consent to go naked, live out of doors all the year round, have no amusement or recreation, and want nothing else but food, and that the lowest, the coarsest, the least nutritious."[47] Indian life expectancy in 1911, as noted by census commissioners in 1921, was 22.59 years for males and 23.31 years for females.[48] Much of the Indian population was dying even before the full maturation of their youth. Out of a hundred thousand males born alive, the survivors between the ages of 30 and 40 numbered between 35,831 and 27,136. India had 18,658 people at the age of fifty, surviving out of a lakh born alive. Most fell to the "diseases of poverty".

It was a population that largely lacked remunerative employment. Yet every Indian in 1915 paid annually, on an average, two rupees towards the import of foreign cloth, while the majority of Indians earned daily anything between 0.04 to 0.20 paisa.[49] As a result, devastating famines were a recurring

(contd.)

in the hands of one-third of the population, and the balance in the hands of the rest (S. Daves, *Gandhiji and some of his thoughts*, 1948, xi).

46 Dutt., op. cit., 31.

47 Shah and Khambata, 1924, *The Wealth and Taxable Capacity of India*, 253.

48 S. Daves, op. cit., xi.

49 This was unofficial. Basing his calculation on the prices of 1946–47, A. Heston, draws a decadal per capita income chart from 1871 to 1946. In the 77 years, for which figures are given, India witnessed an increase of per capita income by 44 rupees (1871: 133.6; 1946: 177.4). It is a notorious fact that the figures for per capita incomes are drawn to serve vested purposes. According to Lord Curzon, then viceroy of India, the per capita income at the beginning of the century was 30 (base year

(contd.)

phenomenon that had led to increasing idleness of the rural population. The dying traditional occupations were not replaced by a new generation of employment opportunities. Gandhi repeatedly drew attention to this abysmally low income of Indians and to their dire straits.[50] "Today the most tragic result of the British rule has been that over 20 millions of the people of India remain in enforced idleness for six months in the year."[51] His aim was to provide employment to this idle population as a

---

(contd.)

1897–98). These however are only a gross average income, not the actual income of the overwhelming majority. Economists Shah and Khambata in their *Wealth and Taxable Capacity of India* (1924) showed that one per cent of the population got one-third of the national income, while 60 per cent of the population got 30 per cent of the income. This meant that for the 60 per cent or majority of the population any gross figure of the average national income per head must be exactly halved to represent what they actually got. Then the Lord Curzon's per capita income figure of 30 becomes 15. Thereby, it could be safely concluded that Indians in Lord Curzon's time received a daily income of 0.04 paisa. That was in the beginning of the century. In 1921, taking the base year of 1946–47 and drawing from A. Heston, the daily income of the majority of Indians came to 0.20 paisa. Now, even that too is an optimistic figure. From per capita figures one has to deduct the exorbitant Home Charges that were being siphoned off every year from India. While the majority of Indians earned anything between 0.04 to 0.20 paisa daily, only through the import of cloth were they made to pay two rupees every year. The Simon Commission in its official report quoted a highly inflated figure for the same. According to the report, published in 1930 but that based its calculation on the prices of 1921–22, the per capita income was about 116 rupees. That figure was not only fallacious but misleading, too, given its base of a post-war period, a decade prior to report writing. The prices immediately in the post-war period had witnessed a boom which was clearly not the case afterwards. Later, agricultural prices too collapsed bringing further hardship.

50 Gandhi advocated his stand for supplementary work through the saying, "an idle man ruins himself and his country" (*CWMG* 19: 131).

51 "Interview to Delhi Express", 15 September 1921, *CWMG* 21: 109.

supplement between the agricultural cycles. "I propose to utilise this spare time of the nation", Gandhi wrote to Paranjapye, "even as a hydraulic engineer utilises enormous waterfalls."[52]

Gandhi faced strident opposition to his attempts at reviving, as some said, the "rusticated spinning wheel".[53] Comrade M. N. Roy pilloried the khadi movement, asserting that it was a sheer "waste of energy".[54] Roy's critique contended that the peasant never got any idle hours for himself. "What leisure he has he needs." The peasants' four-month break was a much-needed respite from the toil of the previous eight months. Gandhi was accused of harbouring anti-industry ideas. His opposition to textile mills, machinery, and his occasional outbursts against the "material civilization" of the West gave credence to this opinion. Gandhi presented khadi and the charkha as an answer to the evil in industrialism. "I am hoping in faith that the Charkha will be universal in India, and that it will correct many evils of industrialism."[55] His opposition to industrialism was not taken kindly to by India's educated class. The Allahabad journal, *Leader*, contended that Gandhi was "putting back the hands of the clock of progress by attempting to replace mill-made cloth and mill-spun yarn by hand-woven and hand-spun yarn".[56] *The Servants of India*, a journal brought out by Gokhale's society, was constantly censorious of and sniping at Gandhi's arguments.[57] Many educated people, even some active khadi workers, thought industrialism as inherent to the inevitable march of superior technology. In the face of such a determined world force, the spinning wheel and all the sciences associated with it seemed incongruous. In intellectual circles, the charkha was disdained

52 "Letter to R. P. Paranjapye", 14 July 1919, *CWMG* 15: 459.

53 "The Music of the Spinning Wheel", *YI*, 21 July 1920, *CWMG* 18: 71.

54 "Waste of Energy?", *YI*, 21 August 1924, *CWMG* 25: 20–23.

55 "Interview to the Press", 13 November 1927, *CWMG* 35: 231.

56 "Swadeshi", *YI*, 18 August 1920, *CWMG* 18: 176.

57 "The Mists", *YI*, 20 April 1921, *CWMG* 20: 16.

for its monotony. It was intellectually unchallenging and was also insufficient to meet the challenge of import-substitution.

Gandhi's unstinted faith in the capacity of the spinning wheel to win swaraj did not carry sympathy with the intelligentsia. For Gandhi, a resolute India spinning with a purpose had political implications. For many in the intelligentsia, however, this relation was not so obvious. They saw in his insistence an attempt to foist *Hind Swaraj* on India as a manifesto of development. They ridiculed Gandhi's attempt to relate spinning to attainment of swaraj. "It is like running after a mirage", an exasperated critic contended.[58] A nationwide acceptance of the spinning wheel may bring in cloth sufficiency, but how would it change the claimants of power? The assumption that the universal adoption of khadi by the Indian population would sterilise British economic interest was misplaced. Only the fulcrum of interest would shift in Britain.[59] Gandhi's attempts to bend gender roles did not meet with much success either. In social consciousness, spinning was a womanly vocation. To men, its very mention insulted their sense of masculine self. In a society with deeply entrenched norms of gender roles, spinning would rightly be successful in crossing boundaries. Gandhi compared spinning to cooking, which in many homes men undertook though ordinarily it was conceived to be women's work. "Similarly, though the spinning wheel may be ordinarily for women, occasionally men also can work on it", he said.[60] If not for anything, it could be plied just for recreation, for "innocent pleasure", as a relief from pressing engagements.

On the charge of being opposed to textile mills, Gandhi said, "I have no quarrel with the mill." He was never direct in attacking mills and yet his strategies endangered their existence.

[58] "Some Doubts", *Navajivan*, 24 April 1921, *CWMG* 20: 31.

[59] "My Notes: Swaraj through Spinning Wheel", *Navajivan*, 8 May 1921, *CWMG* 20: 79.

[60] "What Should I Do?", *Navajivan*, 20 June 1920, *CWMG* 17: 495.

"With the success of Khadi the supremacy of the mill will surely end." Building new textile mills was not the solution. Indian mills would not solve India's curse of poverty; they would only accentuate it. Gandhi's main criticism against industrialism was its potential to accumulate wealth in few persons. He averred that his opposition to machinery was nothing to do with his pronounced antipathy to modern Western civilisation. "Here the question of West and East does not arise."[61] As khadi grew in its production and market penetration, Gandhi increasingly began to hit not only at "Manchester or Japan" but also at "Ahmedabad or Bombay". Mill textiles were to be shunned, whether they were produced abroad or were indigenously manufactured. For the record, he said, by advocating hand-spinning and hand-weaving, he was merely attempting to supplement mill production and achieve cloth self-sufficiency. The mills were not in a position to meet this challenge. Building new mills required a long gestation period and heavy investment, and made Indians technologically dependent on foreign powers. In contrast, hand-spinning and weaving had a short gestation period, required little capital investment, and needed only common sense expertise. Hand-weaving and mill-weaving were not complementary propositions. They were mutually antagonistic, for the tendency of weaving mills, like all machinery, being always to displace the product of hand. "I am not against the handloom", Gandhi said. "It will progress automatically if the spinning wheel succeeds. It is bound to die if the wheel fails."[62]

Gandhi's views on machinery have attracted reams of critical appraisal. He has been accused of being backward looking as far as science and technology are concerned. Gandhi's own opinion

[61] "Interview to Delhi Express", 15 September 1921, *CWMG* 21: 109.
[62] "Handloom V. Spinning Wheel", *YI*, 11 November 1926, *CWMG* 32: 23–26.

was that the increased application of machinery would keep the human race in "permanent slavery".[63] Gandhi envisioned a time when machines would fall to disuse owing to man's own weariness from its "maddening speed". His opposition to machinery was more to do with the quality of its end-use—"...whether these machines will be such as would blow off a million men in a minute or they will be such as would turn waste lands into arable and fertile land."[64] He was categorically opposed to labour-saving machinery that endangered livelihoods of people. His opposition too was India-specific. In answering the charge that he was conspiring against mills and manufacturing industries, Gandhi said: "Opposition to mills or machinery is not the point. What suits our country most is the point."

Keeping this ideal in view, Gandhi did not favour alteration in the design or technology of the spinning wheel till it was patiently tried out. This line of argument was misunderstood and he began to be seen as retrograde, as someone abhorring scientific quest. But he was also aware that the success of his movement was dependent on simple and quick-working machines for ginning cotton, making carding easy, and enhancing the yield of the spinning wheel and loom. Gandhi therefore sought to correct the misconception. Technological improvements were inevitable, he argued. But it was to be qualified with criteria of suitability and simplicity. Technological suitability for the spinning wheel required it to increase the quantity for the same revolutions per minute (rpm) so that spinners' income would increase. He commissioned individuals and institutions to introduce improvements. With the money offered by Rwashankar Jagjivan Mehta, his old benefactor, Gandhi instituted an award

[63] "Letter to Maganlal Gandhi", after 1 June 1919, *CWMG* 15: 340.

[64] "Pure swadeshi is not at all opposed to machinery. I am not opposed to the movement of manufacturing machines in the country. I am only concerned with what these machines are meant for" ("Swadeshi V. Machinery?" *YI*, 17 September 1919, *CWMG* 16: 135).

of Rs 5,000 for the best invention of a "suitable" spinning machine.

In July 1920, Ganesh Bhaskar Kale of Dharwar, announced a new spinning wheel that met the specifications required by the prize. Gandhi was excited at the prospect. He reached Ahmedabad to meet Kale who had come from Dharwar. Later after a week Gandhi wrote to Maganlal, "I am simply in love with the spinning wheel and Kale". "In a short-time", Gandhi declared enthusiastically, "India will possess a renovated spinning wheel—a wonderful invention of a patient Deccan artisan."[65] Kale said that it was made of cheap and simple material, was uncomplicated, yielded more yarn per rpm, and was suitable for any age group or gender. Gandhi instructed Maganlal to write a biographical note on the inventor, name the wheel "Gangabai Spinning Wheel" (and in case of any disagreements to be named after Kale himself) and apply for a patent. "Do not delay the application for the patent", Gandhi wrote to Maganlal somewhat impatiently.[66] Gandhi hoped to employ Kale's invention to enhance the quality of yarn produced. He wished to experiment with its efficiency and its capacity to run for eight hours at a stretch. Euphoria, however, was short-lived as a later report indicated the shelving of Kale's machine.

In the 1930s, a prize was again announced for the most suitable charkha. This time the prize money offered was for Rs 100,000, and the competition was open to all, including foreign nationals. The condition for wining the contest lay in the invention of a faster charkha, but it would also have to fulfil other specified criteria. The conditions were: easy portability, capable of being worked by hand or by foot in an ordinary Indian village home, availability at a price not exceeding Rs 150, and a working life of about twenty years. The replacement charges

[65] "The Music of Spinning Wheel", *YI*, 21 July 1920, *CWMG* 18: 72.
[66] "Letter to Maganlal Gandhi", 18 July 1920, *CWMG* 18: 62.

of worn-out parts per year were not to exceed five per cent of the cost of the machine. In response, in 1934, Kale' again made a bid with the backing of Kirloskar. Gandhi was reluctant to entertain this but was persuaded by friends to test the machine himself. Gandhi wrote to Kirloskar to send the machine. The machine while having longevity was lacking in easy mobility and portability. This effort too was abandoned midway.[67]

Even in 1921, prior to the institution of the award, there were sporadic reports of artisans working to improve the wheel. Some aimed at durability and portability, while others worked to improve the yarn output per rpm by increasing the number of spindles. In Broach, two-spindle spinning wheels were being used. In Punjab, a craftsman from Ludhiana made a ten-spindle spinning wheel. But its drawback, despite being "simple and cheap", was that it could not spin simultaneously on all the spindles.

In the beginning of 1921, Gandhi found a machine in Surat invented by a school dropout. The model used less wood and was capable of more revolutions. While touring Punjab, Gandhi found decorated spinning wheels made of a variety of ebony. Their handles were skilfully and artistically designed and painted. Expensive models had handles inlaid with ivory. Some had small mirrors in their wheels while others had small bells. Gandhi advised Maganlal to consider the size of the Punjab spinning wheel, which seemed to be the ideal one to him. Shankarlal made the Gandiva spinning wheel, which at first drew unfavourable comments from Maganlal. On further trials, however, it was found to be as efficient as the ashram model. The model cost only one and a half rupees.

In September 1921, a spinning wheel exhibition was held at Calcutta's National College. There were about fifteen types of

[67] "Letter to Satish Chandra Dasgupta", 13 November 1934, *CWMG* 59: 336; also, "Letter to Kirloskar Brothers", 24 November 1934, *CWMG* 59: 399.

spinning wheels. The ingenious devices they displayed were endless. Some were so small that they could be carried in a little box. One could be put in a chest, while another was fitted with a musical instrument. Yet, they lacked the capacity to produce as much yarn as the conventional type. An improved spinning wheel with many spindles was exhibited at the Ahmedabad Congress in 1921. It was perhaps the most successful of all the efforts hitherto made.

The only consolation from the spate of spinning wheels that were being exhibited all over the country was that the spinning wheel now had become popular and that improvements in the existing type were exercising the ingenuity of many minds. The price of the spinning wheel had doubled within six months. Generally a good painted spinning wheel carried a price tag of about fifteen rupees. Gandhi however warned the public not to waste their energy in waiting for a "revolutionary Charkha". Instead, he called for all energy to be devoted towards making "the ancient pattern more durable and cheap and portable".[68] But that did not exclude innovation or scientific quest. Maganlal was told to "find out the difference between the method of spinning which Lakshimdas teaches and that which you do, and adopt the one which is scientific."[69]

[68] "Notes: New Spinning Wheel", *YI*, 19 January 1922, *CWMG* 22: 226.
[69] "Letter to Maganlal Gandhi", 16 March 1921, *CWMG* 19: 439.

5 Clothing the Congress

A Mobilisational Relevance: Self, Sacrifice, and Society

On the eighth day of February 1929, Rasik, Gandhi's grandson, died of typhoid in Delhi. Rasik was Gandhi's eldest grandson, the child of his derelict son Harilal. Rasik died at the age of seventeen in Delhi where he had gone to assist his uncle, Devdas, Gandhi's youngest son, who was then teaching a course in spinning at the fledgling Jamia Milia Islamia. While Rasik's father had turned into a tragic but fallen rebel, his mother had died when he was a toddler. Rasik had been nurtured in the ashram, imbibing what Gandhi had thought was the best education. He had become an expert spinner and carder and had won accolades for his skills during the national spinning week. In Rasik, a grandfather saw the embodiment of his own childhood, reviving many memories of Gandhi's adolescence. Gandhi's childhood friend, Sheikh Mehtab, who later also came to stay with him in South Africa, occasionally wrote poetry but under the pseudonym "Rasik". Gandhi had great hopes for Rasik and in his tribute to him wrote that he was "a boy of much promise".[1]

When Rasik died, Gandhi was in Sind, campaigning for the charkha and khadi fund. Since his release from jail in 1924, Gandhi had been ceaselessly travelling across the country as an ambassador of khadi, exhorting people to spin, organising sales, inaugurating exhibitions, straightening hurdles, massaging egos, collecting funds, and writing in his "viewspaper" all that he saw, thought, and was informed about. In the beginning of 1927, Gandhi wrote to his ashram inmates that he "must wander about in the interest of khadi".[2] He travelled third class in trains, which he had resumed after a stint of travelling second class during the heady days of non-cooperation. His needs were frugal; he ate and dressed minimally. There were times when his exertion brought him to the edge of death. Yet, he recovered to undertake more travels, more speeches, and more of everything. His excesses upon his body were proportional to the pain that his immediate surroundings inflicted upon him. Upon hearing the news of Rasik's death, Gandhi refused to alter or abandon his tour programme. "My day's work goes on uninterrupted", he wrote to Mirabehan informing her of Rasik's untimely demise.[3] He conceded the pain but termed it "selfishness".

In embracing death, Rasik was not alone. Many khadi workers perished while engaged in campaign and operational work. Driven by Gandhi's moral call, young people took to working for the cause of khadi. Not only were the working conditions difficult, depressing, and demanding, but most of the work was meagerly paid. It was only idealism coupled with inspiring leadership that kept their spirits high, but that often cost them their

[1] "A Boy of Much Promise", *YI*, 21 February 1929, *CWMG* 40: 13.

[2] "Letter to Ashram Women", 24 January 1927, *CWMG* 33: 6.

[3] "Letter to Mirabehan", 9 February 1929, *CWMG* 39: 431.

health. Diseases such as malaria could easily strike their weak bodies. To the young men who succumbed to exhaustion and inhospitable conditions, Gandhi paid glowing tributes and wrote their obituaries. He devoted considerable space in his journals to commemorate the sacrifices and steadfast devotion of the khadi workers. They were Gandhi's silent workers, scattered all over the country, carrying out his bidding in utter anonymity. "No country", Gandhi wrote in one such tribute "possesses a record of the names of its noblest sons." There are many young people who die in the service of their country and yet remain unknown. "They", Gandhi further wrote, "are known only by their works like the authors of the most valuable ancient books."[4]

Gandhi advised the workers to be without worry. He was particularly concerned about the health of his Bengali colleague, Satish Chandra Dasgupta, who prior to his involvement with the Khadi Prathisthan had worked as a chemist and had earned a handsome salary. But after he had joined the khadi movement, the pressure of slow-moving work weighed heavily upon him. He often sank into sad and sullen moods. Gandhi wrote to him advising restraint and asking him to read the *Gita*. "Whatever the cause, you dare not be moody or morose. You and I and several others have embarked upon a work of service the equal of which I do not know in the whole world. The greater the service greater the suffering required...do you know the song 'Cheer, boys, cheer, no more of idle sorrow?'".[5] Then another time Gandhi wrote, "What does it matter if Khadi lives or perishes?".[6] "Do not be anxious about Khadi or the Pratishthan". After Maganlal's death in 1928, Dasgupta offered to take his place though his own health was fragile. Gandhi declined the offer saying, "Best service you can render today is to build up

[4] "Notes: A Silent Worker", *YI*, 26 November 1925, *CWMG* 29: 274.
[5] "Letter to Satish Chandra Dasgupta", 1 January 1926, *CWMG* 29: 370.
[6] "Letter to Satish Chandra Dasgupta", 19 July 1927, *CWMG* 34: 200.

your body so as to spare me another shock".[7] Dasgupta's own son died in 1934 and, as Gandhi said, "he did not give up spinning on his Charkha for a moment even when he heard the news of the death of his son."[8]

When the going got tough or the task seemed uphill, the Mahatma fought to reinstate faith in khadi as much in himself as in his colleagues. "Do not admit defeat", Gandhi wrote to a despondent co-worker, "this work is a kind of *tapascharya*".[9] He said the spinning wheel was "a gateway to my salvation". Despite being ridiculed by the critics, he persisted and reiterated, "I think of the poor of India every time that I draw a thread on the wheel".[10] He saw in khadi a force of truth worth pursuing despite barriers and frustrations. "We do not give up our faith in truth, or forsake its practice or its propagation, even if the whole world habitually speaks untruth", he wrote in a letter to a colleague.[11] When Mirabehan requested the English translation of the *Gita*, Gandhi refused her and said spinning was the "applied translation" of the *Gita*.[12] She had tried many experiments to develop a suitable spinning wheel.

Gandhi's travels throughout the period were in the cause of Daridranarayana, the poor. Khadi was the instrument of propitiation. Most of his travels after 1926 were "purely a business and businesslike tour".[13] Each leg of his national tour began with the proclamation: "I have come here to do business—to

[7] "Telegram to Satish Chandra Dasgupta", 25 April 1928, *CWMG* 36: 260.

[8] "Speech at Kendrapara", quoted in *Anand Bazar Patrika*, 29 May 1934, *CWMG* 58: 39.

[9] "Letter to Mathuradas", 20 June 1927, *CWMG* 34: 31.

[10] "My Kamdhenu", *YI*, 20 May 1926, *CWMG* 30: 308.

[11] "Letter to Mathuradas", 20 June 1927, *CWMG* 34: 31.

[12] "Letter to Mirabehan", 14 July 1930, *CWMG* 44: 20.

[13] "Speech at Public Meeting", Vizagapatam, 28 April 1929, *CWMG* 40: 302.

collect money for Charkha and Khadi and to sell Khadi."[14] At his public gatherings, he would ask audiences to contribute to the khadi fund and then invite them to buy khadi from the nearest production centre. In every place he toured, he specifically sought out information regarding the number of working wheels and looms, monthly production of yarn and khadi in quantity and value, monthly sale of khadi produced, the number of habitual wearers of khadi, and the number of self-spinners, etc. Gandhi also carried a quantity of khadi with him to sell at meetings and at railway stations. "Empty your pockets for the poor", was his short message. People came to his public meetings, walking miles and carrying their charkhas in a show of solidarity. He held himself "a humble trustee for the millions of paupers of India". In his public meetings, he spoke of the "skeletons" of Orissa and its "death-like quiet", which reminded him of his first introduction with the real India at Champaran. He exhorted his audience to adopt khadi, as that would establish their bond with the "dumb millions". Chettiars of Madras were requested not to "wear wealth so loudly", and he pleaded for their acceptance of khadi. He implored his audience for the speedy acceptance of khadi in order to relieve him from "*bania*" work.[15] According to him, its tardy acceptance was consuming his energy and undermined his actual potential.

The clothing needs of different cultures became an obsession with Gandhi. The inferences he drew in scrutinising cultural codes of dress helped him to further the cause of khadi. Gandhi saw an opportunity in the frugal clothing needs of the people of Malabar. In Sri Lanka he compared the dress of its inhabitants with those of Malabar. "Women's dress here is very simple", his ashram women were told. "It may be said that men and women dress practically in the same way. Only, the dhotis here are dyed

[14] *YI*, 1927–28, 29, quoted in *Freedom Movement in Bihar*, vol. 1, 476.

[15] "Speech at Public Meeting", Vizagapatam, 28 April 1929, *CWMG* 40: 302.

and have various designs on them. Both wear jackets, though there is a slight difference in cut. Women are never without jackets, whereas men are content often to come out with only dhotis on. These clothes are bound to be very cheap. Only if people begin to take a liking for khaddar, there will be no difficulty for them to adopt it." Lajpat Rai was told of the role khadi played in breaking caste segregation. "I want you for Khadi", he wrote to Rai, "I know what a gain it would be."[16] He wished to enlist Rai as a convinced "fellow-worker who would be working for the cause of Khadi to the best of his ability". At another time he wrote that he needed Rai "not as a distant admirer", but someone who gave his "heart and soul" to the khadi movement.[17] To Viceroy Lord Irwin, Gandhi sent Gregg's *Economics of Khaddar*. He humbly wrote in an enclosed letter, "you were good enough to say that when you had more leisure you would like to discuss the potency of Khadi with me. If you have the leisure and still the inclination I am at your service."[18]

The ambition to influence both "the classes and the masses" is an oft-repeated phrase that remained with Gandhi forever. His nationwide tours and speeches, his writings in his journals, which were now three in number and published in English, Hindi, and Gujarati were some of the tools of publicity. He used self-edited journals from a very early stage, as the editor of the *Collected Works* notes, for "establishing an intimate and clean bond between the editor and the readers".[19] Imperatives of the movement made him launch journals exclusively devoted to khadi. It was Maganlal Gandhi who primarily supervised this work. The *Khadi Samachar Patrika* was one such journal edited by Maganlal and published from the Sabarmati ashram. Then, there

16 "Letter to Lajpat Rai", 29 April 1928, *CWMG* 36: 283.
17 "Letter to Lajpat Rai", 12 May 1928, *CWMG* 36: 311.
18 "Letter to Lord Irwin", 26 April 1928, *CWMG* 36: 272.
19 Preface to volume 4, *CWMG* 4: viii.

was the *Khadi News Centre*, which issued leaflets with relevant data about khadi production and sales. "Publicity is of the greatest importance for stimulating production as well as sales", Gandhi wrote.[20] There were special drives for the production and sales of khadi during such nationally recognised periods as the Sataygraha Week that fell in April or the Gandhi Month that began with the Mahatma's birthday in October. In these periods, concentrated efforts were made to increase production and sales of khadi throughout the country.

In March–April 1930, a sixty-year-old Gandhi, weighing forty-five kilograms, marched out of the Sabarmati ashram to Dandi, a seaside village on the western coast, with a bamboo shaft in hand, two cloth bags dangling on either side with straps crossed over his bare chest, and eighty-one of the ashram inmates as walking companions. This was the famous Dandi March that culminated in the breach of the salt law and that launched the civil disobedience movement. Of the eighty-one companions, the majority was associated with the work of khadi; twenty-five were khadi students. "The army was dressed in a uniform of sorts—one denoting humility. The clothes were of Khadi, and included the familiar *Gandhi cap*."[21] In most villages, marchers were accommodated under a canopy made of khadi. A bullock cart accompanied the march, acting as a mobile khadi sales office. It also carried charkhas used by marchers for their daily spinning. The charkhas, as Weber shows, were large and cumbersome and of the Bardoli make. Daily spinning by the marchers was part of their discipline. At every village he halted at on his way he enquired of its record on khadi. He expected the marchers to collect information related to khadi from each of the villages where they halted. A questionnaire had to be

[20] "Accused Judging", *YI*, 21 June 1928, *CWMG* 24: 439.

[21] For detailed study of day-to-day progress of the March see *On the Salt March* by Thomas Weber, 1997.

answered on the number of spinning wheels available in the village, monthly consumption of khadi by villagers, number of people exclusively wearing khadi, etc.

Gandhi required such information to be given to him immediately after his arrival in the village. These statistics, besides the general issue of the grievous salt law, formed the starting point of his speeches. At many of the villages he was disappointed that there was no consumption of khadi, no habitual wearers of khadi, nor even any spinning wheels at work. He openly criticised the villagers for the dearth of users of khadi and spinning wheels among them. "Those of you", he said, "who do not enlist as soldiers of Swaraj should at least wear Khadi." Later, however the momentum generated by the march brought an increased consumption of khadi. The mobile khadi shop began doing good business. Khadi during these tumultuous days regained its rebellious and fashionable symbolic status. Soon, however, as its demand peaked, its supply reduced, and Gandhi had to ask the people to buy less and consume less.

Having released an unprecedented flood of popular energy, which was still rising at the time of his arrest on 5 May 1930, Gandhi showed no further concern for the subsequent course of the movement and concentrated his thoughts on spinning. He felt that he had been slack outside the jail in mastering the art and science of spinning, which he regarded as a "daily *maha-yajna*", a supreme collective effort. Spinning was a part of his "spiritual discipline"; it was an "applied translation" of the *Gita*, his spiritual reference book.

The Yeravda Jail, called a *mandir*, a temple, by Gandhi, became after his arrest in 1930 a spinning abode. Once there, he religiously spun a fixed quantity of yarn every day. Spinning a targeted quantity of yarn required Gandhi to sit in the same posture for hours at a stretch. At the age of sixty-one, Gandhi found it physically strenuous to accustom his body to the demanding schedule of spinning. First his elbow caused him some trouble. Doctors diagnosed it as a case of "tennis-elbow", the result of continuous spinning for years, and they advised rest. His comrades sent him different kinds of wheels to ease the strain. But none matched his requirement of a wheel that yielded the designated amount of yarn and that, at the same time, reduced his hours of spinning. He began to use the paddle charkha that could be run by foot. It gave rise to rumours that Gandhi had taken to using a sewing machine after being disillusioned with the slowness of the charkha.

His passion was also to spin finer counts to reduce the consumption of slivers. He, however, was unable to meet his own expectations. "I am a lame duck in so far as spinning is concerned", Gandhi admitted in exasperation to an ashram colleague.[22] His spinning was slow. "I love it, I work hard and pay great attention to it but the speed simply does not increase." But, soon Gandhi reported to Mirabehan, with whom he always exchanged ideas on spinning, that though his mastery over the wheel was increasing, yet there was much room for improvement. "The Charkha, the takli and the bow have become a fascination with me".[23] Later he wrote, "I am making daily progress and do not know what fatigue is on the wheel".[24] At yet another time he wrote her, "The wheel and thinking about it make the time fly".[25] Gandhi also made many discoveries relating to the spinning process. He discovered that a good carding did not necessarily result in even yarn. The drawing of even yarn was dependent not on carding alone but it was also an art by itself. Hand-spinning was dependent on the deftness of one's fingers. A part of the yarn that Gandhi spun while at Yervada was used for weaving Kasturba's sari.

[22] "Letter to Narandas Gandhi", 3–5 August 1930, *CWMG* 44: 68.

[23] "Letter to Mirabehan", 7 September 1930, *CWMG* 44: 127.

[24] Ibid., 28 September, 178.

[25] Ibid., 14 September, 145.

With such intense industry, sacrifice, and suffering, not only was the khadi movement built but mass consciousness, too, was aroused. It was a unique way of bringing mass participation to a culture that traditionally scorned such a show of communal industry. It was a way to political mobilisation in a socio-cultural context that reserved the domain of macro-polity, governance, and economics primarily to elite manoeuvering. Gandhi drew the masses into building the destiny of the nation. In this conception, swaraj was not limited to traditional elites but was raised from below. Its prime beneficiary was the Congress, which was transformed into a movement from that of a debating club. It is another matter that circumstances conspired to marginalise not just the Mahatma but also the grassroots mobilisation on the issue of livelihood rights. In post-independence India, the mobilisation came to proximate a shriller rhetoric and was borne out of the creation of the otherness.

Gandhi and the Congress: Contrary Agenda, Conflicting Mores

In early 1924, Gandhi was released from prison owing to ill-health. His release coincided with the raging issue of the day: elections to the council. He was against the Congress's participation in the elections; doing so was in contravention of the principles of non-cooperation, he argued. There was a section of Congress politicians who were opposed to this viewpoint. They drew their legitimacy from the fact that they were headed by Motilal Nehru and Chittaranjan Das. They were politicians who, earlier, during the non-cooperation movement, had at first adopted a wait-and-watch policy and later had triumphantly declared the movement a failure. Now, they wanted to effect swaraj from within the legislatures. For this purpose, and faced with opposition from Gandhi loyalists, they had formed a separate Swaraj Party. The manifesto of the new party, which was issued in October 1923, projected the party as "a party within the

Congress, and as such an integral part of the Congress".[26] The No-changers, as Gandhi's loyalists to this issue were known, were said to have supported Gandhi's views on the course of the national struggle. Gandhi was against lending the name of Congress to the Swarajists' cause. He wanted a continuation of the Congress agenda of non-cooperation, whereas the Swarajists wanted its repeal. He talked of the "fundamental difference" that existed between him and the Swarajists. "The Swarajist method", he said, "cultivates British opinion and looks to the British Parliament for Swaraj. The No-change method looks to the people for it."[27] Gandhi did not completely deny the importance of the council. His premise, however, was that it was of no consequence to the masses. Subsequently, a compromise was worked out. In reality, it was what Gandhi wanted. He asked the dissidents to work out their council-entry programme through the Swaraj Party, while, the Congress was to be left alone for carrying on with the khadi programme.

He proposed four resolutions to that effect at the All India Congress Committee (AICC) meeting in Ahmedabad in the last week of June 1924. The first of the four resolutions was the spinning resolution, which asked each delegate to the representative Congress bodies (such as the AICC, CWC, or provincial Congress committees) to spin daily for half-an-hour. And, to "ensure that appearance corresponds to reality", the handspun yarn (at least two thousand yards) was to be sent to the manager of the Khadi Board.[28] The frequency of dispatch was on a monthly basis, failure of which attracted a penalty of voluntarily giving up membership. The second resolution further tightened the noose. It prohibited any dereliction of central instructions by provincial Congress members. The third resolution

[26] Quoted in Bandhu, 2003, *History of Indian National Congress, 1885–2002*, 108.

[27] "Defeated and Humbled", *YI*, 3 July 1924, *CWMG* 24: 339.

[28] "Maha Gujarat's Duty", *Navajivan*, 8 June 1924, *CWMG* 24: 209.

was to cleanse Congress executive bodies of members who neither spun nor wore khadi. Only those who believed in the creed of non-cooperation and khadi were to remain in the Congress; it facilitated efficient functioning, he argued. Those who lacked faith in khadi were to resign of their own volition. Why cling to a position if the efficacy of the programme laid out by the Congress was doubted, he asked? The three resolutions effectively defined Gandhi's aggressive posture in the face of "camouflage and make-believe". It was an attack on "lip-loyalty".[29]

It was, however, the fourth resolution that showed how deep the wedge was. It was concerning Gopinath Saha, a revolutionary, who in his patriotic zeal had murdered an English officer. Saha was later condemned to death. Bengalis eulogised his act and Chittaranjan Das blessed a resolution in the provincial Congress paying homage to the hanged revolutionary. It was a direct challenge to Gandhi's creed of non-violence. He had been asserting that the phrase "peaceful and legitimate" in the Congress constitution effectively meant "non-violent and truthful". But none had heeded his repeated entreaties. There were other Swarajists who were raucously belligerent. Some insinuated the inevitability of "fratricidal struggle" in the Congress given Gandhi's hold on the organisation.[30] Gandhi did not relent. At Ahmedabad, in his fourth resolution, he condemned the culture of political violence. All four resolutions were potentially divisive. Not since 1920, did the Congress have such a face-off with its destiny. It was the moment of denouement, a time of trial.

Gandhi continued with his relentless pursuit for the acceptance of his agenda. Just prior to the meeting of the AICC, he wrote an open letter to its members.[31] At the very outset, he declared: "I believe in Khaddar. I believe in the spinning wheel". He went on to repeat what he had been saying since he had begun to

29 "Notes: An Appropriate Query", *YI,* 12 June 1924, *CWMG* 24: 233.
30 "Interview to *The Times of India*", 5 June 1924, *CWMG* 24: 203.
31 "Open letter to AICC Members", 26 June 1924, *CWMG* 24: 285.

unfold his "primary aims". Khadi's adoption would obliterate foreign self-interest. It would sensitise the educated about the starving millions. In short, "It is life giving." The resolutions, he said, were a "mild minimum" for the attainment of swaraj. He said that as leader of the movement he needed to employ such measures. His iron fist was shown but in the same polite way. If the resolutions meant mutual bitterness, if it meant parting of ways, he would accept these with equanimity, he said. But if he must lead the Congress then he must have his "instruments". Congressmen "must either choose another leader or accept my condition". If he was not given his way, he was ready to form another organisation outside the Congress to work out his programme. He was prepared to leave the Congress but not abandon khadi. The game was checkmated, and the Congress caved in. The threat brought a laboured truce, but the division was very apparent.

Politics is nothing if not a game of brinkmanship; it is also one of biding one's time. Soon, Gandhi was outmanoeuvered. When it came to the penalty clause attached to the spinning resolution, Swarajists abstained from voting, exposing chinks in Gandhi's armour. Though Gandhi's resolution was carried in by 67 votes against 37, with Swarajists protesting through absence, his vulnerability was obvious. If the Swarajists had voted he could have been easily outnumbered. He bowed to their demand and with some chivalry rescinded the penalty clause from the spinning resolution. The Swarajists had extracted their price. The spinning resolution no longer had any teeth. It became a mere policy statement worth not even the paper it was written on. Gandhi was left in the lurch.

But it was really the fourth resolution over Gopinath Saha that brought alive what Gandhi had been writing about: that the difference between him and the Swarajists was "fundamental" and not just related to "details".[32] Speaker after speaker from the

[32] "Statement to Associate Press of India", 22 May1924, *CWMG* 24: 109.

podium of the AICC spoke in defence of Saha. When it came to voting, only eight votes separated violence from non-violence. While 70 opposed, 78 supported Gandhi's resolution. Gandhi's eyes welled up and tears flowed down his cheeks. But he went on. "I for one wish to deal only with straightforward men. All of you are not that", he was bitter and yet compassionate.[33] "If you wish to be true to yourself, leave the Congress and work in the villages. You can take a donkey's work from me, but do that in a straightforward way, not in a cunning way."

Gandhi was "defeated and humbled". Although all his resolutions scrambled through, in reality, he had a series of defeats. It was clear it was not his day. It was a time of "darkness invisible".[34] The drubbing left him dumb. This was a revenge of the politics of old that had been simmering much before the Bardoli resolution and his imprisonment a month after in 1922. It had been there from the time he had swept aside the established Congress structure to install a new creed, a new agenda, and a new constituency. With his power, physical as well as political, seemingly crippled, the dormant but not dismantled politics of old took centre stage. But Gandhi recouped with characteristic resilience and resolve. The momentary frustration had made him contemplate retirement from politics and take up the khadi work independent of the Congress. But now his name began to be circulated for the Congress incumbency for the year 1925. It consoled him that the masses stood steadfastly by him and his agenda. He would drink of the "bitter cup", swallow his pride, and then work towards his agenda within the Congress, as long as he was not driven out by being turned into an actual numerical minority. He will be a party-man and yet work as a no-party man. In spinning lay his solace. With renewed vigour he clung to khadi.

33 "Speech at AICC Meeting", 30 June 1924, *CWMG* 24: 331.

34 "The All India Congress Committee", *YI*, 3 July 1924, *CWMG* 24: 341–44.

It was an AICC meet that exposed the Congress's claim of scrupulousness. The factions had indulged in fake recruitment to swell their support base. The electoral rolls were tampered with. Every tactic from financial inducement to intimidation was adopted to make delegates support a particular agenda. The phase of "organized dishonesty" took over. It was too early for a national organisation to degenerate but symptoms were starkly evident. The changed constitution had caused the Congress's interface with mass mobilisation. It also inaugurated factional politics. Since its inception, the Congress actually was never free from factionalism but now mobilisation became the bulwark of the Congress edifice. It reduced healthy ideological dissent and debate into a degenerated power game of political one-upmanship. Gandhi had initiated grassroots mobilisation for a national and non-sectional agenda, but the Swarajists brought into being a Pandora box of power struggle with their participation in the electoral fray. Throughout the remaining period of the freedom struggle, the Congress remained tainted in one way or the other and yet held aloft high ideals. Its career was to be marked by political corruption as well as patriotic sacrifice. This beginning was not the end but the end had begun.

The battle between Gandhi's realism and the Congress's exigent pragmatism could determine India's future, which it did. The battle had begun with Gandhi's ascendancy; it gathered steam after Gandhi's imprisonment, was feted in his absence, and sprang dynamically to life when he was released. Gandhi's realism had made him "often wonder whether it is sufficiently realized that our movement is not one for mere change of personnel but for change of the system and the methods."[35] This was incomprehensible to the exigent politics of the Congress. The spinning resolution was the first resolution in the career of the Congress that was directed inwardly. Gandhi's attempt was to

[35] "Is It Non-co-operation?", *YI*, 8 May 1924, *CWMG* 24: 13.

make the Congress "Khadi-minded".[36] However, this was not Gandhi's maiden venture. At Nagpur, in December 1920, he had introduced a constitution that brought into being the legendary "four-*anna*" membership of the Congress besides other far-reaching changes. This had invited uncharitable remarks and notable resignations of members. But, when Gandhi attempted to dig deep he precipitated an avalanche of opposition. It deflated the organisation of the Congress whereby Gandhi was forced to retreat or so it appeared.

Gandhi's attempt at reconstituting the Congress was borne out of his experiences after his release from jail. At the time of his release, the Congress was deeply exercised over the council-entry programme. The 1923 election under the reform package of 1919 was held in his absence. It bore ill for the Congress. The elections had given rise to bitter controversies, jealousies, and hatred amongst Congress workers. The political dissensions and conflict had taken a toll on national morale. With Gandhi at the fore, the Congress was making a determined bid to mobilise mass consciousness. Through his emphasis on the khadi agenda, he sought to bring a shift among its constituents. New parameters for Congress leadership were being set, as when Gandhi's mass politics had displaced lawyers from their unquestioned leadership. There was no opportunity for those who continued their law practice and expected positions of importance in the Congress hierarchy. Khadi was one programme that bonded masses with the Congress. With Gandhi's imprisonment the nebulous khadi organisation suffered a setback. The Swarajists had never accepted khadi wholeheartedly and gave it up once civil disobedience was called off. His own loyalists wore it on only ceremonial occasions.

[36] What Gandhi meant by being "Khadi-minded" was explained thus: "Until we realize that Khadi, even if expensive, is in reality cheap and other cloth, even if offered free, is expensive, we shall never become completely Khadi-minded" ("The Forthcoming Conference", *Navajivan*, 11 May 1924, *CWMG* 24: 28).

The sale of khadi was further reduced after his release.[37] A Congress worker vented his frustration by observing that it appealed "neither to our workers nor to the villagers nor to the public".[38] In many parts of the country, Congress memberships fell to abysmally low figures. In Gandhi's conception, popular desertion began when political battles received primacy over the khadi agenda.

If the Congress was to survive, it had to reassert its constructive identity and don the garb of khadi. Immediately after his release, Gandhi openly expressed his desire to fill Congress executive bodies with leadership from artisan and agricultural sections of the population. In an organisation thus conceived, privileged classes had no place in the executive. Instead educated classes were asked to stay in the background and "push into public life those who have hitherto kept aloof".[39] Gandhi's resolutions implied that the Congress must cater to only those who believed in non-cooperation.

The purpose of the spinning resolution was to politicise the "mercantile, artisan and agricultural classes". Though its conditions were relaxed, it made the thirty-minute spinning an obligation upon all Congress delegates. In accordance with the spinning resolution, every delegate had to send at least 2,000 yards of well-twisted even yarn per month. It was in the nature of a subscription. No personal use of the yarn was allowed. The implementation of the spinning resolution was the responsibility of the provincial Congress organisations. For instance, the Gujarat Provincial Congress Committee took stringent measures to implement the spinning resolution. It also set some of its own targets. It reinforced the penalty clause and also raised the amount of yarn that its members were supposed to spin and send.

37 "Is Bombay Asleep?", *Navajivan*, 29 March 1925, *CWMG* 26: 382.
38 "A Heart Searcher", *YI*, 8 May 1924, *CWMG* 24: 9.
39 "Notes: My Position", *YI*, 10 July 1924, *CWMG* 24: 358.

The spinning resolution was to transform the Congress into an organisation of skilled spinners. Such a calculation was based on the number of delegates in executive positions at provincial, district, *taluka*, and village Congress organisations in each of the twenty provinces. Even if a minimum figure of five hundred representatives were taken, it added to ten thousand delegates for twenty provinces. The spinning resolution bound them to send 2,000 yards of yarn of ten counts every month. Ten thousand members sending their quota would have brought to the Khadi Board, the collection centre, every month some 2,500 pounds of yarn. This would have clothed five thousand poor people. "Apart from every other consideration, is this labour not worth taking for the sake of the poor", Gandhi asked?[40] Further, it was hoped, spinning Congressmen would be infectious, inducing a similar spinning culture among the poor. The prescription was to revive a waning khadi with redoubled force. "I must reiterate my belief that, without hand-spinning becoming universal, there will be no Swaraj *in terms of the masses*", Gandhi said.[41]

The objective of the spinning resolution was to make the middle class spin as most of the Congress delegates were from the middle class. The protagonists believed that only the middle class could make the revival of the craft possible.[42] Their participation could inaugurate a sacrificial spinning movement as a mark of middle-class solidarity with poor compatriots.[43] Their voluntary spinning could make khadi a cheaper commodity. A skilled middle class could remove khadi's technological and organisational bottlenecks. The middle class was the single largest source of the skilled cadre that could contribute to the

40 "Spinning Resolution", *YI*, 10 July 1924, *CWMG* 24: 371.

41 "In fulfillment of Promise", *YI*, 24 July 1924, *CWMG* 24: 431.

42 "My Notes: Khadi Association at Amreli", *Navajivan*, 17 August 1924, *CWMG* 25: 11.

43 "Notes: Non-Representatives", *YI*, 11 September 1924, *CWMG* 25: 113–14.

development of the science of spinning. Their role in the colonial context was equivalent to that of the government in an independent India. Ruled as India was by a colonial metropolis, voluntary sacrifice from her middle classes was a substitute for tariff protection. By adopting khadi as the sole garment, the educated could "set the example" and promote consumption. It was a necessity if khadi was to gain a competitive edge over mill textiles. "Khaddar is a people's programme, for success in which all, high and low, rich and poor, Hindu and non-Hindu must take part," Gandhi wrote.[44]

The second related aspect was Gandhi's desire to make every province self-sufficient in food and clothing requirements.[45] "Self-sufficiency in food and clothing—this was Swaraj", was his constant refrain.[46] But because of the initial need to reach out to the provinces with no production base of its own, khadi had as much mobility as any other commodity. With the ambition of leaders to bring import-substitution into being and with Indian mills having capacity constraints, the khadi movement

[44] "Is It Non-co-operation?" *YI,* 8 May 1924, *CWMG* 24: 14.

[45] The role of khadi was understood but its limitations too were obvious. Subhas Chandra Bose, in a presidential speech delivered at the Maharashtra Provincial Conference, Poona, on 3 May 1928, said: "If we view the programme of the Congress during the last few years we shall find that only in our Khadi programme have we been able to offer to our masses something which means bread and butter to them. Khadi, I am glad to say, has brought food to thousands and thousands of hungry mouths all over India. Given money and organization there is plenty of scope for pushing on Khadi. There are lakhs and lakhs of poor Indians living on the verge of starvation to whom Khadi can offer a means of subsistence, but the appeal of Khadi cannot be universal. We find from bitter experience in some parts of Bengal that as soon as the masses are a little better off, their Charkhas lie idle and that the peasant who gets a better return from paddy or jute cultivation refuses to cultivate cotton" (Sisir K. Bose and Sugata Bose 1997, 84).

[46] "Speech at Mass Meeting", Bombay, 29 May 1921, *CWMG* 20: 154.

was an attempt to supplement mill manufacture. It created a network of cotton growers, individual spinners and weavers, and consumers to implement this strategy. It entailed a huge mobilisation of men, money, and machinery for universalising khadi. It was in this context that Gandhi desired to harness Congress to his agenda.

The third consideration was to make political work self-supporting. Khadi was its ambitious axis. The Congress had traversed a long distance from its club-like confines to the domain of the masses. The class composition of its workers had markedly changed. The workers were now drawn from mainly the rising lower middle class, a product of the colonial educational apparatus but afflicted with financial insecurity owing to the restricted colonial economy. The leaders, too, had felt stifled with the continued ideological embargo on law practice and employment in agencies with government patronage or affiliation. This was threatening as physical survival was at stake. The political workers faced coercion from those intimidated by a movement that could change course from being one against foreign rulers to one confronting domestic elites. It was Gandhi's idea to offer financial support to the political workers in their engagement with the khadi process. He aimed at creating a dedicated cadre to impart "efficiency and swiftness" to khadi work, unaffected by political vicissitudes.

The political fallout of such a programme was to knit the country into an organisation. A flourishing khadi network would demonstrate India's capacity for self-government. A successful execution of khadi work would be proportional to the development of national consciousness. "If India can demonstrate her capacity for such an achievement by voluntary effort she is ready for political Swaraj."[47] The spinning wheel did not contribute remuneratively to an individual's income. Yet, the

[47] "Interrogatories Answered", *YI*, 29 January 1925, *CWMG* 26: 49.

same activity performed communally appreciably increased national prosperity. Last, but not least, khadi was an indispensable preparation for civil disobedience, the uncontested weapon of the non-violent struggle. The spinning resolution meant a charged national consciousness and a contribution by every individual to definite constructive work. "In my opinion, the most important constructive activity is hand-spinning," Gandhi declared.[48] "Its possibilities are immense."[49]

With the spinning resolution, the Congress took a step forward from collective action to individual responsibility. At the same time, implementation of the spinning resolution required a monumental network. The collection, transmission, and classification of subscription yarn required a large organisation and much organisational ability. The All India Khadi Board (AIKB) established a most elaborate and uniform scale for classification of the subscription yarn. It instituted a committee of experts to scrutinise the quality of yarn. The yarn was to be "good, well-twisted and uniform".[50] The fifteenth of every month was the deadline for receiving subscription yarn at the board's central office in Ahmedabad. The board insisted on clockwork regularity. Provinces were asked to make one complete delivery from month to month. The members were required to send their self-spun yarn in labelled hanks. The label contained information on length and number of strands, its weight in *tolas*, the count of yarn, kind of cotton used, etc. Hanks were of uniform size and bulk. The sliver reel circumference was uniform for the purpose of standardising the count of yarn. Such data was useful to classify varieties of cotton available in the country. The fifteenth of August 1924 was the first date set for the delegates to send their first batch of self-spun yarn.

[48] "Maha Gujarat's Duty", *Navajivan*, 8 June 1924, *CWMG* 24: 209.
[49] "Notes: False Pride", *YI*, 10 July 1924, *CWMG* 24: 362.
[50] "Inviolable Pledge", *Navajivan*, 27 July 1924, *CWMG* 24: 459.

When the yarn came from across the country it revealed a stark situation. The majority of delegates despite voting their approval at the AICC had failed to abide by the resolution. In the twenty provinces that had sent their returns, there were around 12,202 eligible delegates but only 1,746 of these had sent their self-spun yarn; only fourteen per cent had complied. A scrutiny of the subscription yarn revealed that most delegates had spun indifferently. Despite elaborate instructions, members had not taken care to spin or send the yarn properly. The return figures were also a reflection of the mentality of the Congressmen. It was proof enough that the members found it easier to pay than work for Congress membership. An existing resolution had asked the members to at least learn the art of spinning but it was met with apathy.

The individual yield from each province exposed khadi's spatial spread. Gujarat with a 42 per cent compliance rate had the highest; Bengal took second position, though her success was due mostly to the work of the Khadi Prathisthan and not the Congress organisation. Bombay's redeeming feature was that its list included more female than male spinners. Bihar, despite promise, had failed to reach the minimum mark in quantity and quality. A similar situation prevailed in the Punjab. Gujarat and Tamil Nadu showed uniformly practiced spinning. This regional study showed that yarn delivery was directly proportional to the intensity of khadi work in the region. In terms of religion, over 40 Muslims and Parsis sent in their quotas.

Many individual members did put in a valiant effort at spinning. Jawaharlal Nehru not only sent his quota of yarn but sent the most. Rajendra Prasad spun the best yarn in Bihar. Mohammad Ali, the then Congress president, learnt to spin. "Big Brother" Shakaut Ali, with his heavy body, found spinning difficult but still managed to meet his target. Dr Ansari soon achieved enough proficiency in his Khilafat office to be called an expert spinner. Sarojini Naidu, despite suffering from a bad heart, struggled "with her spinning wheel, with a determination to learn it and do it regularly".[51]

Although the AICC resolution had made it obligatory on only its delegates to spin regularly, it was also an invitation to the country to adopt the same. People were exhorted to organise spinning clubs in their respective regions. The day was clearly won by the non-members who overwhelmingly outnumbered the official delegates. While 104 members of the AICC sent in their yarn, only 3 members of the Congress Working Committee did the same. Of the most noted ones outside the AICC to send in yarn were Maulana Abdul Bari and P. C. Ray. Most of those who had sent in their quota had direct links with and were loyal to Gandhi's khadi programme. It was notable that the highest count reached was 100 (the higher the counts the finer the yarn). Even Indian textile mills then did not spin more than 40 counts. The next month's figures of yarn showed some improvement as the number of those who had sent their quota had almost doubled. There were a total of 4,908 people compared with the earlier month's 2,780, who had fulfilled their obligation.

But as a "measure of discipline", the spinning resolution failed to register with the consciousness of the Congress. Some of the Congress delegates had not hesitated to send mill-spun yarn as part of their constitutional obligation. Still others asked permission to send yarn spun by proxy spinners. None of the leading Swarajists, including Motilal Nehru and Chittaranjan Das, sent any yarn as part of the constitutional obligation.

The returns disheartened Gandhi. "If delegates do not fulfil their pledge, what hope should be entertained from the general public", Gandhi said.[52] "Is it much use my presiding if the returns remain as poor as they are", he wrote to Rajagopalachari, referring to the talk of his impending presidency of Congress.[53]

51 "The Half-Hour Drill", *YI*, 25 September 1924, *CWMG* 25: 189.
52 "First Test", *Navajivan*, 24 August 1924, *CWMG* 25: 31.
53 "Letter to C. Rajagopalachari", 24 August 1924, *CWMG* 25: 149.

There was marked despondency in his tone when he further wrote, "Will it not then be better to retire from the Congress...? Is it any use having a vote for the wheel from persons clad in foreign stuff?" He conceded that he had no fight left in him and wished retirement. The biggest battle that Gandhi faced was from the Swarajists who relentlessly pursued their idea of council entry. It was a piquant situation. The Swarajists, as Gandhi wrote to Jawaharlal Nehru, neither spun nor agreed to Gandhi's withdrawal from the Congress.[54] "They do not realize that I shall cease to be useful as soon as I cease to be myself." Gandhi craved for Swarajist solidarity and their conversion to his agenda. In an article "When Will it End?" Gandhi showed his cards. He said, "I do not propose to fight the Swarajists at the forthcoming Congress. I have no terms or my only terms are the beggar's bowl. I ask the Swarajist, the Moderate, the Liberal, the Conventionist to throw into it yarn of their own spinning."[55] It was a wartime programme. He was a soldier and he knew his strategy best. His weapon, the Congress, needed whetting, and khadi was the whetstone.

The spinning resolution unfolded with unintended consequences. Gandhi's persistence inaugurated a slew of resignations from the Congress committees. Some others protested exasperatedly. A delegate wrote back in disgust, "Today it is the spinning wheel or the resignation. Tomorrow it may be 'cook your own meal or resign', or it may be 'shave your heads clean or resign'. I distrust the philosophy of the Charkha. I distrust it just as much as Mahatma Gandhi trusts it. It is his hobby. I am not going to submit to the resolution nor am I going to resign. Let the committee expel me."[56] The results of the spinning resolution showed that Congress members preferred to resign than to spin. Inevitably, it led to bitter rivalries among

[54] "Letter to Jawaharlal Nehru", 15 September 1924, *CWMG* 25: 148.
[55] "Notes: When Will it End?", *YI*, 4 September 1924, *CWMG* 25: 76.
[56] "Two Sides", *YI*, 28 August 1924, *CWMG* 25: 50.

the factions. The political atmosphere became laden with mutual suspicion and distrust. Rival groups derided one another's political sagacity and integrity. The schism debilitated the Congress organisation. Its electoral college shrank; the Congress constitution collapsed; the functioning of the committees worsened. Gandhi was unperturbed: "I do not care how small that organization is", he vented.[57] The Congress still had leaders but, as Gandhi said in an article, "We are a self-appointed electorate and self-appointed representatives."[58] The intransigence had its political limits however. Gandhi needed a "compact disciplined Congress" and "no more domestic wrangling" before national struggle could be waged. It was a challenge to trim Congress into a political organisation that was sharp, swift, and effective. With the schism widening, he began to contemplate surrender to the Swaraj Party, though not fully, as yet.

He wrote to Motilal Nehru, the leader of the opposing party, inviting a truce and offering to surrender "almost" on the latter's terms.[59] The "almost" was necessary, he said, because there were a few things he held "dearer than life and all the ties of the world". Khadi was one of those few things. He offered to suspend the moribund non-cooperation programme and lift the embargo on council entry and law practice. His second proposal was to abolish the four-anna franchise. The alternative he suggested was a more stringent spinning franchise. It required a monthly contribution of self-spun yarn as a qualification for membership. Further, each Congress member had to wear khadi compulsorily. The Swarajists could canvass in council elections as an arm of the Congress. The parent body itself was to remain committed to the three-fold programme, with khadi leading the list.[60]

[57] "Letter to Motilal Nehru", 30 October 1924, *CWMG* 25: 270.

[58] "Notes: When Will it End?", *YI*, 4 September 1924, *CWMG* 25: 76.

[59] "Letter to Motilal Nehru", 30 August 1924, *CWMG* 25: 53–55.

[60] The other two proposals were forging of communal unity and eradication of untouchability.

However, his offer of truce appeared more conditional than concessional. Gandhi had not yet given up his idea of an ideological cleansing of the Congress. During the year of his presidency, he wanted no action but those revolving around khadi. The suspension of the non-cooperation programme restored freedom to practice professions, particularly to lawyers, who also wanted political engagement. The proposal of the spinning franchise, however, was to debar from primary membership those unwilling to spin. The majority of those affected by this twist in the franchise were the Swarajists. They could legitimately fight council elections and claim Congress membership, but for such a claim to hold they had to endure the ordeal of spinning. Gandhi's truce offer made sure that khadi retained its primacy. He expected some obstacle to his proposed alteration in the basic franchise of the Congress. "I hope you will see that", Motilal was told, "if *we all* believe in khaddar even as an economic necessity, the acceptance of my proposition is a necessity."[61]

The proposal to initiate spinning on a national level, as expected, found many detractors.[62] He was told that he was putting the cart before the horse; India needs preparation before it can adopt such a franchise. Even his closest friends, such as Andrews, were sceptical of his arguments. Gandhi's insistence, Andrews said, could open a new dogma, a creed with spinning and wearing khadi as its essential elements. Gandhi argued that the system of franchise, by its very nature, was exclusive. His proposal was neither original nor ridiculous, he protested. There were precedents, he said, such as the Soviets who had "no work, no vote" formula enshrined in its constitution. The French had compulsory military training for her citizens. He asked for labour contribution—that is, a thirty-minute daily spinning schedule. He was prepared to offer free cotton to members who objected

61 "Letter to Motilal Nehru", 30 August 1924, *CWMG* 25: 53–55.

62 "No Work, No Vote", *YI*, 25 September 1924, *CWMG* 25: 205.

to the increased liabilities. "The nation", he said, "is not dying for want of raw products, but it *is* dying for want of labour and minimum skill." The spinning franchise was "the widest intelligent franchise the world has ever seen", for it gave statutory recognition to the dignity of labour.[63]

The Congress saw khadi as an instrument to transform its character from a political to a reform organisation. The Swarajists, the "politicized class", were not sympathetic to such a conception. They were impatient with Gandhi's attempt at limiting the national agenda to khadi alone. Their argument was that it would be a long wait for freedom if the liberation struggle and the implementation of the constructive programme were to be led simultaneously. Gandhi differed and said that khadi would give people "political education of a high type".[64] "I see no other way of making the Congress organization a real and living thing", he argued.[65] It was his intention that "day by day the Congress should become a purer and a stronger organization".[66] It was not for nothing that he was called the Mahatma. "You regard me as a Mahatma.... on account of my deep attachment for the poorest of the poor.... That is why you feel that Gandhi counts for something."[67] His argument was that "this is the work of internal development without which there will be no effective external political pressure".[68]

After protracted negotiations, in November 1924, Gandhi signed a pact with the Swaraj Party represented by Nehru and Das. As laid down in his letter to Nehru, the statement of truce declared suspension of the non-cooperation movement and acceptance of the spinning franchise. It seemed as if Gandhi

63 "Comments on a Letter", *YI*, 25 June 1925, *CWMG* 27: 243–44.
64 "How to Do It?", *YI*, 1 January 1925, *CWMG* 25: 529.
65 "The Realities", *YI*, 11 September 1924, *CWMG* 25: 121.
66 "First Test", *Navajivan*, 24 August 1924, *CWMG* 25: 31–34.
67 "Speech at Excelsior Theatre", Bombay, 31 August 1924, *CWMG* 25: 59.
68 "Letter to Motilal Nehru", 30 August 1924, *CWMG* 25: 53–5.

had had his way. But the biggest setback for him was on the franchise itself. The statement freed all those who feigned "illness or unwillingness" from franchise obligations. For such persons could send the required quantity of yarn spun by a proxy. Khadi was to be worn on Congress occasions, but at other times, accountability, self- or institutionally imposed, could fade into the hazy rationality of moral compulsion. It was a compromise formula that would create dishonesty in an honest endeavour. The pact rendered the spinning franchise as toothless as Gandhi's earlier compromise a few months ago when the spinning resolution was stripped of its penalty clause. Unwillingness to spin on as vital an aspect as franchise was all that was needed to sabotage an organisation. The pact reduced the wearing of khadi to a ritual, a ceremonial dress. Like all rituals, would not pretension, fraud, and a priestly hierarchy surround khadi in due course? The Congress would never be the same again. The battle of proxy had begun; the baser instincts and lofty intentions would mix and blend, conform and coexist. Its grassroots workers would be relegated to being flag-bearers, but its power would be wielded by those who could disguise their worst instincts with ostensibly the best of intentions. It was from here that khadi began to gain stature as an apparel of power.

If Gandhi was "caught in a whirlpool of doubt", his close comrades found his compromise an appalling capitulation. His bending over backwards had legitimised opposition to khadi. They could now refuse to spin and still legitimately occupy positions of importance in the Congress hierarchy. Gandhi had unwittingly introduced an element of sabotage within his programme even before it was brought into practice. By admitting the right to council entry and law practice, Gandhi was legitimising that which had attracted much of his ire during the non-cooperation movement. His duty, Gandhi said answering the charge, was to sacrifice his cause to an extent to force/shame his opponents into submission. It was Gandhi's "ethics of giving": give till the receiver is shamed. Was it equivalent to inducing piety in the opponent through self-flagellation? Or was shame, here, a revolutionary sentiment?

But the question here is the historical relevance of this pact: What was the need for Gandhi to surrender if he already reigned over the people? Why did he stoop to conquer those who would not have materially affected his programme anyway? Answers to such questions lie in the unenviable context of his leadership and politics. Gandhi was torn by the possibility of split, fragmentation, and dissipation in the nationalist alliance. He carried the campaign only as far as to bring to the fore the festering council-charkha conflict. He refused to extend the conflict to the threshold of a split. Historical memory was still fresh. In 1920, liberals and the followers of Annie Besant had left the Congress with an agenda contrary to that of non-cooperation. Now, the followers of Tilak formed the main bulwark of the Swaraj Party. They represented a strong body of public opinion in favour of council entry. Its leadership comprised educated people, "the best intellect". And, this influential section that shaped public opinion was ranged against Gandhi's khadi, his "sword". The national struggle, Gandhi confessed in a pragmatic mood, was impossible unless "the intellect" actively supported it. If breach led to severance, it could retard the national movement. The pact provided equality of status to the two wings of Congress. The Swarajists' agreement on khadi as a ceremonial dress satisfied Gandhi. "I have affection for the spinning-wheel", Gandhi explained in defense of his climb-down, "but there are other countrymen of ours who have real disinclination to spin."[69] It was this historical responsibility that explained the pact and the sacrifice, and the "ethics of giving".

[69] "Speech at AICC Meeting", Bombay, 23 November 1924, *CWMG* 25: 351.

He regarded the pact as the "boldest experiment" in non-violence. "I must convert or be converted or retire."[70]

The pact was not governed by purely moral considerations. There was a practical side too. In introducing compulsory wearing of khadi, even if limited to Congress ceremonies, and the spinning franchise, even if watered down by the "unwillingness" clause, Gandhi was actually moved by two concerns. Khadi's sagging quality and consumption had been a continuing concern for its proponents. In some little way, his move was to spur the production and consumption of khadi beyond the periodic upsurge during phases of national struggle. He still got his yarn whether members spun by themselves or bought it from others. And The members still had to buy khadi even if it was worn only on ceremonial occasions. Each aspiring person had to send 24,000 yards of self-spun yarn annually to retain the Congress membership. If the momentum caught on, an enormous amount of yarn could be collected every month and that too free of cost. Gandhi hoped for just two lakh enfranchised members of the Congress as opposed to the crore that he had targeted in Vijaywada in early 1921. On an average, each province would register ten thousand spinner-members. At first glance, the figure was not extremely discouraging. It was pregnant with a "living Congress organisation". Thus the spindle could very well spur an organisation. From the days of vain vows, the movement had come to a stage when spinning and khadi-wearing were conditions for franchise. He had stuck to basics and was contented. It also mollified the aggrieved loyalists.

The pact was a statement of truce and needed ratification in the general assembly of the Congress. The annual Congress conclave was held at Belgaum in late December 1924. Gandhi presided over the session. The man who was at the periphery in 1919 was now at the apex of the organisation. It was not through

[70] "Letter to C. Rajagopalachari", 14–15 November 1924, *CWMG* .25:324.

anyone's charity that he was there. He was there because of the single-point agenda, most determinedly pursued since 1919. It was to achieve swaraj for the millions, a swaraj that meant not just freedom to indulge in political demagoguery but in which economic freedom held equal importance. Gandhi's agenda of khadi had played a stellar role in bringing him to where he was. It was a mutually beneficial relationship; his establishing the fabric and khadi making him the Mahatma.

Gandhi presided over the annual Congress when, as he said, "a gulf seems to be yawning between educated India and myself". Vithalbhai Patel asserted that the majority of the Congressmen (90 per cent in Patel's opinion) were not in favour of the new franchise. Patel told Gandhi that he (Gandhi) was taking a fatal step. Gandhi called for a straightforward rejection of his proposed changes if such was the majority opinion. "I must warn you against accepting this change simply to please me. You must vote according to your conscience", Gandhi said in the Congress Subjects Committee at Belgaum.[71] It was his last attempt to gain positive acceptance from the Congress. He wanted active allegiance and not passive acceptance. "Reject it if it does not appeal to your reason. I do not want to appeal to your heart. I want to appeal to your cold reason."[72] But when he grew desperate by their cold shouldering he pleaded, "Accept it even for the sake of discipline. Accept it as an article of faith." He hoped that someday his advocacy of khadi would be seen as "shrewd, wise and enlightened".[73] The khadi programme was not just "Gandhi's toy". He was firm and hopeful when he said, "First it was hailed with ridicule, then came scorn, and presently

[71] "Speech at Subjects Committee Meeting", Belgaum, 23 December 1924, *CWMG* 25: 451.

[72] "Speech at AICC Meeting", Bombay, 23 November 1924, *CWMG* 25: 352.

[73] "Opening Speech at Kathiawar Political Conference", Bhavnagar, 8 January 1925, *CWMG* 25: 565.

it will be received with joy."[74] Yet the political environment was not very conducive, as Chittaranjan Das had to issue a party whip to influence the voting of the members. Eventually, the number game was won, but implementation of the resolution remained a daunting task.[75]

Gandhi had one year to prove himself. With the spinning franchise coming into effect, he was on his last wicket as far as making the Congress "Khadi-minded" was concerned. He had asked that the Congress be relieved of its political ambitions, at least for the year he was at its helm. He had persisted in transforming the Congress mainly into a production and consumption house for khadi. He altered some elements of the franchise, but the signs were not wholly encouraging. At least they were not commensurate with his ambition. The Congress had been built by people that Gandhi now wanted to be replaced by his village rustics. The Congress recoiled, its membership fell, and Gandhi retreated. In just about a few months' time the old franchise was reinstated.

To realise his plans, Gandhi left no stone unturned. He took to travel and tour with unparalleled energy and conviction. While he was being opposed in the boardroom, his popularity among the masses had remained virtually intact. He had not toured since his release in early 1924. That he would do now with a vengeance. If in 1920–21 he asked the country to be prepared for jail, now he was asking the same people to devote all their energy to spinning and spreading khadi. Persuading

74 "Speech at Samaldas College", Bhavnagar, 9 January 1925, *CWMG* 25: 577.

75 It was decided to fix the venue of the next Congress in that province, which, on the basis of its population, showed the best results in connection with khaddar and boycott of foreign cloth. But, it was held in Kanpur, which fell in the United Provinces. This province, as a recent book shows, was un-Gandhian and it was where khadi was least visible (Menon 2003).

and enrolling people as members and coaching them in spinning became a part of Gandhi's busy schedule. As a salesman of swaraj, he asked each of the Congress volunteers to be self-accountable and daily assess oneself with a list of the following questions: "How many yards of yarn have I spun today? How many people today did I persuade to adopt spinning? How many people did I persuade today to adopt Khadi?"[76] Each volunteer was to maintain a diary.

Throughout 1925 Gandhi toured extensively. He carried his spinning wheel even while travelling. He planned tours with khadi in view. He plied the charkha while he delivered speeches. No gifts of money, garlands, or coconuts satisfied him. Rather, he scrutinised his audience's garments and chastised them if he discovered that they were wearing the foreign or mill-made clothes. His face brightened up when he saw people wearing khadi. In every public meeting, he made a passionate appeal for the adoption of khadi. At Cochin, he spoke of "character and not clothing" as a mark of dignity.[77] He was responding to the criticism that Indians had outgrown khadi.[78] "Were our mothers mad that they used to spin?", Gandhi asked in a meeting of women at Sojitra in Gujarat almost exasperatedly.[79] In some places he was received with pieces of handspun, handwoven quality cloth as a gesture. He would immediately auction the cloth to the crowd at a premium. He asked for contributions for the khadi fund, urging people to "give the most that you can and not the least you have". He was good at exhorting an

[76] "To Salesman of Swaraj", *Navajivan*, 11 January 1925, *CWMG* 25: 578.

[77] "Speech in Reply to Municipal Address", Quilon, 12 March 1925, *CWMG* 24: 292.

[78] "Speech at Public Meeting", Cochin, 8 March 1925, *CWMG* 26: 258.

[79] "Speech at Women's Conference", Sojitra, 16 January 1925, *CWMG* 26: 3.

adoring crowd. But it was just that; most of the time the crowd's adoration did not really translate into action.[80]

In March, while in south India, Gandhi visited khadi centres, addressed public meetings as the ambassador of khadi, or inaugurated khadi and spinning exhibitions. Tiruppur, known to be a "khaddar capital" received the "khaddar king" with great fanfare. Tiruppur khadi was famous for varieties in checks and colours. Women here were capable of spinning finer counts of twenty and more. Although Tiruppur khadi was dearer than mill textiles, its high durability discounted the high price. Yet the district had only a few thousand wheels and looms plying.

In mid-1925 an ailing yet energetic Gandhi toured Bengal. Gandhi stayed for four months in Bengal (May to August). He had come to investigate the extent of khadi in Bengal. His first comments were addressed to "the millionaires...the barristers, the MLAs and the MLCs ...the women of Calcutta". He asked them to spin "half an hour, in the name of God, for the sake of perishing and famishing humanity of India".[81] In such dire circumstances there was no substitute for the hand-spinning industry. It suited the village requirement of low investment and simple technology, easy availability of raw material, and a ready local market. Gandhi compared the charkha both with Kamdhenu as well as Sudarshan Chakra. As Kamdhenu it gave plentifully to Indians, and as Sudarshan Chakra, the charkha opened the political door to swaraj. Swaraj was to come through the trinity of the constructive agenda: Khadi, Untouchability

[80] He passed through the Central Provinces during his journey and he narrates one encounter with the public at Nagpur railway station: "Instead of a forest of white khaddar caps, I see everywhere the provoking black foreign caps on almost every head. My name on the lips and black caps on the heads—what a terrible contrast! What a lie! I could not fight the battle of Swaraj with that crowd" ("Illuminating Documents", 30 April 1925, *YI*, 7 May 1925, *CWMG* 26: 574–78).

[81] "Speech at Public Meeting", Calcutta, 1 May 1925, *CWMG* 27: 7.

and establishment of Communal Unity. The communal question proved too intractable for him.[82] The issue of untouchability was till then very much diffused. It was khadi that his tour brought alive. These were not hardcore political issues as politics was left for the Swaraj Party to handle. The Congress was for the constructive work alone.

The visit to Bengal was occasionally depressing.[83] Politically, Bengal was a Swarajist citadel. The Congress organisations were under Swarajist control. Gandhi's khadi had few takers. The Congress membership, owing to the spinning franchise, had fallen drastically. There was an undercurrent of a campaign to abolish the spinning franchise. The Bengal strongman, Chittaranjan Das, was perceived as a man opposed to the spinning franchise. Deshbandhu was not particularly enamoured by the spinning wheel as testified by his biographer.[84]

Gandhi was keen to convert Chittaranjan Das to his cause. "I do want you to learn spinning both at the wheel and the takli", Gandhi wrote around 13 June , extolling the virtues of spinning.[85]

82 Fragmentation was the story of the day. Communal riots that had arisen since the Moplah disturbances refused to abate and recurred with eerie regularity and ferocity. At Kohat, a town in the North-West Frontier Province, marauding crowds indulged in violence. But as Gandhi admitted, "Unfortunately the non-cooperation never became actively non-violent." He confessed, "I put away in my cupboard this Hindu-Muslim tangle….I can not persuade either the Hindus or the Mussalmans to accept my solution."

83 "Spinning in Bengal", *Navajivan*, 31 May 1925, *CWMG* 27:179.

84 A biographer of C.R. Das writes, "Chitta Ranjan had never pinned his faith to the cult of the Charkha, and this led to the formation of the Swaraj Party in 1922 to carry on the non-co-operation campaign more effectively from within the council" (Ray 1927).

85 "If the Governor said, 'Spin and take what you want', you will work at the wheel for twenty-four hours and master it. Well, it is not the Governor who is saying it; but one who loves you and loves India does say: 'Spin and take swaraj'" ("Letter to C. R . Das", 13 June 1925, *CWMG* 27: 229).

He even arranged an expert spinner to teach Das. But soon, on 16 June, Das collapsed owing to an illness. He did not learn spinning, though in the end it was said he tried valiantly to satisfy Gandhi. It was Das who was the figurehead of those who opposed Gandhi on his charkha ideology. Yet, immediately after his death, Gandhi constituted a Memorial Fund in his honour for propagating khadi. Das was appropriated suitably not only to mollify his faithful but also to further the khadi cause by brandishing him as a convert. Gandhi gave prominent space in his speeches and writings to the last-minute conversion of Das. Das, Gandhi said, regularly wore khadi and his whole family knew spinning even if he did not learn it. Now though alone, Basanti Devi, widow of Chittaranjan Das, drew solace from spinning. This tactic was reminiscent of how after Bal Gangadhar Tilak's death Gandhi had claimed to have got Tilak's approval for the non-cooperation programme. Tilak had laid the foundation of the national aspiration when he had belligerently stated, "Swaraj is my birthright". If that was the end, Gandhi provided the means for it. "The spinning-wheel and Khadi are the means of obtaining it." Tilak's followers however disagreed with this logic and remained estranged till the end. The death of Chittaranjan Das was an opportunity to bring followers into Gandhi's camp. Gandhi did not meet with much success even here, what with one of Chittaranjan Das's followers putting a blot on Gandhi's sense of fair play. He was none other than Subhas Chandra Bose, the expelled Congressman who became a leader in exile.

Since the acceptance of the spinning franchise at Belgaum, the political air in the Congress was laden with palpable tension. By mid-1925, the muted resistance against the spinning franchise turned into an open demand for Gandhi to retire or revise the spinning franchise. The operational result of the spinning franchise was grim. In April, a total of 4,862 members had sent self-spun yarn towards the fulfilment of the franchise condition. Another

4,441 members had sent their yarn subscription under the secondary category of those who did not spin by themselves. In the month of May, the numbers fell drastically. There were 681 members in the first category and 1,884 members under the second. In May only 6 out of the 20 provinces furnished information. No explanation was offered by the recalcitrant provincial committees. Neither was there any provision for strictures against them. This non-compliance meant that Congressmen were reluctant not just to spin but also to buy handspun yarn to submit the required quantity. Many district Congress committees claimed to have voted for the change in franchise for the sake of "discipline or unity", but later showed their inability to fulfil the conditions. Workers found the task of recruiting voluntary spinners far more difficult than getting four-anna members.

Gandhi concluded that the Congress's defiance of the spinning franchise was more to do with their lack of faith in the charkha than in logistical bottlenecks. Gandhi confessed his inability to command discipline. For Gandhi, the principal causes of failure were: idleness, lack of proficiency, and apathy to the miseries of the poor.[86] He laid the blame on workers who suffered from "sheer laziness and ignorance". "Harvest" was good though "labourers" were few.[87] His assessment was not entirely correct, for he himself received many complaints about the unavailability of spinning tools from even the diehard enthusiasts. He reported one such complaint: "A lover of the spinning-wheel from Bombay with great difficulty found a shop selling spinning wheels. He got one after waiting for two and a half hours. He paid Rs 4 for it and, on returning home, found that the spindle was bent. The spinning wheel moved by fits and starts and even now it does not work well."[88] Gandhi was aware of the difficulties but

[86] "Causes of Failure", *Navajivan*, 14 September 1924, *CWMG* 25: 141.
[87] "Notes II: An Oasis in the Desert", *YI*, 5 March 1925, *CWMG* 26: 227.
[88] "A Spinner's Difficulties", *Navajivan*, 5 April 1925, *CWMG* 26: 466.

said, "to me the value of the spinning franchise consists in its difficulty."[89]

With all their institutional limitations, the Satyagraha Ashram and the All India Khadi Board (AIKB) attempted to give the spinning franchise a semblance of organisation. Following the successful passage of the spinning franchise resolution at the Belgaum Congress, it had begun to receive orders for spinning wheels and its accessories such as spindles, slivers, etc, from across the country. The Congress committees at various levels were asked to organise depots for these items. For efficient functioning of the spinning franchise, the AIKB organised its own network of provincial boards. It provided Congress members with spinning wheels and slivers, and supplied cotton to provinces deficient in cotton. It provided training to members on carding, spinning, etc. The board even took upon itself to provide those "unwilling" members with handspun yarn at a suitable price to prevent them from buying spurious yarn from the open market.

Congress dissent had an important lesson for Gandhi. It proved its open hostility to khadi. Many in the Congress viewed khadi "as a mere mahatmic freak or fad". The remaining members had begun to devise ingenious schemes to wreck the spinning franchise. The rule that permitted the purchase of yarn for membership led to an increased "hypocrisy and falsehood".[90] Congress committees were accepting money in lieu of yarn for membership. It was illegal. "The Congress ledgers", Gandhi wrote, "can only contain yarn receipts, not monetary subscriptions." Even among those who sent self-spun yarn, spinning was of indifferent quality. The spinners were more concerned about fulfilling their obligation than about the quality of their spinning. The insufficient twisting made the yarn weak

[89] "Notes: Remember 1st March", *YI*, 19 January 1925, *CWMG* 26: 163.

[90] "Civil Disobedience in the Congress", *Navajivan*, 2 August 1925, *CWMG* 28: 16.

and unreliable for weaving. A large quantity of yarn therefore went waste. It also affected the earnings of weavers.

Gandhi attributed his failure to his inability to convince the educated class of India, in particular the Congress, which he admitted was a product of educated Indians. He could, therefore, not foist his own convictions on it without inviting mass withdrawal or at best a reticent adherence. He invited the Swaraj Party, as representative of the politicised, educated Indians, to reject the spinning franchise but not before he had appealed to them to make "wheel propaganda a success". The revolving wheel was the only thing that could impart "substance to any big political move that the country may make".[91] The spinning franchise was the only method to sieve genuine members from the false ones, he said. But demand for the revision of the franchise condition only became more shrill. Gandhi refused to roll back the conditions of the franchise on his own and invited open revolt. He himself however was unavailable for anything other than khadi, undaunted, "hardened criminal" that he was.[92] Though Gandhi was slighted he refused to abandon the spinning franchise. "Mine is the beautiful condition of the mother who hugs her child more closely to her bosom the more the others dislike and slight it", he wrote while accepting that the franchise had been reduced to a mockery.[93] As for retirement, Gandhi had contemplated this step earlier but had withdrawn the idea. Oscillating between persistence and withdrawal, he argued that for a public man to retire he must first cease to be popular. It was a delicate matter. His was a voluntarily chosen service. His opponents must create conditions against continuation of his ideas, methods, and personality.

91 "The Revolving Wheel", *YI*, 15 January 1925, *CWMG* 25: 593.

92 "Are We Ready?", *YI*, 18 June 1925, *CWMG* 27: 258.

93 "My Notes: Franchise Reduced to Mockery", *Navajivan*, 31 May 1925, *CWMG* 27: 176.

Within the span of a few months, Gandhi would capitulate. He was forced to yield the Congress to the Swarajists. From a position that desired securing the Congress for khadi work alone, Gandhi now desired conversion of the Congress into a political body. From a position of enforcing ideological cleansing, he conferred ideological parity to the two warring factions of the Congress. "I do not wish violently to wrest the Congress from the educated India. The latter must grow to the new thought, if such it is", Gandhi said wondering why it was that while he constantly grows others stagnate.[94] Towards factional conciliation, he proposed the formation of a separate body, the All India Spinners' Association (AISA) to undertake khadi work, under the aegis of the Congress. He also proposed a duality in the franchise to accommodate those who had refused to spin or send even off-the-shelf yarn. In his attempts to wrest control of the Congress for village India, Gandhi failed miserably. The Congress committees had witnessed a gradual painful shift in the Congress, from being debating bodies to activity-centred associations. Now, however, khadi shops and depots, were abruptly closed and the Congress reverted to its earlier status.

The AISA was organised to provide subsistence employment to the poor. It also employed the educated in remunerative occupations of building a network, that is, an organisational web of khadi production and sales centres. Only those who believed in the efficacy of the spinning wheel were invited to join. Gandhi relied on the fund collection under the All India Deshbandhu Memorial Fund to give a headstart to the enterprise. By anointing himself as chairman of the fund, Gandhi took total responsibility for its collection and administration. Gandhi hinged the second phase of massive organisation building through the AISA in memory of the legacy of Deshbandhu Das.

94 "Why Not Surrender Completely?", *YI*, 20 August 1925, *CWMG* 28: 86–88.

In December 1925 at Kanpur, where the Congress met for its annual ritual of baton passing, Gandhi's tenure as president of the Congress came to an end. Here, strong opposition to the spinning franchise surfaced. There was opposition even to its introduction as an alternative franchise. Congress members asked for the total abolition of the spinning franchise. Gandhi argued for the continuation of franchise through monetary payment of four annas or supply of 2,000 yards of self-spun yarn. "Why don't you have a resolution permitting everyone to become a member of the Congress?", Gandhi said at the AICC.[95] Then with a heavy heart, in a tone reminiscent of his prior face-off with the Congress at the Ahmedabad AICC meet in 1924, he went on to warn prophetically, "Today you may oppose me, but the time is near when all of you will say that Gandhi was right." Earlier while touring Bengal, Gandhi had said he was sure how history would judge him. "The finest testimony that will be given to me will be that I revived the cult of Charkha—that he spoke in terms of Swaraj for the masses when he delivered the message of Charkha".[96] Gandhi had then warned Congress volunteers "Take up the wheel betimes, or perish".

Gandhi's proposal for a "Khadi Clause" in the constitution did not find many takers either. According to the clause, if a member was not "a constant wearer of Khadi" he was debarred from participation in the work of the Congress, its committee or subcommittees, and could not speak, vote in or contest the elections of any of its committees. The earlier condition of wearing khadi on ceremonial occasions had given rise to an "atmosphere of cant, hypocrisy, and humbug". A "constant wearer of Khadi" literally meant one who habitually wore khadi irrespective of the consideration of space, occasion, and time. Gandhi asked for the

[95] "Speech on Franchise Resolution", AICC, 24 December 1925, *CWMG* 29: 353.

[96] "Speech at Bengal Provincial Conference", Faridpur, 3 May 1925, *CWMG* 27: 32.

clause to be altered into making "habitual wear of khaddar" a qualification for franchise.[97] Despite verbal veneration, it found widespread opposition at the annual Congress in December 1926.[98] While granting the right of the Congress to alter its constitution, Gandhi refused to budge from his position. "My own opinion is emphatically that it will be wrong for the Congress, if it is to have an organic connection with the starving millions, to break this one and only bond between the classes and the masses."[99] Stiffening of the clause from "ceremonial wear" to "habitual wear" was his final resort to keep khadi in the Congress franchise. The clause inserted in the Congress constitution at the behest of Gandhi was however abrogated.

"Swaraj in terms of the hungry millions"

Throughout 1926, Gandhi was confined to the Sabarmati ashram. All through his year-long seclusion, he worked to organise the AISA "on a sound businesslike basis", managed his three "viewspapers", wrote *An Experiment with Truth*, his autobiography, and gave weekly sermons on the *Gita* to his fellow inmates. Spinning was done with "religious punctuality". He filled pages of his journals with accounts of khadi work from centres sprouting all over the country.[100] He was to produce extensive documentation on khadi, giving details on the processes leading to khadi. He was unsure of the utility of such statistical publications, but the

97 "The Congress", *YI*, 6 January 1927, *CWMG* 32: 523.

98 Srinivasa Iyengar, the 1927 Congress President, said "Khaddar is at once the radiant symbol of our self-reliance and of our power of resistance" ("The Congress", *YI*, 6 January 1927, *CWMG* 32: 519).

99 "Khadi Franchise", *YI*, 9 June 1927, *CWMG* 33: 457–59.

100 There was also a counter-view about Gandhi's journals. A correspondent wrote in his criticism: "*Navajivan* has become like a monthly magazine because it contains uninteresting and depressing articles on the spinning-wheel and Khadi" ("Concerning *Navajivan*", *Navajivan*, 15 March 1925, *CWMG* 26: 312).

motive behind such a publication was to give an idea of the khadi work to the outside world. He read the *Gita* more to find solace than to gain spirituality. Adopting the dictum of detached action gave him personal contentment but it robbed the national movement of vitality. Increasingly, it was the momentum of the national movement that drew Gandhi to it rather than his willingly leading it. In a letter to Motilal in 1928, he showed how distanced he had become from politics as generally understood. "I know that that part of the national work is also useful, but my heart has gone out of it and I become more and more inclined to give my time to what is consciously understood as constructive work".[101] It was in organising the khadi network that he concentrated his energy.

The imperial government's decision to send in 1927 a statutory commission comprising all white members to review the constitution brought the underlying currents of politics into the foreground. In the interregnum of one year, between the Calcutta and the Lahore Congress, boycott of foreign cloth as a measure of protest gained renewed emphasis. Congress constituted a Foreign Cloth Boycott Committee for the purpose. It had a full-time secretary in Jairamdas Doulatram, a Congressman from Sind, and Gandhi was its chairman. Gandhi offered to provide "an illimitable quantity of Khadi if cost and quality was not given consideration".[102] Khadi's success was linked to the intensity of work put in by the politicians. It relied on revolutionary change in the mental outlook and sartorial choices of political India. Though, in a letter to Motilal Nehru, Gandhi admitted that the "only thing that hampers the progress of Khadi is the want of demand and want of capital". Initial attempts of the nationalists were to depend on the combined strength of indigenous mills and khadi to effect the boycott. The negotiation

[101] "Letter to Motilal Nehru", 30 September 1928, *CWMG* 37: 318.
[102] "Letter to Motilal Nehru", 12 April 1928, *CWMG* 36: 220.

with mill-owners ended without tangible success. The mills tended to compete with khadi itself. The mills manufactured coarse cloth similar to khadi to take advantage of the niche market created by the movement. The mill-owners formed their own Swadeshi League. Nehru was decidedly against the Swadeshi League. In 1933, he was reported to have said: "I have no time to waste over Swadeshi League exhibitions...I do not subscribe to the policy of encouraging exhibitions where mill-cloth is allowed either for sale or for display. I have no sympathy for mill-owners. They try to fill their pockets at the expense of labourers".[103] Gandhi did talk of resorting to satyagraha against the mill-owners but never initiated it. The mills therefore were "severely" left alone. While burning was revived as a form of people's aversion to foreign cloth, boycott was to be achieved by wearing the AISA-branded khadi alone. The programme of public bonfire of foreign cloth had to be stopped earlier when people had resorted to tearing the clothes off people who wore foreign-made cloth. A worried Gandhi had to recall the weapon. Now, however, on 4 March 1929, Gandhi himself lighted one such bonfire in disregard of a police notice declaring it an unlawful activity. The incident did raise the political temperature.

Even while negotiating with Lord Irwin in 1931, Gandhi remained uncompromising on the issue of boycott of foreign cloth. This issue in the programme had affected English material interests and was having a significant effect on its textile industry. It, therefore, easily lent itself to misunderstanding and misinterpretation of Congress policy. As a result of the Settlement with Lord Irwin, the Congress lifted the boycott of British goods, which had been adopted as a purely political weapon, but the boycott of foreign cloth, including British cloth, remained "an economic necessity for the semi-starved millions".[104] Writing

103 "Speech to the Kanpur Swadeshi League", 6 December 1933, *Selected Works of Jawaharlal Nehru*, 6: 78.

104 "Interview to the Press", 6 May 1931, *CWMG* 46: 102.

in *Young India* on the "needlessly bitter and unwarranted agitation" launched against the movement in England, Gandhi asked the Lancashire mill-owners to "realize that India to be free from chronic starvation must for ever banish foreign cloth whether English, Japanese or any other…Let all the foreigners understand that this boycott movement is a mass movement, it is a humanitarian movement…". Gandhi admitted that the Lancashire workmen might have to suffer during the transition stage. "But can it be any reason", he asked, "for India's millions starving themselves". "Lancashire did wrong in killing India's cottage industry", he said, and it must now "turn to a less injurious industry".[105] In order to assuage aggrieved feelings, Gandhi readily accepted an invitation to visit the Lancashire working community during his visit to London in 1931.

After the 1929 Lahore Congress, Gandhi firmly resumed active leadership of the freedom movement after a gap of nearly eight years. With his foot march to Dandi in March 1930, the civil disobedience movement was launched. The movement was launched with a plank that linked all Indians and sought to position itself above the thorny communal issue. The movement was launched purportedly to break the government's "illegitimate monopoly of salt". The salt law was chosen as "the independence movement" and was "essentially for the poorest in the land". Gandhi's letter to Viceroy Irwin on the eve of the launch of Dandi march was a long list of economic grievances under which India was then suffering.[106] What distinguished the civil disobedience campaign from the non-cooperation movement of 1920–21 was the stress Gandhi laid during the former on the economic grievances of the masses and the meaning of political freedom for them. "I have," he claimed, "endeavoured to give a new orientation to the national demand," which consisted in

[105] "Letter to Emma Harker", 5 June 1931, *CWMG* 46: 324.

[106] "Letter to Lord Irwin", 2 March 1930, *CWMG* 43: 2–8.

"familiarizing the nation with the contents of independence". Whereas the non-cooperation movement was launched to secure redress of offences in Punjab and the Khilafat wrongs, this time Gandhi emphasised the economic, political, cultural, and spiritual ruin of the country under British rule and pleaded for immediate relief to the masses from what he described as "the killing weight" of an expensive, top-heavy administration. Unless, he argued, "the motive that lies behind the craving for independence" was constantly kept in view, "there is every danger of independence coming to us so changed as to be of no value to those toiling voiceless millions for whom it is sought and for whom it is worth taking". This seemed all the more necessary because, as Gandhi was aware, "those who are engaged in the war of independence are not, it is obvious, moved by the economic wrong."[107] There were moral and spiritual wrongs but what was most important was to fight the economic wrong of British imperialism.

That Gandhi was distancing himself from the political formation of the Congress[108] is evident from the character of the civil disobedience movement. Another indication was the fact that he launched the movement not with Congress workers but with eighty-one of his closest ashram volunteers. In a prayer meeting, on the very morning of the march to Dandi, Gandhi told the assembled volunteers: "We hope to become the representatives of the poorest of the poor, the lowest of the low and the weakest of the weak".[109] He had miserably failed in

[107] "Preface", *CWMG* 43: vii.

[108] As early as 1908, Gandhi expressed his feelings when he wrote the "Story of a Soldier of Truth"—"I think I hear a divine voice whispering into my ear, telling me not to take part in politics. He who would approach every question from the standpoint of justice had better stay out of the bother and bustle of politics" (*Indian Opinion*, 2 May 1908, *CWMG* 8: 218).

[109] "Some Questions", *YI*, 20 February 1930, *CWMG* 42: 483.

setting such a goal for the Congress. The civil disobedience movement was seen as the "last throw of a gambler". This was more so in his struggle within the Congress than in the war for independence. It would also be his last attempt to convert Congress into a vehicle for constructive work.

The march to Dandi meandered through Gandhi's backyard, his home state. The residents of each village that the marchers halted at were asked to provide basic information on the village. There were very few who wore khadi or plied the charkha. Most of the villages showed that there were no habitual khadi wearers. For Gandhi this was disheartening. "How shameful that your village shows a zero against the columns for the number of spinning wheels and Khadi-wearers!"[110] In every village on the route to Dandi, Gandhi enquired in detail about the progress of khadi and exhorted people to start spinning so as to accelerate the manufacture of khadi to meet the increased demand. He suggested that khadi be sold not for money but only against handspun yarn. This was, he said, "the only way to make it clear to people that Khadi is not a mere commodity…but …a symbol of the nation's strength and aspiration".

Khadi's career was interwoven with political crests and troughs. Immediately after Gandhi undertook his march to Dandi, khadi's consumption peaked and brought on an acute scarcity. Khadi's stock dwindled nationally. "The demand for Khadi", in March 1929, a concerned Jawaharlal reported to Jairamdas Doulatram, secretary of the Foreign Cloth Boycott Committee, "is increasing so rapidly that we are hard put to meet it." "Our bhandars have got little stocks left and our production centres cannot supply the demand. Every considerable town writes to me asking for a bhandar." Nehru asked the central office of the AISA to give a loan to the United Province branch of the AISA to increase production. If khadi was to be so closely linked with the political

[110] "Speech at Vasaṇa", 16 March 1930, *CWMG* 43: 76.

course, its production must surge with the rising political temperature. The experience during the civil disobedience movement was such that as politics brought a greater number of people to its rebellious ambit, the first thing that they did was to don khadi. During the non-cooperation movement, khadi was in a nascent stage. Its production was quantitatively as well as spatially restricted. When the civil disobedience movement was launched in 1930, production though nothing close to national consumption potential had reached a respectable level from the standards expected from voluntary effort. This limitation in production and the fallout of its inevitable political association were among some reasons that brought a reorientation in the programmae of khadi in 1934.

6 A "Clear Clash of Ideals"

THE FINAL CONTEST: EXHIBITS AND EXHIBITIONS

The proximity of the Congress to concerns of the masses was an outcome of a decade long hegemonic contention between Gandhi and Congress politicians. At any point of time during the decade the contention had not yet yielded to a single-party control over the political organisation. The battle between aspiration for council and advocacy of charkha would continue. This battle was abundantly reflected in the conduct of exhibitions during the annual sessions of the Congress. The idea of having an exhibition simultaneously with a Congress session had originated with Gandhi. The exhibition, being "predominantly and progressively of an educative character" was a distinctive feature of Congress sessions. A small entrance fee was charged initially to separate the genuine from the idle sightseers. But, slowly, exhibitions became a source of considerable revenue for the Congress management. Not only were visitors charged an entrance fee but an exhibition fee too was collected from those who put up their exhibits.

For Gandhi, the exhibition was an autonomous space where the country's strengths and progress could be shown. But the exhibits to be displayed had an agenda of creating ideological dissensions. Gandhi wanted Congressmen to see the exhibitions with "my eye". He was against any complicity in any form with the government. On the part of the organisers, however, they were often tempted to invite government and private-sector participation. That this was a possible source of revenue made Congress organisers fall prey to the temptation of inviting participation from government and private-sector parties.[1] Initially, in the face of surging patriotism, such inclinations were restrained. But just as it waned in the wake of the suspension of the non-cooperation movement, organisers began to clamour for government participation.

Since the Ahmedabad Congress session in 1922 where khadi was at the centre of swadeshi exhibits, a tradition was set to exclude not only foreign cloth but also all other foreign commodities from Congress exhibitions. At the Madras Congress session in 1927, the tradition of holding a primarily swadeshi exhibition was breached, and foreign textile specimens and machinery were conspicuously displayed.[2] Not even British exhibits were excluded. Moreover, the organisers not only invited government and private-sector patronage but remorselessly relegated khadi to an obscure enclosure outside the main all-India pavilion. It was rumoured that the government had asked for the exclusion of khadi-related exhibits if the organisers desired its participation.

Further, in the khadi pavilion, too, the exhibits went against khadi's proclaimed mores. The AISA had been emphasising the need to use handspun yarn both in the weft and warp of the cloth. They found it difficult to convince the weavers to do this,

[1] "Letter to Dr B. C. Roy", 3 November 1928, *CWMG* 38: 8.

[2] "The National Congress—The Elephant and the Ant", *YI*, 5 January 1928, *CWMG* 35:439–40.

as handspun yarn was weaker compared with the mill-spun one. The practice of weaving mixed khadi was catching on. Mixed khadi cloth was that whose warp was made of mill yarn. Though manufacture of such mixed khadi was against the precept of the Congress resolution, many Congress organisations supported it. It was the use of yarn in the warp that was a test of its quality. If the practice caught on, it would hamper improvement in the quality of handspun yarn. But the exhibition banner boldly proclaimed its intention in ingeniously written couplets. One such couplet said:

> Feed the poor and work the able,
> Let the Charkha spin the weft,
> And the mill the warp,
> In this combination lies the solution.

In the same vein was another poster, which mischievously advocated:

> To force a weaver to use handspun warp yarn
> Is like forcing him to fight a battleship with a knife
> To cut a weaver off from the best methods of work
> Is like cutting off his thumbs.

Gandhi was cut to the bone. The attack was directly on his ethos and agenda. He charged the exhibition with harbouring an "anti-India-spirit".. It betrayed "venomous prejudice" against khadi, he said. The second poster accused Gandhi of doing to weavers what he had accused the East India Company of having done in their trade: cutting the thumbs of the helpless weavers. In Gandhi's view, even the partial use of mill yarn meant eventual burial of both the khadi enterprise and handloom sector. Gandhi took to heart this open defiance and wrote aggressively about it.

In 1928, at the Calcutta Congress, the model of exhibition remained the same with the exception that British exhibits were not displayed as a concession to Gandhi's protest. But before the actual event, a protracted correspondence took place between

Gandhi and the organisers of the session, Dr B. C. Roy and Subhas Chandra Bose. Gandhi opened communication lines with the organisers when he was informed that the exhibition was to comprise machinery and textiles of foreign make.

The departure from a tradition painstakingly established hurt Gandhi. His position was that mill cloth or foreign merchandise did not deserve the Congress platform. Congress exhibitions must primarily cater to swadeshi and that too the basic enterprise of khadi. While Gandhi was vocal about his criticism of the exhibition at Madras, about the Calcutta Congress he kept his criticism to private letters. Gandhi gave vent to his frustration when he wrote to Motilal Nehru, "They are evidently inviting local Governments' co-operation. The exhibition will be a more spectacular display than an instructive effort designed to educate the poor cultivator and the other public."[3] Khadi was mentioned but just in passing. In their indiscriminate invitation to the government, Gandhi said that the organisers were betraying a "clear clash of ideals" between them and him.

As mark of its protest, the AISA categorically refused to participate in the exhibition at the Calcutta Congress. An aggrieved Gandhi too expressed reluctance to attend the Congress and wrote, "What shall I do there?" The AISA by threatening non-participation was attempting to obviate a recurrence of such a possibility in the future. Gandhi's concern was to maintain khadi's exclusive brand-equity and unique identity separated from the melee of other exhibits. Jawaharlal Nehru attempted to mediate between the Calcutta organisers and the AISA. He wrote a letter to Shankarlal Banker, secretary of the AISA, offering an alternative out of the impasse: "Could it not be possible for you to have an entirely separate Khadi exhibition? The Reception Committee might be induced to give you some land and some money and leave you a free hand. The Bengal people will certainly

[3] "Letter to Motilal Nehru", 30 September 1928, *CWMG* 37: 318.

not convert you to their way of thinking and I doubt that you will convert them for the present at least".[4] The AISA was eventually persuaded to participate, but the whole affair displayed contending hegemony even on seemingly innocuous matters such as content of the exhibition. The AISA consented only when they had extracted a ban on mill textiles being exhibited.[5]

The AISA refused participation in swadeshi exhibitions that permitted stalls for mill textiles, though there was "a good sale of Khadi". From the perspective of khadi's uniqueness, it was thought that it was better that the exhibitions should incur some financial loss by not having mill textiles, than for khadi to go unnoticed in the melee of textiles when mill textiles were also exhibited. As Gandhi said, khadi and mill textiles were on two different planes. "The aims are opposite. It is not intended to supplement, it is intended to supplant mill textile. Khadi gives work to all; mill cloth gives work to some and deprives many of honest labour. Khadi serves the masses; mill cloth is intended to serve the classes. Khadi serves labour; mill-cloth exploits it." These exhibitions were visited by floating customers who occasionally bought khadi and did not distinguish between the real and spurious varieties. AISA's non-participation would not exclude the presence of spurious khadi in such exhibitions. People were beguiled into buying spurious khadi, adversely affecting AISA's name and quantum of khadi sales. Nehru advised the exhibition of khadi in swadeshi exhibitions with certain caveats. He asked for a clear distinction to be maintained between khadi and mill textile and, secondly, to keep away foreign textiles from such exhibitions. But he advised against the AISA's exclusion from such exhibitions. For Gandhi, however, it was dangerous to juxtapose khadi with mill textiles as that could confuse the people.

[4] "Letter to Shankarlal Banker", 13 July 1928, *Selected Works of Jawaharlal Nehru* 3 (1972): 269–70.

[5] "Telegram from Dr B. C. Roy", *CWMG* 38: 93 (ft2: Roy's reply).

The AISA contemplated even organising independent khadi exhibitions during the annual Congress conclave, but this was opposed by the political body. The AISA, however, came to experiment with the idea of organising an independent all-India exhibition every year. Such an exhibition gave a striking demonstration of the entity and identity of the khadi enterprise. The idea of holding an independent exhibition was also demonstrative of the strength that the AISA had succeeded in accruing. It no longer needed to flaunt its political paternity. It was ready to forsake the obvious advantage that its connection with the Congress provided. Its acceptance among the population had reached a depth that gave it an independent identity.

At Lahore, in December 1929, where Jawaharlal Nehru gave the clarion call for *purna swaraj*, complete independence, the Exhibition Committee desired to charge even the AISA for khadi stalls.[6] The AISA refused to pay the required subscription. Here, Gandhi introduced two important resolutions to bring the Congress closer to grassroots' reality.[7] One was about the content of exhibitions and another was about the timing of the Congress session itself. The exhibition, Gandhi proposed, must be conducted mainly to boost khadi. Conducting them was made the responsibility of the AISA, and thus he ended a recurring controversy about the content of the exhibition. Khadi and the spinning wheel were to be the centre round which all the other exhibits were to find place. Gandhi's second proposal was to rid the Congress of its fixation of holding sessions in December. The winter sessions of the Congress involved considerable expenses for delegates. At a time when the Congress goal was passionately announced to be that of complete independence,

6 "Letter to Satish Chandra Dasgupta", 19 October 1929, *CWMG* 42:19.

7 "Draft Resolutions for AICC", Lahore, 26 December 1929, *CWMG* 42: 321; "Speech at Subjects Committee, AICC-I", 1 January 1930, *CWMG* 42:35; also, "What Not To Do?," *YI*, *CWMG* 42: 400–02.

the shifting of the annual session from the colonial winter date to a sub-continental spring was an effort to bring the Congress closer to people's concerns and to wean the organisation away from any colonial excrescences. He proposed holding sessions in grass sheds with half walls rather than building a mini, temporary town of tents. This was one more attempt of Gandhi's to change the character of the Congress. His last attempt would be when he suggested the dissolution of the organisation itself, just three days before his assassination.

With the formation of the All India Village Industries Association (AIVIA) in 1934, it was decided that all future Congress exhibitions would jointly be organised by the AISA and AIVIA. At the Lucknow Congress in March 1936, for the first time an exhibition was held under the joint responsibility of the AISA and AIVIA. It was for the first time also that a conception of a true rural exhibition became a reality. Congressmen acted as "voluntary advertising agents" so as to attract crowds to its precincts. But khadi exhibitions were not confined to Congress occasions alone. Some exhibitions helped convert khadi occasions into a Congress affair. Khadi exhibitions were a means of contact with the masses for the Congress. The exhibitions were advertised by means of notices, placards, etc. Educative demonstrations, lectures, and distribution of leaflets accompanied exhibitions. A prominent local person was invited to throw open the exhibition to the public. During the exhibition, lantern-lectures were held, illustrating the course of the khadi movement and the freedom struggle.

Khadi exhibitions also aided sales. Khadi was hawked in places where exhibitions were held. Exhibitions were one way to clear the piling stocks of producing centres. They showcased and sold khadi and other village crafts. The spinning wheel was the central theme of village exhibitions, and other village industries specific to the locality revolved round it.

INTELLECTUAL RATIONAL: "WILL HE FACE AN ARMY WITH HIS CHARKHA?"

"To me" recalled Nirad C. Chaudhuri in 1921, "all these demands of Mahatma Gandhi seemed not only extreme, but even crude and irrational. It appeared to me that his entire ideology was driven by a resolve to abandon civilised life and revert to a primitive existence."[8] Nirad C. Chaudhuri was often called the last of the Englishmen, residing as he was at London's Oxford Street. In *The Autobiography of an Unknown Indian*, he analyses the national movement with ingenuity and insight. Like most English-educated intelligentsia in India in the 1920s, Chaudhuri saw both retrogressive and progressive elements in Gandhi. If the intelligentsia found itself "not only out of sympathy with the ideas, aims, and methods of the movement but also violently opposed to them", it also saw the Gandhi-led movement as tending to "transform the middle-class nationalist movement into a mass nationalist movement". If "certain particulars about his character, ideas and methods...jarred" with the intelligentsia, Gandhi was also the harbinger of "a new kind of nationalism". As Chaudhuri writes, "I did not understand the nature of Gandhism, and I do not think there was better understanding of the tremendous phenomenon of Gandhian politics anywhere else". In the 1920s, Chaudhuri, then "an obscure and immature student" was not the only man to have doubts about the Gandhian way, and incomprehension and ambivalence were writ large.

Aurobindo Ghose, the rebel recluse, was another such person who would not reconcile to Gandhi's method. Ghose had fled to Pondicherry unable to bear the heat of British prosecution for his militant activities during the anti-partition agitation of 1905–8, and had taken the mantle of spirituality. Since then, Aurobindo, from the safe confines of the French territory of

[8] Nirad C. Chaudhuri, 2000, *The Autobiography of an Unknown Indian.*

Pondicherry, repeatedly ridiculed Gandhi's views on khadi and charkha. In 1939, Aurobindo said, "What a tremendous generalizer Gandhi is! Passive resistance, charkha and celibacy for all!" He called the spinning franchise "a tremendous waste of energy". In 1940, amidst the raging world war, he asked, "Will he face an army with his charkha?"[9] Jinnah viewed Gandhi's insistence on winning swaraj through the spinning wheel with the same streak.[10] Charkha became the butt of jokes among Gandhi's opponents. But even among his close comrades, such as Jawaharlal Nehru, it remained an irritating element.

Jawaharlal Nehru was "bewildered" owing to the incomprehensibility of Gandhi's strategic planning. It was at the Madras Congress held in December 1927 that differences between Gandhi and the young Nehru came to the fore. There, the mighty Congress, Gandhi averred, was reduced to a "school boy's debating society" that drew resolutions that were "hastily conceived and thoughtlessly passed".[11] The resolution that he was critical about was the one on complete independence, which was passed at the behest of Jawaharlal Nehru who had just returned from a European tour and who had imbibed many socialist ideas. Gandhi's criticism of the independence resolution passed at Madras in 1927 "very much troubled" Nehru. Gandhi had asked Nehru to behave and reign in his "hooligans" and was critical of the "propriety" of resolutions passed. In response, a peeved Nehru reminded Gandhi of the Congress discipline and wrote a letter that almost brought their relationship to an end.

The letter dated 11 January 1928 that the young Nehru wrote to "My Dear Bapuji" was devastating in its indictment of Gandhi's personality and ideals.[12] The content of the letter

9 Sri Aurobindo Ghose, "India's Rebirth", 1994.

10 P.C. Roy Chowdhury, *Gandhi and his Contemporaries*, 1986.

11 "The National Congress: Unity", *YI*, 5 January 1928, *CWMG* 35: 435–41.

12 "Letter from Jawaharlal Nehru", 11 January 1928, *CWMG* 35: 540–44.

betrayed long dormant and stifled feelings of the writer. Gandhi's *Hind Swaraj*, Nehru wrote, was a superfluous "little book" that had failed to find any intellectual agreement in Nehru. Gandhi, in criticising the West and its industrial civilisation, Nehru wrote, was akin to Katherine Mayo, who had drawn a malicious "drain-inspector's report", Gandhi's own words, based on statistics of unsavoury aspects of Indian life. As Gandhi was very critical of Mayo's characterisation, such a comparison was a cutting accusation for him.[13] Nehru talked of utopias and social theories that would eventually rid industrialism of its capitalist defects. He was emphatic in stating that if India has a future, it is in industrialism alone. Gandhi's prescription of the khadi regime was an avoidance of the real cause of Indian poverty, according to Nehru. Why was Gandhi not attacking the "semi-feudal zamindari system" or "capitalist exploitation" that really kept the people poor?

Khadi could never open the door of freedom as even the Congress had spurned it as its franchise, Nehru wrote. He disapproved of Gandhi's attitude towards the boycott of British goods. "You must have read about the wonderful effectiveness of the boycott in China", he wrote. Nehru then touched the most sensitive chord. "Has our boycott of foreign cloth by khaddar succeeded so remarkably? Has our spinning franchise succeeded? They have not but you do not hesitate to press them on the country and the Congress..." And, the khadi workers on whom Gandhi showered so much attention, energy, and hopes were a bunch of apolitical workers. The least could be expected from them. Nehru was impatient for a political plan and expected

13 In his rejoinder to Mayo's book, *Mother India*, Gandhi wrote: "The book is cleverly and powerfully written. But the impression it leaves on my mind is, that it is the report of a drain inspector sent out with the one purpose of opening and examining the drains of the country to be reported upon, or to give a graphic description of the stench exuded by the opened drains" ("Drain Inspector's Report", *YI, CWMG* 34: 539).

Gandhi to provide the lead. But it was rarely forthcoming. "I have asked you many times what you expected to do in the future. All you have said has been that within a year or eighteen months you expected the khadi movement to spread in a geometric ratio and then some direct action in the political field might be indulged in. Several years and eighteen months have passed since then and the miracle has not happened", nor shall it happen in future. If India were to wait for freedom till the time khadi became universal in India, Nehru wrote a bit exasperated, it shall be a long, darkened wait, "till the Greek Kalends". Khadi might grow in due course but there was no sign that freedom was "coming in its train".

Nehru in 1927 was a busy man. The Congress at Madras, in December 1927, was the culmination of a busy year-long schedule. In his ideological development, a visit in this year to Europe proved to be of decisive importance. In February, he attended the International Congress on Colonial Oppression and Imperialism held at Brussels and came into contact with communists and anti-colonial fighters from all over the world. Quoting S. Gopal who emphasised that "the turning point in Jawaharlal's mental development" came with active participation in the Brussels Congress, Sarkar writes that it gave him a vision which he often did not live up to but never totally abandoned.[14] The same year, he visited the Soviet Union and was deeply impressed by the new socialist society. On his return, he published a book on the Soviet Union, on whose title page he wrote Wordsworth's famous lines on the French Revolution: "Bliss was it in that dawn to be alive. But to be very young was very heaven". Jawaharlal returned to India, in the words of his biographer Gopal, "a self-conscious revolutionary radical".[15] Thus, when with all his revolutionary enthusiasm the young Nehru returned to India, Gandhi's criticism of the Madras Congress

[14] Sumit Sarkar, 1983, *Modern India-1885–1947*, 252–53.

[15] Bipin Chandra, et al. *India's Struggle for Independence*, 1988, 248.

caused Nehru considerable "mental agitation", which made him write to Gandhi the letter quoted above.

In response, Gandhi wrote that Nehru's letter made him aware of the "terrible extent" of the differences between them. The differences were so "vast and radical" that Gandhi was now prepared to free him "from the humble, unquestioning allegiance" that he had given him all these years. He asked Nehru to unfurl his banner. "If careful observation of the country in the light of your European experiences convinces you of the error of the current ways and means, by all means enforce your own views, but do please form a disciplined party".[16] That brought Nehru to seek a truce. In response to Gandhi's "unfurl your banner", Nehru replied he had "no particular banner to unfurl". Nehru wrote almost pleading with Gandhi for truce: "...No one has moved me and inspired me more than you...But even in the wider sphere am I not your child in politics, though perhaps a truant and errant child?"[17]

If Nehru was disillusioned with khadi workers, Gandhi's khadi cadre was no less disappointed with the Congress. P. C. Ghosh of the khadi-producing Abhoy Ashram was blunt enough to state that "Humbuggism is writ large on the Congress".[18] He considered the Congress "a place for bluffers". While Gandhi agreed with much of the criticism, he, at the same time, asked for the "tenderest feeling" towards the Congress. He exhorted khadi workers to counteract the Congress's "talkative activities and falsities by silent, dignified, un-revengeful work and that alone". There was, as Gandhi noted in a letter to Nehru, "utter absence of seriousness and disinclination to do any concrete work demanding sustained energy" on the part of Congressmen.[19]

[16] "Letter to Jawaharlal Nehru", 17 January 1928, *CWMG* 35: 469–70.

[17] "Letter to Mahatma Gandhi", 23 January 1928, *Selected Works of J. Nehru* (1972) 3: 18–20.

[18] "Letter to P. C. Ghosh", 22 February 1928, *CWMG* 36: 42.

[19] "Letter to Jawaharlal Nehru", 17 April 1928, *CWMG* 36: 237.

The importance of the Gandhi-Nehru debate lay in Gandhi's troubled relationship with educated India. This India was impatient with Gandhi and saw his constructive programmes including khadi as a painful distraction from the main task of political liberation and self-rule. Nehru's *Selected Works* contains a letter that he wrote to a woman who was seeking some financial support from the AICC to start an ashram intended for social service. Nehru wrote declining support, "The Congress is a political organisation seeking political change in India. No number of ashrams of the kind you mention will transfer the power from the foreigner to Indian representatives."[20] But the attacks were not just indirect ones. "The fateful 1st of January 1930 is approaching fast", Gandhi was bluntly told by a correspondent, "but you are still harping on your incantatory [sic] formula of 'Khadi, Khadi, again Khadi', and refuse to give any effective lead to the country".[21] There was perceptible impatience with Gandhi's emphasis on constructive activities than on the political course. Gandhi was aware of this impatience as apparent by the refusal to buy the requisite yarn to fulfil the qualification for Congress franchise. His writings in his journals attracted derision from the politically inclined public who did not find any politics in his articles.

Such objections arose from differing perspectives on the content of swaraj. As Gandhi would repeat, his swaraj did not mean a mere transfer of power from British to Indian hands. Gandhi's swaraj was "regulated power in the hands of thirty crores of people". He succinctly described it through the mythical phrase of "Ramarajya", a rule of "dharma".[22] In the political arena his symbolism was a potent force, and he could show the effectiveness of his symbolism and thus silence his critics. But on the

[20] "Letter to Sakarben K. Vyas", 6 December 1929, *Selected works of J. Nehru* (1973) 4: 112.

[21] "Bitter as Poison", *YI*, 5 September 1929, *CWMG* 41: 275

[22] "Anarchy of Thought!", *Navajivan*, 20 October 1929, *CWMG* 42: 23.

constructive programmes he could not carry conviction among his critics. It required a long gestation period to show any substantial results and needed a dedicated band of workers. Educated India was full of scepticism when it came to Gandhi's "inner voice" determining the national agenda. It was his "inner voice" which would bring salt into the epicentre of the national upsurge. It sprang from a knowledge base that had been acquired through wide travel and sustained introspection. It was like an exercise where data was collected, inferences were drawn, and then posited against the unfolding situation. Conclusions thus drawn became the foundation of his political action.

"Snares of Satan": Insider as a Critique

Criticism of khadi had continued to mount, and now Gandhi faced flak also from an entirely new genre of critics—those who had worked with him and had parted company when yield did not match their enthusiasm. George Joseph was one such comrade reconverted into a critic who now thought that khadi would not survive the creator of the movement.[23] Gandhi's khadi did not serve "the fundamental need of this nation", George said. Khadi was afflicted with "fundamental economic defect". He argued:

> It costs far too much to produce and to buy, and is, consequently, unjust to the consumer. My experience of khaddar is that it results in injustice to the producer also. The women, the spinners, who are at the root of khaddar, working for 10 hours a day, have got to be content with a wage less than sufficient for her physical maintenance. It is no answer to say that the country is stricken with famine, that there are millions of people without occupation. I refuse to accept that argument. Wages would not be sufficient to maintain the worker, much less her family. That is to my mind the hopeless ineradicable and inexorable vice that attaches to khaddar. That is why today, in spite of 7 or 8 years of labour by Gandhiji, and in spite of lakhs of money poured like water into the

[23] George Gheverhese Joseph, 2003, *George Joseph: The Life and Times of a Kerala Christian Nationalist.*

> organisation of the industry, the production of khaddar is infinitely small compared to the magnitude of the problem that has got to be solved.[24]

Gandhi termed such criticism as signs of "impatience". Gandhi said Joseph brought no new argument in support of his summary rejection of khadi, "but quotes as facts what he himself used to refute as fallacies". Khadi did not cost more than mill textiles, as ideally its producers were to be its consumers too. "The earning from spinning", Gandhi said while asserting that women took to spinning only in their spare hours, "is waste turned into wealth." Spinning was not conceived as a full occupation. The khadi organisation was built on minimum financial inputs. "No organisation on a nationwide scale has been known to cost less in organising than this has", he wrote while asserting that the charkha had no alternative.

S. Ramanathan, secretary of the Tamil Nadu branch of the AISA, was another of those insider critics. He was extremely harsh in his criticism of khadi once disenchantment took hold of him. Both George Joseph and Ramanathan disapproved of khadi and advocated khaki, representing militarisation, as a political weapon. In most cases, a journey from khadi to khaki was one of traversing a value distance from non-violence to violence. For Gandhi, freedom won through military might was a negation of the democratic spirit and people's empowerment. Khadi was the spirit of "unarmed resistance before which the bayonet runs to rust and gunpowder turns to dust". His ideal was to have a government that did not draw its legitimacy from its coercive apparatus. "If it is a change from white military rule to a brown, we hardly need make any fuss. At any rate the masses then do not count. They will be subject to the same spoliation as now if not even worse", Gandhi cautioned. Ramanathan's critique is important as it repeats everything that

[24] "A Military Programme", *YI*, 19 December 1929, *CWMG* 42: 293.

had been said before and it came in the 1930s, more than a decade after the movement of khadi was started.

Ramanathan's was an insider's criticism. A close confidant of the father of the Self-Respect Movement in Tamil Nadu, E. V. Ramaswamy Naicker (who himself was the president of the Provincial Khadi Board in 1925), Ramanathan was, as he said, "intimately connected with Khadi since its very inception". During the early days of the non-cooperation movement he had acted as a salesman at the "very first Khadi sale depot" that was then established in Tamil Nadu. He had been the secretary of the Provincial Khadi Board, and when the AISA was founded, he was again appointed its secretary, a position he retained for the next three years. During these years, as he said, "I wandered through the villages carrying the charkha on my head coaxing the women to take back the wheel which they were slowly discarding. I scoured the countryside in search of weavers who would tackle the coarse handspun yarn which they had long since rejected in preference to the easy weaving mill twists. I toiled at improving the quality of khadi. I tried to rationalise the industry by controlling the prices, creating reserves and eliminating competition." After all these efforts he was, in 1931, a disillusioned man, so disillusioned that, now, he termed khadi a "superstition of recent origin", which was doubly dangerous as it donned a "patriotic garb". "After long and arduous practice", Ramanathan had discovered that the spinning wheel was dead and surviving on "artificial respiration" provided by Gandhi. Now, his task was to rid India of the "superstition of khadi". On 31 May 1931, at a public meeting held at Lalgudi, Ramanathan gave vent to his feelings. It was a hard hitting speech, rhetorical in tone.[25]

The theory on which the khadi movement based itself, Ramanathan observed in his speech, later published in

[25] S. Ramanathan, Pattabhi Sitharamyya, and N.S. Varadhachari, 1931, *The Superstition of Khadi: A Discussion* 3.

"Swarajya", was unsound. Its programme embodied "primitive individualism" and was inversely proportional to the progress of machinery. "Hand-spinning implies in theory not merely the discarding of cotton mills but the rejection of all machinery." It was a pull to primitive times. Civilisation is a march of human beings from individualism to collectivisation of lives. "Civilisation is but the process of transforming men who lead individual disconnected lives into a society of men who lead a collective life each toiling for the sake of others and each enjoying the fruits of labours of others." He went so far as to say, "The austere, self-sufficient, self-absorbent individualist is hardly a likeable being....Human lives inter-depend; they interpenetrate; hence their beauty, hence their joy."

Machinery, Ramanathan contended, was a necessity of the times. It was the fruit of the progress of science and science was the offshoot of human intelligence. Scientific discoveries are pooled into a common heritage of all humanity.[26] Any attempt

26 By 1947, however, Ramanathan had realised that scientific discoveries were not a common heritage of all humanity, but business secrets which nations guarded jealously. In the preface to his book *Gandhi and the Youth*, published in February 1947 in a second, much mellower edition, Ramanathan wrote about the "sinister attempt to deprive vast sections of humanity of economic and social equality which they justly lay claim to. Exploitation is sought to be carried on not merely by the might of the arms...but by a more sinister and ingenious method of secreting knowledge and science under the purdah." But the remedy he suggested was equally sinister and unethical. Continuing in the same vein he wrote: "Discoveries of science have to be stolen so that they may be distributed to those who have been kept out of them. Comparatively backward nations like Japan in olden days and Russia today have instituted widespread system of espionage to steal knowledge from the archives within the closed doors of science. That is the task, which faces the Indian Youth if they would see their motherland enjoy equal rights with other nations." Little wonder that even in its mellower and refined version, if anything that was notable about the book, it was the intensity of the vitriolic outpouring on Gandhi and his ideologies.

to discard machinery would write India's obituary. The economic crisis is not due to "overproduction but (due) to unequal distribution". It is the wrong use of machinery and not its introduction that causes unemployment. Ramanathan provided an ingenious way to solve the displacement caused by mechanisation. If the introduction of particular machinery had the potential to displace people from the occupation then the solution lay not in shunning the machine but in reducing the work hours so as to accommodate all. "If we reconstruct society so that machinery is made to function for the benefit of many and not for the profit of few, we shall find machinery to be a great blessing." So he recommended mechanisation of agriculture. It was to be on the lines of "machine farming" as in America and "collective farming aided by machine" as in Russia. Indian farming practice bore nothing but cruelty. "The sight of bullocks being goaded by boys who are themselves knee-deep in the mire challenges description. Often the bullocks finding themselves unequal to the task, lie down, prostrate and perform satyagraha....The plough boys grow desperate, twist the tails of the animals and begin to bite them." After graphically detailing the "horrors" of Indian farming, he almost temptingly asked his audience whether they would not like that the same land could be "ploughed by a machine like the motorcar driven by you with all the ease and comfort with which you drive the motor car"? India's salvation lay, Ramanathan said, in throwing the takli away and in adopting the tractor. Machinery had its danger, but "Let us be masterful and learn to enslave the machine".[27]

If khadi was theoretically untenable then, Ramanathan asserted, it was practically unviable too. Self-spinning with the purpose of making one's own cloth was tried out and then given up. The professional spinners had neither the inclination nor the means to wear khaddar. "The outstanding fact about the

[27] S. Ramanathan, 1931, op. cit., 10.

khadi situation today is that those who spin do not wear khaddar and those that wear khaddar do not spin". It was contrary to the principles around which khadi was sought to be organised. The slogan of symbolic spinning—the classes to spin to induce masses do the same—had made "spinning a farce". All efforts to make Congressmen spin had gone in vain. Amongst the professional spinners, it was only the women—"the sex that has been brought up in the tradition of suffering and servitude"—who spun. Again, in the agriculturally rich regions, Ramanathan contended, there was no tradition of spinning. It was only in the parched up deserts where one would find the charkha being plied. "The charkha is an alternative to suicide. The beggar's bowl is another alternative to suicide. Their economics are identical. You feed the spinner out of a sense of patriotism. You feed the beggar out of divine compassion. It requires only a slight alteration of the slogan and no change in the spirit, instead of 'Be patriotic and buy' you have simply to say, 'Be merciful and give'".[28] Khadi could show no improvement in its quality, Ramanathan said. "The fault is not in the spinning but in the tools employed." The right way to prevent exploitation and enforce boycott of foreign cloth, Ramanathan proposed, was to establish more mills. He even alleged that the figures purported by the AISA were fudged.

Such arguments coming from a man of Ramanathan's stature, and that too from Tamil Nadu, provoked a response from the khadi establishment. Ramanathan had been secretary to the Tamil Nadu branch of the AISA for years. The province of Tamil Nadu, as noted by *Khadi Guide* of 1927, when Ramanathan had been at its helm, was foremost both in khadi production and sale.[29] Out of the total production of khadi in the country, nearly half was produced in Tamil Nadu. The goods produced

[28] Ibid., 12–13.

[29] All India Spinners' Association's *Khadi Guide*, 1927, 70–79.

at Tiruppur were in great demand in all parts of India. It was this province that was meeting the needs of less developed provinces. About forty per cent of the production of this province was exported to other provinces and overseas. The quality and the prices of the cloth produced in Tiruppur compared very favourably with those produced in other parts of India. The superior cotton used by expert weavers gave the cloth produced an unusual softness and attractiveness not found in cloth produced in other provinces. The AISA had a direct investment of Rs 318,144 in the province. There were thirteen centres of production and nineteen centres of sale, run directly by the AISA. The bhandars, departmental as well as certified, sold only Tamil Nadu khadi. The production activities of all the centres, run directly by the provincial branch of the AISA, furnished work to 12,829 spinners and, 1,138 weavers. There were 63 workers in the AISA. Of this number, fourteen of them were workers who gave up their practice of law or their studies in college during the non-cooperation movement in 1920–21. Would Ramanathan contend that the figures supplied by him in his capacity as secretary of the Tamil Nadu branch of the AISA, based on which *Khadi Guide* was published, were fudged? Ramanathan's knowledge of the spatial distribution of hand-spinning too was misplaced. Punjab with a rich agricultural tradition was also where the most voluntary spinning took place. Orissa with maximum poverty had the least spinning activities.

Ramanathan's scathing critique of the khadi movement succeeded in eliciting responses from two well-known khadi workers. Pattabhi Sitaramayya and N.S. Varadachari, both secretaries to their respective provincial branches of the AISA in Andhra and Tamil Nadu, wrote their rejoinder to Ramanathan. The critique of Ramanathan contained no new points, they said. During its tenure, khadi had faced many such criticisms and Gandhi had patiently refuted them. Pattabhi wrote in his rejoinder that a response to Ramanathan was necessitated not for the novelty of argument, if any, that his criticism contained, but because it came from the horse's mouth.

Pattabhi's rejoinder lacked the bite of Ramanathan's.[30] It lacked lustre, perhaps emanating from the sentiment, as he wrote that it was "too late in the day to attack the cult of khaddar on fundamentals". "Khaddar is really the beacon fire." Pattabhi defended khadi on the pretext of its being *the* handicraft. "Machinery has its place in life but not to displace artistic crafts", he argued. "Craft promotes creative energy and gives man the joy of making whole not parts, of being an artist not a mechanic, of being a master not a coolie", he wrote.

Gandhi, while advocating khadi, had been constantly saying that his campaign was not against mills as there was enough space for both to grow as long as foreign cloth continued to be dumped in the country. It was his concern for idleness in the villages that had him think of khadi. It was however, not a permanent solution.

> If ever the time comes when the people of this country will have another, more honest occupation [other than spinning and weaving], then the vow of swadeshi cloth may serve no useful purpose. If future generations, reading the literature of this age, regard this vow as an immutable principle and even at that time apply the principle of swadeshi to cloth, they will show themselves as foolish and will be acting like people who drown themselves in their ancestral well instead of swimming across it.... My reason cannot conceive of such a time ever coming. Whether it comes or not, there can be no two opinions that in our present condition, khadi is the purest form of swadeshi...."[31]

What was India's condition then? Three-fourths of the Indian population was dependent solely on agriculture without any other supplementary occupation.[32] The organised industries had

[30] Dr Pattabhi Sitaramayaa, "A Reply to Mr S. Ramanathan", in S. Ramanathan (1931), op. cit., 18.

[31] B. R. Nanda, 1990, *In Gandhi's Footstep: The Life and times of Jamnalal Bajaj*, 56.

[32] *Khadi Guide*, 1927, 3.

not absorbed more than one per cent of the population and had not been able to fill up at all the gap left by the extinction of almost all the old indigenous industries. Agriculture was still the only source of living for three-quarters of the population. It yielded, even in normal seasons, a poor and precarious living. The holdings were too small and very often scattered to make cultivation profitable.

Pattabhi wrote in his "On Khaddar" answering the allegation that spinning was not a paying proposition.

> It is not. It has never been claimed to be such. At best it cannot fetch more than one *anna* eight pies a day but what is the average income of the Indian? It is one-*anna* nine pies per day and that including the millions of the millionaire. Is it wrong then for these millions who are earning nothing to be provided with an occupation which yields them as much as the average income in India without dislodging them from their homes and families? [33]

But these criticisms from insiders would not go unnoticed, as shortly after the civil disobedience movement, remedial measures began to be formulated, and much of the criticisms were answered not in words but by suitable actions in reorienting khadi's course.

Conclusion

Khadi's brand-building exercise appealed to the heart, the base for Gandhi's political and social philosophy. A firm believer in man's capacity to transcend limitations, Gandhi's technique of social change aimed at the transformation of the human heart. Gandhi left no "stone unturned" to practice what he preached. In September 1921, he adopted the loincloth. He spun daily with a "religious punctuality". In pursuance of his method, he wrote open letters to ruling Englishmen. He said that he had discovered that the man is superior to the system that he

33 Pattabhi Sitharamayya, 1931, *On Khaddar,* 25.

propounds.[34] Therefore, to G. D. Birla, a textile magnate, Gandhi sent a charkha, "specially made for you"[35] although, ironically, he also expressed his desire to "watch the condition of labourers [at your mill] with my own eyes"[36]. It was also ironical when his financier and "fifth son", the cotton merchant Jamnalal Bajaj, negotiated a deal to buy a textile mill in 1934.[37] It "shocked" him as Bajaj had played an important role in the khadi organisation. Faith, the only capital with which he had begun the khadi movement, could not enlighten the intellect of and induce industry in his co-workers. So much so that in 1934 he was poignantly admitting, "It is not possible for a single human being to change the heart of a fellow being. I know that I cannot do it."[38] In order to fight this fatal realisation of his failure he resorted to a spate of dangerous fasts, starting with "the epic fast" of September 1932.

Throughout the decade of 1924–34, Gandhi kept harping that the educated India, the politicised India, did not understand him or his agenda. Imbuing the masses with faith in khadi and charkha could not be done without the aid of the educated class. "Masses... lack the heart to do what their mind approves... If the strength was in my gift, the masses would have been transformed by now. But I know my helplessness in that direction".[39] Gandhi maintained, "If the middle class take to khadi, people will take to khadi very soon." To the educated, charkha seemed an anachronism. The acceptance of khadi among

[34] "To Every Englishman in India", *YI*, 13 July 1921, *CWMG* 20: 366.

[35] "The charkha that I got specially made for you has arrived. It is certainly very fine to look at. I have tried it; it works very well" ("Letter to G.D. Birla", 28 February 1925, *CWMG* 26: 210).

[36] "Letter to G.D. Birla", 7 June 1932, *CWMG* 50: 17.

[37] "Letter to Jamnalal Bajaj", 27 September 1934, *CWMG* 59: 85.

[38] "Speech at Public Meeting", Trivandrum, 20 January 1934, *CWMG* 57: 24.

[39] "About Educated Classes", *YI*, 15 October 1925, 331.

the educated remained tardy. Plying the charkha was seen as retrogressive. Despite his failure, he persevered with the educated to convert them from their hearts. Referring to the Swarajists he said, "I must wait for their conversion before the Congress can become a purely spinning association".[40] Making the educated the carrier of his ideas was fine as long as people of this class could relate to the poor. Gandhi did achieve notable success in collecting exceptional people who were, though city bred and educated, magnificent in their dedication to the cause. But it remained limited to exceptional people.

Doubts over the efficacy of the idea of khadi endured. "Can it work? Can it succeed? Can we now plant again the charkha in its old place of sanctity in every home? Is it not too late? Can India even if she wants to, isolate herself and get out of the clutches of industrialism".[41] It could be argued that on the technological scale the educated had moved higher even as the masses had remained technologically stagnant. There was widespread scepticism about the longevity of the charkha. Most of the intelligentsia thought that khadi would not survive the creator of the movement.

There were debates over priorities too. The educated were impatient with Gandhi's insistence on the "Khadi First". Instead, they advocated the "Independence First" rationale. Once India won her freedom, they argued, her government could bring legislation to favour khadi. In Gandhi's conception a "decent show" of khadi was required before India could achieve her swaraj. An ideal government for him was one that governed the least. Gandhi wrote in an article, "Hookworm and Charkha", that legislations were important in issues such as unsanitary village living, but the same method of legislation did not apply to the charkha.

[40] "Why Not Surrender Completely?", *YI*, 20 August 1925, *CWMG:* 87.
[41] "Snares of Satan", *YI*, 6 August 1925, *CWMG* 28: 30

On the contrary, the charkha was the precursor of every reform. Only if the nation could concentrate its energy on the charkha, would it pave the way for legislation where legislation was required. The bane of the country was not the drain of wealth; it was not even the poverty; it was the enforced idleness, which then became a habit for the peasantry. Idleness was the root of all the ills. "A nation that is starving has little hope or initiative left in it." Only plying of the charkha could result in the country's re-invigoration. The energy required could only come from the people. Gandhi desired harnessing the power of society and self for khadi. But it is strange that while Gandhi believed in building the khadi movement at the people's level, without government intervention, he needed active participation of the educated Indians in taking the charkha to the real target, the poor. In his design he failed, though not completely.

7 Authentic Khadi: Agency, Activism, Agendas

Making a Choice: Sense, Sensibilities, and Sales

The khadi movement was as much about the production and consumption of handspun, handwoven cloth as it was a moral critique of consumerism and development. It was a political statement as well as an enterprise in philanthropic commerce. Gandhi's aggressive espousal gave khadi an identity and popularity, but its commercial viability required it to have an organisation. The AISA or the *Charkha Sangh* was an agency built to cater to the commercial aspects of the enterprise, such as the production, brand-building, and marketing of khadi. If khadi had to spread, it needed a dedicated and decentralised channel. Founded in late 1925, the AISA directed its efforts towards building an identifiable brand and a commercial network. Its immediate impetus lay in Gandhi's failure to make the Congress "Khadi-minded". It was with equal desperation and bravado that Gandhi founded the AISA as a substitute for the inability of the Congress to transform itself into a spinning organisation or a khadi warehouse.

Khadi's association with political campaigns had made it a cloth of exceptional occasions. Even the Congress constitutional arrangement had facilitated its evolution into a clothing of compulsion, a garb to create an effect externally. Its consumption, inadvertently, was linked with the vicissitudes of the national political course. Thus, during moments of political upsurge it signified certain abstract notions and its sales surged, which cleared stagnant stock. Khadi was then bought and worn with nationalistic pride. The sentiments of consumers on these occasions subordinated the sense and sensibilities of normal times. But such sentiments were short-lived. During the nationalist troughs, the phases purportedly for calm constructive work, the demand for khadi declined, stocks piled up, and complaints about its doubtful durability, dearness, and lack of variety came thick and fast. It was heavy and got dirty and crumpled quite easily, and therefore it needed high maintenance. Its inherent defects had a sagging effect on its popularity and sales. It never ever became a commodity of general consumption. All the nationalist efforts and campaigns did not lead to the material progress of khadi. What it gained by its association with the nationalist agitation, it lost through its own inadequate infrastructure. This spoke volumes about the organisation and the quality and reach of khadi. Its detractors, such as *The Times*, referred to khadi as the "Congress grave clothes".

The AISA was preceded by other efforts to organise the khadi network. In July 1921, for the first time, a Congress resolution asked for information on khadi work. In May 1922, a Department of Khadi was sanctioned by the Congress Working Committee under the management of Jamnalal Bajaj. The department comprised three divisions—technical instruction, production, and sales. The Department of Technical Instruction was located at the Satyagraha Ashram and was under the supervision of Maganlal. It conducted a six-month course in the processes of khadi production. Students trained here were sent to organise khadi centres or similar training institutes in their respective provinces. The inter-provincial work was coordinated by the Department of Production under the stewardship of Lakshmidas Purshottam. It had a number of travelling inspectors to facilitate its work. The Sales Department under Vithaldas Jerajani opened khadi stores in places where Provincial Congress Committees were unable to do so.

In January 1924, an All India Khadi Board (AIKB) was established. It was sanctioned by the AICC held at Cocanada. Its term of office was for three years, and its headquarters were at the Satyagraha Ashram. Bajaj was appointed its president-cum-treasurer and Shankarlal Banker, the secretary. Among the six members on the Board were Shaukat Ali, Vallabhbhai Patel, and Maganlal Gandhi. Bajaj's appointment as the president-cum-treasurer of the board was significant. In the absence of Gandhi, who was then undergoing a six-year jail term, his appointment showed the confidence that Gandhi reposed in him. An adopted heir to a rich marwari merchant of Wardha, then a nondescript town in central Maharashtra, Bajaj, was attracted to Gandhi, as his biographer avers, by his ethical and spiritual outlook. "He was one of the first and few businessmen who burnt their boats to join Gandhi."[1] This perhaps is not entirely true, for while Bajaj was the treasurer of the AISA, he remained a textile magnate, who supported Gandhi's cause; the council of the AISA had sanctioned a sum of rupees fifty per month for his office at Bombay. It was a personal loyalty to Gandhi which drew Bajaj into the political arena and which gave him immense social capital. Bajaj played a significant role in the making of Wardha as a laboratory for village-reconstruction experiments by donating chunks of land for Gandhi's ashrams.

[1] Bajaj was made the chairman of the Reception Committee for the Nagpur Congress session. Soon after, he was nominated as one of the two treasurers of the Congress (Nanda 1990).

Organising structures of a Philanthropic Commerce

The AISA was established in September 1925 to undertake a systematic propaganda for khadi and to promote its production and commerce. It was the year of Gandhi's presidency of the Congress. It was also the year when his unwavering bid to establish khadi more firmly in the Congress culture was met with an equally resolute resistance from the Congress organisation. The Congress opposition had a definite and conclusive impact over the character and contour of its political organisation. At the Patna AICC, a much disillusioned Gandhi proposed the founding of the AISA under the aegis of the Congress, but unfettered by the encumbrances. Ironically, the founding of the AISA marked the beginning of the end of Gandhi's political influence in the Congress organisation. It would eventually take a decade before Gandhi resigned his primary membership in 1934, though signs of the same were unmistakably evident even in 1924. Between 1924 and 1940, Gandhi devoted himself mostly to concerns that were largely considered by his political colleagues as non-political.

The AISA was an association not of but for the poorest. It was conceived as an organisation "unaffected and uncontrolled by politics, by political changes or political bodies". Though "an integral part of the Congress organization", the AISA had an "independent existence and powers", and an independent constitution. Whatever its political ambitions, the AISA primarily fashioned itself as an economic enterprise catering to the poorest. Its organisational objective was to provide subsistence wages to "living skeletons". By offering to engage the poor and idle in a productive scheme, its aim was to provide an opportunity to earn at least a minimum subsistence wage.

The first Governing Council meeting of the AISA was held at Patna on 25 September 1925, immediately after it was accorded independent organisational status by the AICC. Besides Gandhi, Jawaharlal Nehru, Shankarlal Banker, Jamnalal Bajaj, Satish

Chandra Dasgupta, Maganlal, and Rajendra Prasad attended the inaugural meet. The AISA's only Muslim face was the "big brother", Shakaut Ali. Gandhi often referred to the tepid approach of Muslims to khadi. The Muslim attitude to what he termed the "much needed national work" was not overtly enthusiastic. Not many Muslim organisations were devoted specially to khadi work, although the weavers generally belonged to the Muslim community. Gandhi was candid about Shakaut Ali's appointment as a member of the AISA council. His sole qualification, Gandhi said, was his being a Mussalman. This was also a factor for his eventual resignation from the council when their relationship soured owing to their differing interpretations of the Kohat communal riots. Kohat's communal massacre that they had investigated together, but on which they were at tangential paths, brought an end to their political comradeship.[2] Shaukat Ali, who formally resigned from the AISA board in 1928, himself never attended its board meetings.

The AISA's Governing Council comprised people who were close to Gandhi. At the beginning of its career, the AISA council had equal representation from both the political and constructive work streams of the Congress. In December 1928, after Maganlal's premature demise, the AISA's reconstituted council comprised 12 members. If members such as Jawaharlal Nehru, Vallabhbhai Patel, Rajendra Prasad, and Rajagopalachari were

[2] In September 1924, at Kohat in the North-Western Frontier Province, a communal riot destroyed Gandhi's cherished dream of utilising the glue of religion to forge Hindu-Muslim unity. Kohat was not the first chink that had appeared in the armour of Hindu-Muslim unity. Earlier, murderous Moplas had mercilessly exposed the limitations of this unity. Kohat, therefore, was a tragedy. A tragedy not in the sense that the town was caught in the melee of massacre. It was a tragedy in the sense that it put the final nail on Gandhi's attempt to draw religious backing to his action agenda. It brought to an end an unprecedented political comradeship that Gandhi had forged with the Ali brothers.

from the political stream, Jamnalal Bajaj, Gangadhar Deshpande, Satish Chandra Dasgupta, Shankarlal Banker, Manilal Kothari, and Konda Venkatappayya were diehard constructive workers and fairly apolitical. All these members, whether political or distantly apolitical, were those who belonged to Gandhi's loyal inner circle. Yet, it would be erroneous to assume absence of friction between the factions.[3] There are recorded instances of ruffled feathers between Nehru and Kumarappa, the executive president of the All India Village Industries Association (AIVIA) another organisation founded by Gandhi. In the Nehru-supported Planning Committee, as Partha Chatterjee notes, Gandhi's representative, J. C. Kumarappa, was humiliated and ousted.[4] Nehru even went so far as to declare that Kumarappa was a "worthless man".[5] Gandhi reacted sharply to this and asked Nehru for an explanation. In his letter of 3 January 1940, Nehru wrote to Gandhi, defending his Planning Committee members who, according to him, had approached Kumarappa "for certain information in regard to cottage industries".[6] Nehru accused Kumarappa of refusing to cooperate with them. Gandhi, in his letter of 5 January 1940 wrote to Nehru that his assessment of Kumarappa was on the "flimsiest testimony".[7] Gandhi termed it "ignorant or interested criticism" which did not influence

[3] Many of the elected district boards controlled by the parties cooperated with the AISA in promoting the khadi movement, but some did play truant under misplaced notions of loyalty. A schoolteacher of Arcot was dismissed from his employment by the North Arcot Board for collecting subscriptions for the Khadi Fund from students. Similar dismissals also took place in Moradabad where a circular was issued by the board that forbade teachers from raising funds for khadi ("Elected Boards", *YI*, 24 October 1929, *CWMG* 42: 37–38).

[4] Partha Chatterjee, 2000, "Development Planning and the Indian State", in *Politics and the State in India*, ed. Zoya Hasan, 115–41.

[5] "Letter to Jawaharlal Nehru", 5 January 1940, *CWMG* 71: 77.

[6] "Letter to Jawaharlal Nehru", 3 January 1940, *CWMG* 71: 77.

[7] "Letter to Jawaharlal Nehru", 5 January 1940, *CWMG* 71: 78.

him. As the time for freedom approached, political participation in the AISA council fell. Patel and Prasad both resigned from the council in October 1946. Nehru had resigned even earlier. In the circumstances, an advisory body was proposed but soon the idea was shelved.

The AISA's career had spanned over 25 years (1925–53). Its council alone was empowered to amend its constitution. In the second council meet, held in November 1925 at the Satyagraha Ashram, a sub-committee was appointed to frame rules and instructions for organising work in the provinces to encourage voluntary spinning and to enlist members. The council met with religious regularity and even political upheavals seldom obstructed the frequency of its meetings. By 1941, the AISA council had held about 50 meetings, interrupted only by the quit India movement. Considering the frequency of the AISA council meetings, which were always held under Gandhi's eagle eyes, and also considering the fact that some of the provincial agents of the AISA were active political leaders, it appears that Gandhi had succeeded in harnessing the Congress's manpower, energy, and resources to the khadi cause. Yet, just four members were the quorum required for council meetings. Maganlal, Bajaj, Banker, and Gandhi were regulars till Maganlal's death in 1928. All the four held important positions in the central command structure of the AISA. In December 1928, the AISA began to enrol life members in its central council. Some insinuated that this was done under compulsion owing to a paucity of qualified candidates.

Membership in the AISA was conditional. The individual AISA members were expected to adhere scrupulously to the spinning routine and habitually wear khadi. Each of the AISA members was constitutionally required to submit a specific amount of self-spun yarn on a monthly basis. There were two categories of membership. The A-class members were those who habitually wore khadi and voluntarily deposited a monthly subscription of 1,000 yards of uniform and well-twisted self-spun yarn. The B-class members were those who habitually wore khadi and deposited an annual subscription of 2,000 yards of self-spun yarn. No special effort was made to enrol members for the AISA. It was thought that those who believed in khadi would scarcely require enticement. But, the AISA membership remained insubstantial. Even those who had joined in the first flush of enthusiasm withdrew soon after. In April 1929, the AISA took a decision to abolish its B-class membership. Finally, in 1945, even the A-class membership was abolished. In 1926, a category for the children of age below 18 years was introduced. But three years later in 1929 the juvenile category was also abolished. This was dictated by a situation in which members were failing in the discipline required of membership. In 1931, S. Ramanathan, a disillusioned khadi worker, in a polemic said, "The AISA was constituted on a spinning franchise and today its voters can be counted on the fingers' ends". "To avoid a break down of the constitution they have made the executive to consist of life members. Shortly, I expect they will make the offices hereditary." In the later phase, the AISA membership was confined to its paid workers. The limited membership somehow restricted the organisation's desire to adopt a democratic administration. Table 7.1 indicates the membership in the various categories from 1926–42.

The AISA's executive positions were safely in the hands of Gandhi's constructive workers. Even while Gandhi, striding across the divide, was the president of the association, Jamnalal Bajaj, until his death in 1940, held the treasurer's position. Gandhi's travel schedule and health problems repeatedly incapacitated him from attending to the AISA's routine work. In Gandhi's absence, it was Bajaj who was the officiating president. Shankarlal Banker, again till 1940, was the executive secretary of the AISA. Banker earlier had worked in close proximity with Annie Besant and later was converted to Gandhi's cause. He was the son of a

Table 7.1 Membership Details from 1926 to 1942.

Year	*"A" Category*	*"B" Category*	*Children Category*
1926	3,472	942	–
1927	2,195	340	264
1928	1,527	279	205
1929	1,411	In this year, both these categories were removed	
1930	1,928		
1931	1,308		
1932	655		
1933	512		
1934	1,131		
1935	1,206		
1936	1,994		
1937	1,161		
1938	1,836		
1939	2,531	Out of this, 2,274 were AISA workers.	
1940	3,558	Out of this, 2,939 were AISA workers.	
1941	2,914	Out of this, 2,417 were AISA workers and, workers of certified organisations.	
1942		Owing to political upheavals there were very few members and information is lacking.	

Source: Charkha Sangh ka Ithihaas, 150.

professional banker. He wrote an autobiographical chronicle that is a good source book on khadi work.[8] An AISA colleague wrote: "Banker...burnt out his youth in the service of the Charkha."[9] In the 1940s, after Banker had stepped down on the grounds of ill health, Krishnadas Jajoo became the AISA's secretary. Maganlal until his death held sway in the organisation and was its technical director. Rajendra Prasad served as a legal advisor, besides his appointment as the AISA agent in Bihar. The AISA's provincial presence was through the agents appointed by its council. Provincial agents and secretaries played a significant

[8] *Gandhiji aur rashtriya pravartiyan*, 1969.

[9] S. Ramanathan, *Gandhi and the Youth*, 27

Table 7.2: The Names of Agents and Secretaries of Provincial AISA Branches in 1927

Province	*Agent*	*Secretary*
Andhra	Dr Pattabhi Sitaramayya	
Behar	Rajendra Prasad	Laxminarayan
Bengal	Hemaprova Devi	–
Burma	Nanalal Kalidas	–
Karnataka	Gangadharrao B. Deshpande	–
Punjab	Dr Gopichand Bhargava	Kishanchand Bhatia
Rajasthan	Jamnalal Bajaj	–
Sindh	Dr Choithram P. Gidwani	–
Tamil Nadu	–	S. Ramanathan
U.P.	Pt Jawaharlal Nehru	Sitla Sahai
Utkal	–	Niranjan Patnaik

Source: Khadi Guide, 1927.

role in the spread of the AISA network. These provincial agents were Gandhi's closest followers. They took part equally in the deliberations of the council. The names of the provincial agents and secretaries in 1927 are given in Table 7.2. Later there were changes but the table gives an indication of the kind of people who were with the AISA.

Professional Philanthropy and Philanthropic Profession

The AISA was headquartered at the Satyagraha Ashram. After Maganlal's death in 1928, the ashram was dedicated totally to khadi work. Gandhi changed the name of the Satyagraha Ashram to Udyog Mandir. It was thought that while the ashram's inward journey was limited by the potential of its ever-growing inmates, its outward manifestation was visible in its industry and physical work. Hence, the name Udyog Mandir was more suited to its vocation.

In its formative years, the majority of the AISA council deliberations were apparently over applications which came from all over the country, for the establishment of sale and production units for khadi.[10] The AISA council devised certain guiding principles to enable its secretarial staff to sanction the loan applications. Rules were deliberated, formulated, and adopted in its second council meeting held in November 1925. Most of the council minutes chronicle the loan sanctioned and disbursement made to various applicants from across the country. Loans were to be sanctioned only where spinning was to be developed among the poorest people. The AISA was not a legally registered body. However, it made legal registration of the applying organisations a condition for entitlement of institutional loans from it. The AISA council deliberated on the financial viability of each venture. Each application was properly examined with respect to its work-plan, "documents, titles and values", and its "technical and business" viability. The AISA sent its own trusted lieutenants to evaluate various criteria such as the viability of applications, possibilities in a province, fund requirement, etc. before sanctioning the production unit or sales depot. For instance, in 1926, the AISA's Bihar agent Rajendra Prasad was sent to Assam to investigate its potential and recommend its claim to the council. The AISA worked on the principle that noble causes always deserve a closer look. The AISA council usually set individual targets of production and sales for various provincial units. The council ordered, as the occasion arose, investigation of work done under the sanctioned money. They deliberated over the appointment of the provincial offices, financial position of associate agencies, and financial statements received from the provincial departments.

Gandhi was the AISA's roving brand ambassador and fund raiser. Gandhi organised the fund collection drive under the

[10] Details of the AISA's functioning is recorded in the minutes of its Trustees Meet; preserved in micro-films at the Nehru Memorial Museum & Library, New Delhi.

aegis of the All India Deshbandhu Memorial Fund. But there was pronounced scepticism among the contributors of the Khadi Fund about the money being collected. Earlier, the Khilafat Fund had disappeared as, oddly, the banker got liquidated. Though Gandhi had nothing to do with the disbursement of the Khilafat Fund, the upkeep of the Khadi Fund was his responsibility. The council of the AISA was entrusted with these funds and their management. The fund was kept in well-known banks and was audited intermittently.

On account of its not being a legally registered body, the AISA experienced many instances of default from fledgling units. The defaulting units could exploit the fact that since the AISA was a non-registered body, it was not in a position to approach the court of law for redress against any financial violations. Facing many such cases of default and forgery, the AISA on 8 November 1937 got itself registered under the government's Society Registration Act XXI, 1860. It was not as if the nationalists were unaware of the legal requirement. Jamnalal Bajaj had registered an organisation called Gandhi Sewa Sangh under the Act in the year 1923. It was just that with khadi they had had a larger ambition and an overarching design for an autonomous alternative that shunned governmental patronage or recognition.

Khadi Service: Bureaucracy for Philanthropy

"You have come here", Gandhi said in April 1928, speaking to the interns at Khadi Vidyalaya, "not for earning your livelihood but with a desire to serve, to dedicate your life to the cause of Khadi, and for this character will be very essential."[11] The cadres were not to work for a livelihood alone but were also to undertake service. The science of khadi required a different approach from

[11] "Speech to Trainees at Khadi Vidyalaya", before 13 April 1928, *CWMG* 36: 221–24.

that applied at mills. It required cultivation of character in addition to expertise. "We need character in addition to this knowledge." An AISA worker was required to be adept in the science of spinning and other auxiliary processes and also possess certitude of moral character. The commandments for a khadi worker were: lead a pure and chaste life; know laws of health and sanitation; find happiness in a simple and frugal life. Gandhi could not "appreciate, much less adopt" the view that the "character of a public worker ...is his own private concern".[12] It was a community-based organisation and, therefore, character and expertise were of equal importance.

A successful khadi organiser had to possess "skill and love in equal measure". The science of khadi was a list of qualifications in the skills of various processes leading to the manufacture of khadi. It included cotton-growing, picking, ginning, cleaning, carding, slivering, spinning, sizing, dyeing, preparing the warp and the woof, weaving, washing, and the knowledge of different instruments required at each stage. It included the ability to differentiate between cotton varieties. The logistics of khadi work were varied and began with the maintenance of an inventory of spinning wheels. In the early phase of the movement, salesmanship in a worker was a valuable trait. In the organisation of the AISA the smallest details were as important as the macro-strategies of the national campaign.

It was the search for such workers that constrained the expansion of the AISA network. Gandhi thought there was a dearth "more of men than of money". In his scheme of things it was the "human will" that was in short supply and not the "human spindles and human looms" that India had in millions. The recruitment of workers was evidently hard as the AISA was periodically forced to put up advertisements "Wanted Workers" through the writings of Gandhi.[13] The AISA's predecessor too

[12] "One thing needful", *Harijan*, 7 November 1936, *CWMG* 64: 11.

[13] "Wanted Workers", *YI*, 10 March 1927, *CWMG* 33: 152.

had found it difficult to recruit a qualified workforce. In June 1924, Gandhi wrote: "I understand that the Khadi Board is finding it difficult to get the right kind of men to give their whole time to the work".[14] Those who were ready to undertake khadi work showed reluctance to accept payment for such work, as it was an endeavour in patriotism. Such dilemmas were inherent in the career of the khadi movement. The organisation of the AISA based itself on a foundation of voluntary sacrifice, and yet it wanted to attract the best workers on a full-time engagement.

Whether one searched for workers with the spirit of service or whether their service was availed with a high salary is a question of debate in India's voluntary network that remains alive to this day. As voluntary work moves into the domain of professionalism, there is a need to probe assumptions beneath the bipolarity of spirit and salary. Richard Gregg, an American contemporary who wrote many books on Gandhian economics, advocated having trained professionals on a competitive salary. Gandhi, though not disputing the proposition, was under financial constraints with regard to paying high wages to the workers. But more than the pecuniary constraints, Gandhi certainly had a practical reason for opposing the proposition. He would not adopt the business strategies of mainstream commercialism, as it would create the problem of keeping highly paid workers who had joined for only pecuniary gain rather than being attracted by the spirit of the work. Such paid workers, besides being upwardly mobile, were also regarded as being unwieldy in terms of obedience.

Gandhi's arguments betrayed his lack of trust in the educated and skilled though, throughout, he was urging their participation

[14] In July 1921, with a resolution eliciting general information on khadi works, the Congress began its association with khadi. In January 1924, an All India Khadi Board was established. It was sanctioned by the AICC ("False Pride?", *YI*, *CWMG* 24: 361).

in his activities. He recruited them only if they also showed that they had imbibed the right spirit. Salary was secondary; what was primary was that the spirit of the movement should have been inculcated in them. Such a spirit moved one to sacrifice comfort and not demand a salary: it was this condition on which workers were judged. The khadi enterprise, as it was conceived then, was never in a position to give enticing pay and perks to its workers. It was a movement which required a fair measure of continuous sacrifice from those who had become accustomed to city life. The class of workers required for the movement was trained for the specific work of the AISA. No prior acquired skill was the benchmark. Every one had to undergo the grind of minimalist existence. Such workers could not be availed through advertising either. Khadi was not a profit-based enterprise but one of philanthropic commerce. The science of khadi was organised on principles diametrically opposite to that of ordinary business. Its entrepreneurial parameters were different from those generally held in the capital market. The khadi protagonists had devised methods that differed from the demands of the capital market. "The adversary believes in the latest appliances and therefore is bound to adopt the methods of those who are adept in using those appliances; but in the spinning movement, modern appliances are largely discarded and the few that are retained are used in a different way. The spinning movement, so far as I can see, will never afford the high wages that are demanded by good men in such a line of business."[15] It is such a dilemma that continuously stifled the growth of the commodity of khadi and yet, inherent as it was, there was no escaping from the dilemma. Even the formation of a workers' union within the AISA's productive units was discouraged. A workers union within the AISA organisations was considered[16]

[15] "Letter to R.B. Gregg", 27 May 1927, *CWMG* 33: 376–80.

[16] "A Fallacy", *Harijan*, 16 July 1938, *CWMG* 67: 176.

a "fallacy". It went against the philanthropic organisation as well as against the artisans who were "half-starved half-employed persons, mostly women". A worker-related grievance was to be sorted out by the central body and "surely not through unions after the orthodox style". Workers were "part creators and part trustees" and therefore equally responsible for the well-being of the association.

In recognition of its difficulties in recruiting qualified workers and enrolling voluntary members, the AISA council in its eighth meeting, held in December 1926, resolved to establish a Khadi Service. It was colloquially called Khadi Sewa Sangh and was instituted as the AISA's answer to the government's bureaucracy.[17] It was intended to create a dedicated cadre in the service of khadi. An elaborate screening and training process was laid down for recruitment. Only those who had received a certificate of competency from the Board of Studies could be a member of the Khadi Service. Maganlal Gandhi was the secretary of the board. Training of recruits was for a minimum of two years. There were also other shorter courses for specific purposes. Selected candidates from among the applicants were first admitted as probationers at a working centre for three months. Later, they were sent for a two-year course of instruction to the AISA's Khadi Vidyalaya at Sabarmati. The course of instruction included all the processes leading from growing cotton to making khadi. The candidates also had to learn book keeping and account management. Upon receiving a certificate of competency the candidate was sent to a provincial khadi *Karyalaya* to gain practical

[17] "The idea of the Khadi Sewa Sangh was mine. I felt that just as the Government has an organization, its *naukarshahi,* it would be good for us also to have an organization of workers. The Government's *naukarshahi* is called '*shahi*' because its members, although they are servants, function as rulers. But we are not '*shahi*' because we have to do real service" ("Speech to Trainees at Khadi Vidyalaya", before 13 April 1928, *CWMG* 36: 221–24).

experience for a month. The AISA's technical department which ran Khadi Vidyalaya awarded the certificate of eligibility. It was then only that a candidate was recruited into the Khadi Service.

The recruitment of successful candidates was done after signing a contract that bound a candidate to at least three years of uninterrupted service to the AISA. The head of the province could terminate the services of a candidate upon furnishing a valid reason. The council of the AISA was the final appellate authority for redress of any service grievances. A candidate received a monthly remuneration of thirty rupees which was raised to a maximum of fifty over a three-year period. Every applicant who successfully entered the Khadi Service deposited the return fare to his/her original address of residence in addition to three rupees as a return arrangement in the event of his or her being discharged.

The AISA workforce had a male-upper-caste bias. In Tamil Nadu where Brahmin-non-Brahmin contestation was in the forefront, the AISA faced accusations of being under the control of Brahmins. There was certainly a predominance of Brahmins in the khadi organisation, but the large majority of spinners and weavers on its rolls were non-Brahmins. It was argued that such a bias in its workforce was due to the absence of suitable and skilled non-Brahmin workers, but it is difficult to accept this argument. In 1929, the AISA began a provident fund scheme for its workers. It kept a record of its workers through a periodic census. The census made a list of khadi workers with particulars about their qualifications, work, and remuneration. In 1925, there were a total of 148 workers on its payroll. Another 58 were those who worked in an honorary capacity. The maximum a worker got paid was rupees 65 and minimum was rupees two. There were periodic publications of *Khadi Bulletins* giving all kinds of information to khadi workers. It was also to act as a platform for khadi workers. Table 7.3 gives a yearwise list of khadi workers with the AISA.

Table 7:3 No. of Workers on AISA's Roll and the Wages Received

Year	*Numbers of workers*	*Remarks*
1927–28	411	
1928–29	663	Average monthly wage Rs 25.
1929–30	1,145	
1930–31	1,949	Average monthly wage Rs 30.
1932	1,134	Average monthly wage Rs 20.
1933	1,115	Average monthly wage Rs 20.
1934	871	Average monthly wage Rs 26.
1935	1,097	Average monthly wage Rs 21.
1936	1,135	
1937	1,633	
1938	2,221	
1939	2,732	
1940	2,933	
1941–42	3,400	2,188 of these received a monthly payment of Rs 19. 1,122 of these received Rs 20–50. 122 of these received Rs 50.
1942–43	1,935	
1943-44	2,438	
1944–45	2,341	
1945–46	2,136	394 of these received Rs 15. 1,170 of these received Rs 15–30. 408 of these received Rs 30–50. 142 of these received Rs 50–75. 22 0f these received more than Rs 75.

Source: Charkha Sangh ka Ithihaas, 169.

Science of Khadi

"I believe that I have got the mind of a scientist."[18]

In 1941, at Wardha, while inaugurating a Khadi Vidyalaya, Gandhi asked the students to undertake "a scientific study of the charkha and khadi and make improvements by new inventions and serve the villagers". Such a scientific process involved all the

[18] "Letter to W. Tudor Owen", 2 March 1933, *CWMG* 53: 441.

operations from sowing of cotton in the fields to the manufacture of khadi. Gandhi attempted to stop the pandering to the "fancies" of people just to increase khadi's acceptability. Instead, he desired a diligent study of the "science of khadi" to bring about its spread. It would be appropriate for a khadi worker to develop a kind of scientific attitude similar to that which had fostered the discoveries of Newton or Galileo.

The science of khadi was an empirical science as its experiments and conclusions were accessible to the experience of practitioners. It was a science that drew its strength from actual observations and experiments in the field. Its laboratory was the field. Practitioners were its scientists. Its motive was not to aggrandise profit or power of knowledge. The lay as much as the learned had direct experience of and access to it. Everyone involved in cotton cultivation or in plying the charkha was a scientist endowed with acumen. It therefore was a science that bridged the gap between experience and academics.

It was a science that drew not only from the experience of the present generation but also from the knowledge accumulated through previous generations. It harked back to tradition and its inferences were always measured in the backdrop of accumulated traditional knowledge. But tradition was not to be a blind alley. Tradition was sought to be restructured on the basis of new scientific knowledge. Earlier skill-based occupations had disintegrated owing to its overdependence on the passage of knowledge through tradition. The carrying of knowledge merely on the strength of tradition did not lead to scientific growth. It was to be a systematic process of observation, analysis, and new inferences drawn that enhanced the knowledge bequeathed by tradition. There is a great difference between know-how and know-why. While the former is mechanical the latter is ever-generative knowledge.

This field-based science involved all the processes that the conventional laboratory-based science boasted of. What the textile mills did in their laboratories, khadi science did in every home. Testing the strength of cotton, cotton gathering etc., was the first step of the khadi science. It was more complicated, more demanding, more prone to failure as even a little carelessness had negative consequences. There was rarely any wastage in the operational science of khadi. In ginning cotton, it was important that the cottonseeds were retained as the products of each step had multiple-utility values. The cottonseeds after its oil was extracted were fed to cattle. These by-products were as important as the ginned cotton itself. The mill ginning entailed wastage of resources. It was because of these that khadi science demanded greater expertise and a fine-tuned sense of duty.

As science is context-specific, the science of khadi was specific to India. "A scientist can derive all the joy from his particular science, can go on making new discoveries and improving the science", Gandhi wrote, asserting that science is all about enlightened enquiry. The science of khadi asked for joyous engagement with all its processes leading to the fabric of khadi. Maganlal was such a scientist. He was an engaged thinker; he "died thinking every hour of the day and ever inventing something new". Mirabehan was another person like Maganlal. She chose to live in an obscure village in Bihar, and despite facing disease and depression, she experimented with the potentialities of the old spinning wheel and other implements. Gandhi hoped, "Once our people begin to appreciate the great power of charkha, writers and thinkers would also be drawn to it. They would then begin to see in it poetry and art and utility and a great deal more."[19]

Gandhi's method was scientific and ever-watchful. He was not immune to the claims being made on behalf of industrialism. Soviet experiments had certainly caught the attention of India's

[19] "Speech to Trainees at Khadi Vidyalaya", before 13 April 1928, *CWMG* 36: 221–24.

future leaders. He wrote to Kumarappa, on his article, *Public Costs of Centralized Production*, "What we have to combat is socialization of industrialism. You have to show, if you can, by working out figures that handicrafts are better than power-driven machinery products."[20]

The whole reorganisation of the khadi network was based on scientific claims. The AISA's Technical Department carried out experiments in the technology and process of spinning. Maganlal Gandhi was sent to a technological laboratory near Bombay to study the different instruments for testing cotton. Vithaldas Jerajani wrote a booklet on the science of selling khadi just as Maganlal wrote on the science of spinning. In a message to a periodical, *Khadir Katha*, Gandhi desired the publication of a "true record of khadi work from month to month". He wanted the journal to be fully awake to the causes of the decline of khadi by publishing interrogative reports. The AISA undertook "scientific and diligent study" of the growth potential of khadi in provinces. A poverty map of each province was made, indicating regions where grinding poverty prevailed and where spinning activity could be carried out. Three kinds of spinning endeavours were introduced based on the poverty map of a region. In a perpetually scarce area, spinning for wages was introduced, in the remaining villages, irrespective of depth of the poverty, it was spinning for self, and in places, wherever possible, spinning for sacrifice was introduced. The AISA solely concentrated on spinning for wages as it was an organisation "for the poor".

Transparency made the scientific quest more exciting. Since its foundation in 1925, the AISA regularly published its annual report containing detailed analysis of the income and expenditure of the association and its associate agencies. It was part of the pioneering work done by Maganlal Gandhi who built up the science of khadi. *Dev Cotton* published in 1923 showed how

[20] "Letter to J. C. Kumarappa", 12 August 1941, *CWMG* 74: 233.

attempts were being made even in the early stages of the movement to work out a scheme for self-sufficing khadi. Since 1933, *Maharashtra Khadi Patrika* registered the progress of khadi in provinces on a monthly basis. The AISA launched a detailed data collection drive too. To keep in regular touch with customers, the AISA's sales outlet maintained a register of customers with their names and addresses. Even while the customer base was erratic in its loyalty to khadi, such a database proved useful. Every production centre was instructed to maintain a spinners' register giving the names and addresses of the spinners with information about quantity of yarn spun and wages earned by each spinner. Each of the production centres provided information on and samples of its produced cloths. These particulars were used by the Technical Department to make generalisations, draw deductions, and guide khadi producers. Quality control, market survey, efficiency, and cost effectiveness, were the keywords in Gandhi's writings on khadi.

As the movement progressed and paucity of implements became constricting, Gandhi began to propagate the takli as an alternative to the charkha. The takli was a small iron spoke with which one could spin yarn from raw cotton. It was for "wheel-less spinning". In the past people spun even the finest yarn on the takli. It was made of bamboo and was still used by the Brahmins to spin the very fine yarn required for the sacred thread. Making a spinning wheel was an elaborate process, but a takli could be made anywhere. It had no mechanical problems and made no noise. Such an implement solved the problem of the availability of charkha's in schools. It made spinning easier for those who constantly travelled. "If the spinning-wheel is for thousands", Gandhi said, "the takli is for millions."[21] It was a kind of rosary that one could always ply. "Huge mills may arise out of the takli. A spinning mill means a mill containing taklis."[22]

[21] "Letter to Narandas Gandhi", 27 November 1932, *CWMG* 52: 85.

[22] "Culture", *Navajivan*, 5 December 1926, *CWMG* 32: 388.

The AISA considered the takli as best suited to the school environment. The spinning campaign had caught on in schools, particularly those run by various municipalities controlled by nationalist parties. It was through this implement that the acute shortage of charkha was met. It was cheap, portable, easy to make and handle, and spun yarn half as fast as an ordinary spinning wheel. The takli meant practically no cost, no space, and no trouble of breakage of parts. The AISA published an authorised eighty-page booklet, *Takli Teacher*, with illustrations and text prepared by Maganlal Gandhi and Richard Gregg to popularise the idea of takli spinning. The takli was presented as an appliance of production for the masses.

The Brand Khadi

A long and arduous process went into the making of the brand khadi. The brand was built by appealing to the sentiments and patriotism of Indians by recalling the past glory of Indian entrepreneurship and craft and by building a national network of production and retail centres. Although the medium of advertising was seen as "undignified and incompatible with the khadi spirit", the AISA approved of the method. The AISA advertised through loudspeakers, popular gramophone records, etc., to push the sales of khadi. The workers toured giving lectures and visited principal towns in their respective divisions. The Maharashtra branch of the AISA conducted annual khadi *yatras* on foot, during which people were encouraged to buy khadi. Khadi exhibitions were of educational value and aided in increasing sales. Gandhi's birthday anniversary observed as Charkha Jayanti became an occasion to organise *Sutra Yajna* (sacrificial spinning) and khadi sales. It occasioned non-stop sacrificial spinning during the days leading to Gandhi's birthday. Since his sixty-sixth birthday, a spinning spree for days equalling the number of his years was launched.

The AISA's most celebrated advertisement that appealed to the discerning purchasers claimed that 95 per cent of the sales price went directly into the kitty of the primary producers. Only 5 per cent of it went to middlemen, comprising organising associates and sales agents. Gandhi Ashram in Trichur, of which Rajagopalachari was the organising secretary, iterated: dress you must have, but if you choose to buy khadi, you help the reconstruction of rural India.[23] Khadi was not merely a cloth but an idea that could reconstruct Indian economy and ameliorate India's fallen status. "One rupee spent on khadi giveth life, one rupee spent on foreign cloth killeth."[24] The economics of khadi had a soul whereas that of mill textile was soulless. *Majoor Sandesh*, a journal published by Majoor Mahajan of Ahmedabad, gave a breakup of the paid-up price of khadi that was variously distributed to the needy population unlike that of mill textiles which went only to the coffers of the mill-owner.[25] It said that if one bought a pound of khadi:

> Ten annas will go to one of our peasants.
> One-and-a-half to two annas will go to one of our poor carders.
> Four to six annas will go to some poor woman who spun the yarn.
> Eight to nine annas will go to some weaver who wove the yarn spun by those sisters.
> Three-quarters of an anna will go to one of our washermen.
> If you wear Khadi, all this money will remain in our country and will go to some of our poor brothers and sisters.

The most important step in building the brand of khadi was the AISA's power of approval. The AISA was the only body empowered by the Congress constitution to issue certificates authenticating the quality of khadi. Congress committees were debarred from exercising the same power and their persistence

[23] "Khadi Economics", *YI*, 1 December 1927, *CWMG* 35: 356.

[24] "Foreign Cloth Boycott", *YI*, 18 April 1929, *CWMG* 40: 261

[25] *Majoor Sandesh*, a journal published by the Majoor Mahajan, Ahmedabad (*CWMG* 24: 120).

was seen as interference. Khadi with the AISA stamp was certified khadi, the rest were unethical and spurious khadi. A certification process that approved certain cloth and considered the rest spurious was a product of khadi's distinct manufacturing ethos. Khadi was an enterprise with the intention to eradicate poverty in India. It also received its identity and popularity by being associated with the political movement for independence. However, the AISA certified only select retail outlets to sell the authentic khadi.

Writing in 1930, Jawaharlal Nehru observed that the demand for khadi was so great that appeals were made to the public to reduce consumption of the fabric. Gandhi advised his Gujarati readers of *Navajivan* to adopt the dhoti in the style of people from Malabar as that required less cloth. Increased popular demand for khadi was responsible for duplication of khadi, causing its spurious cousins to invade the market.[26] The mill-made textiles, coarse in texture, stamped with "Swadeshi Cloth Mark" and embossed with a picture of Gandhi's face sold in the market as Gandhi cloth. Spurious khadi produced and sold by mills threatened to capture the niche market created by the khadi campaign. "...I should like to warn people against purchasing spurious cloth which is specially made coarse so as to resemble khadi", Gandhi said categorically.[27] "I would appeal to mill-owners to refrain from naming, stamping or styling cloth manufactured in their mills as 'Khadi' and also refrain from manufacturing cloth under 18 counts' yarn." The sale of spurious khadi did assume dangerous proportions as is evident from *Young India* repeatedly publishing warning notes to caution buyers. "Beware of fine cloths", was Gandhi's cautionary note. The intervention of Indian mills to fill the gap had the tendency to jeopardise the potential of khadi to become a commodity produced by the masses. But the piracy was also a recognition of khadi's popularity.

26 "Statement to the Press", 24 September 1941, *The Hindu*.

27 "Notes: Khadi Buyers' Beware", *YI*, 21 November 1929, *CWMG* 42: 92.

In 1934, the AISA took a policy decision to unilaterally raise the spinners' wages. The wage revision was based on the knowledge that the spinners did not get even living wages for their spinning. The raise in the spinners' wage increased the production cost and thereby the sale price of khadi at the AISA-certified shops. But many of the associate production units thought it imprudent to raise the wages and openly flouted the rule. They gave the lower wages and sold khadi thus produced at lower rates. Thus, more than the textile mills, the AISA faced competition from its former associates. It implored the public to buy khadi from an AISA-certified khadi store and recognise such khadi alone as authentic khadi; other khadi even if produced by hand-spinning and hand-weaving was uncertified. "Those who sell uncertified khadi are guilty of theft from khadi-artisans. To purchase such khadi is to acquire stolen property", Gandhi wrote.

But the AISA did not just confine itself to merely issuing appeals. It moved in aggressively and innovatively to protect its brand interest and market share. The AISA claimed a patent for "khadi" and "khaddar" as exclusive to it.[28] It proposed a bill that protected the names of "khadi" and "khaddar" in that it solely denoted handspun and handwoven cloth. Its effort was directed to monopolise the handspun handwoven khadi and exclude all others from selling khadi or even using the name "khadi". Khadi as a brand had begun to take shape. In order to present khadi as a philanthropic and national commodity, it was presented as a commodity with a countrywide presence. The prices of khadi produced in various centres were pooled to bring down the average. The idea was to sell khadi at standard prices nationally with merchants receiving a certain commission on sales. But to standardise khadi production was a difficult proposition. Unlike mill cloth, khadi was not produced in factories with standard spindles, but by illiterate villagers in

[28] "Khadi in the Legislatures", *YI*, 28 March 1929, *CWMG* 40: 187.

poor rural habitats. Its yarn therefore was not uniformly even, inducing variations in cloth quality. These variations added to khadi's distinctiveness and individuality. It was its USP.

The AISA opened sales' outlets all over the country. These stores were given a common name of Khadi Bhandar or Khadi Vastralaya. The practice of having retail outlets named after their owners was discouraged. Existing outlets changed their names to suit the new policy. Each of the sales stores had a franchise from the AISA to call itself Khadi Bhandar. It helped in building khadi's recall value. *Young India* regularly published a list of Khadi Bhandars from where authentic khadi could be bought. In 1927, there were 110 retail outlets owned, certified, or affiliated to the AISA. In 1929, the list increased to 328 production-cum-sales depots scattered all over the country. But these had an uneven spread. Bengal had the highest number of 66, followed closely by Tamil Nadu with 64. Khadi Bhandars were permitted to stock indigenous silk cloth to attract customers and also to offset losses on khadi sales as silk cloth was sold at higher prices.

Commerce and Philanthropy

The AISA was in philanthropic commerce, and profiteering was not its aim. It was a business venture with philanthropic ethics. If its inspiration was altruistic, its compulsion was commercial. From the minutes of its council meeting, it does appear to work like any other business organisation. Khadi was a business venture that played to the rules of the market even while it proclaimed its innocence to common business practices such as "debasing of quality, adulteration, pandering to the baser tastes of humanity". Even while "truth, patience and faith" were the only weapons in the arsenal of a khadi seller, the AISA did introduce mainstream marketing innovations. It made forays into the ready-made garment market and adopted vegetable dyeing of khadi. It recruited the services of businessmen like G.D. Birla to streamline its sales network. It established a chain of retail outlets called Khadi Bhandars and attempted standardising the price.

The AISA tried to set standards in hand-spinning to rival mill-spinning. In one of its evaluations, the AISA noted that, "these yarns have been singled out for neatness and evenness. But even the best does not come up to the mill yarn standard."[29] The AISA aimed at producing yarns that were more even in texture and more durable than mill yarn. Improvement in the quality of yarn—its texture and strength—was a necessity for its being accepted by the weavers. The more even the thread the better it was for weaving. Gandhi wrote to Gangadharrao Deshpande, a Karnataka loyalist and khadi activist, advising greater industry in improving the quality of yarn so as to win the weavers' confidence. "Within limits our wheels do admit of improvement", he wrote.[30]

The AISA was trying to compete with the mill textile's super smoothness and affordable pricing. Making khadi an alternative to mill textiles rather than celebrating its uniquely different texture was what the AISA aimed at, but the exigencies of providing survival wages had a significant impact upon its strategies. Hence the promoters continuously measured their achievement against the standards of the market. Gandhi often distinguished khadi from purely commercial ventures, and yet he compared khadi's growth with other mercantile textiles. "How many shops are there in Bombay which sell mill-cloth both foreign and Indian? And how many khadi shops are there? We shall have to hang our heads in shame if these figures are compared." It was a trap that would beguile the promoters as well as the consumers. It was this trap that sapped khadi's potential in a substantial way. Experiments were conducted to demonstrate that "given good cotton and good carding, it is possible to draw fine thread that would beat the strongest mill

[29] "Notes: Room for Improvement", *YI*, 29 April 1926, *CWMG* 30: 380.
[30] "Letter to Ganagdharrao Deshpande", 27 July 1926, *CWMG* 31: 200.

yarn of the same count". Thus, exigencies were making the promoters cater to market sensibilities. Ironically, khadi was also identified with a movement and brandished as symbolising an ideological severance from the market.

Like any other enterprise, it needed to keep its balance sheet from being in the red. The profit motive was not encouraged; but neither were any loss-making units tolerated. In 1926, The AISA ordered all loss-making Khadi Bhandars to be closed. It stopped all "credit-sales" for retail or wholesale transactions. It discouraged altruistic but amateurish entrepreneurs as their ventures often incurred heavy losses, and the AISA had to buy their badly spun yarn. But it also betrayed its philanthropic core. While it acted as a business outfit, it also gave space for experimentation even if it meant monetary loss in the beginning. Its strategy was to depend on extensive business rather than on high profits on capital invested. Raising the wages of spinners unilaterally was its second most important policy decision that proved AISA's philanthropic or righteous commercial intentions.

Khadi was conceived as the foundation and symbol of *ahimsa*. Gandhi was often prone to equate khadi wearing with virtue and purity. "A real khadi-wearer will harbour no violence, no deceit, and no impurity", he said.[31] Khadi was identified as the fabric of morality; its donning imbued the wearer with virtue. Inevitably, a simple khadi garment was burdened with the conflicting mores of economics and morality. There were complaints that many used khadi as a cloak for their deceit. The self-serving exploitation of khadi's moral attributes made others question the validity of investing it with excessive attributes. Thus, the morality of khadi could jeopardise its economics.

Khadi kept oscillating between altruism and commercialism, and this contradiction in intentions reduced its chances of commercial success. Khadi as a brand was created from its avid

[31] "Speech at Khadi and Village Industries Exhibition", 16 Februray 1938, *CWMG* 66: 372.

association with ideals. It was not merely a commercial brand. It was consciously built on values of purity and patriotism, of simplicity and sacrifice. The khadi movement was the "greatest cooperative effort of modern times" and the AISA "the largest cooperative society in the world".[32] Those involved in the khadi enterprise were "trustees" for the welfare of spinners. "In ordinary commerce the maxim is that we look after ourselves and those with whom we trade have to look after themselves. The position in Khadi trade is reversed".[33] The AISA was against selfish exploitation and personal aggrandisement and advocated instead service to the poor. Khadi was not dependent on the market but "upon the purity of our transaction".[34] These differing aims distinguished the khadi enterprise from other commercial ventures. Yet, its commercial success was dependent on the piety of merchants who ironically were in trade for profit and not altruism.

The commercial exigencies made Gandhi advocate khadi to everyone. "Even a scoundrel has a perfect right to wear it", he said when reported of the use of khadi by people with questionable integrity. "Khadi may be worn by the devout as well as by the hypocrite or the treacherous; by the chestiest of wives as well as by a prostitute."[35] Even a man propagating an ideology contrary to the non-violence struggle could wear khadi. Alluri Shri Rama Raju, a rebel Andhra hero, was one such person who wore khadi. Gandhi himself provided publicity to Raju's uniform. He was not even against the AISA's selling khadi blankets to the military.[36] Non-violence, Gandhi argued,

[32] "Speech at Khadi Vastralaya", Rajatalayam, 4 October 1927, *CWMG* 35: 77.

[33] "Speech at Public Meeting", Rajatalayam, 4 October 1927, *CWMG* 35: 80.

[34] *Khadi Jagat*, *CWMG* 74: 59–60.

[35] "Speech at Khadi and Village Industries Exhibition", 16 February 1938, *CWMG* 66: 372.

[36] "Blankets for Soldiers", *Khadi Jagat*, September 1941, *CWMG* 74: 329.

is much like a geometrical line, which cannot be drawn but only imagined. One must therefore practice non-violence as best as one can. It was such fine-edge policy decisions that made khadi or even the whole of Gandhian dogma fraught with abuse. Dilemmas about taking recourse to legal action was another instance of the AISA's suffering financial loss and embezzlement. Its method of trust in business was the cause of the many unfortunate experiences it suffered. There were cases of embezzlement of the AISA's finances by some of its workers. In one case the AISA suffered loss due to the fudging of audit records. It tried to retrieve the appropriated money but without taking recourse to a court of law, as per its traditional policy. However, this met with little success.

The AISA increasingly targeted public institutions such as hospitals to buy khadi. The King Edward Memorial Hospital under the Bombay Municipal Corporation bought khadi in bulk for their clothing needs. Local governments and municipalities bought their cloth requirements from the AISA-certified institutions. The Assam council successfully piloted a resolution calling upon the local government to make all its cloth purchases in khadi. In 1937, when the Congress ministries were formed, the AISA called for state purchases of cloth to be made in khadi. "The administration of eight provinces is virtually in Congress hands to an extent enough to protect khadi", Gandhi said.[37] He called for taxing any mill cloth that competed with khadi.

Theoretically, khadi had immense possibility for growth. Each of the rural hamlets could be transformed into a miniature-spinning mill requiring little capital investment or technical expertise. Khadi then would not only be produced in every village but it would gain the status of a transnational commodity with an independent momentum. In its most advanced state of

37 "Notes: Khadi as Famine Insurance and Medium of Instruction", *Harijan*, 19 August 1939, *CWMG* 70: 92.

development, after khadi had become a "current coin", as Gandhi envisioned and postulated, "the toiling millions will spin their own yarn and get it woven by the village weaver".[38] It would be a "natural decentralization" of an economic imperative. Such a system would permit the least fraud. It would be like the times before the British merchants had stamped out the indigenous manufacturing system. Yet, this was not merely a re-enactment of past practice, nor a continuation of tradition. It had new manufacturing ethics and a commercial organisation that Gandhi had envisaged. He regarded khadi to be "the shortest route to healthy commercial prosperity of individuals as it certainly will be of the nation".[39] Its slow growth did not dishearten him. "After all, sound commerce", Gandhi said, "is of slow growth". It was for the khadi movement to nurture an alternative understanding of the commercial mechanism. It was potentially a powerful idea of transformation, pregnant with far-reaching consumer ethics. But from a practical point of view it meant the creation of an alternative production and consumption pattern on a massive scale. As it took on an established foreign trade and indigenous textile producers, the odds against it were heavily stacked. Yet the simplicity of the idea was profound.

Khadi and social reform became inadvertently intertwined. Village reform movements almost always arrived in the wake of khadi work in a particular village. R.B. Gregg said khadi provided elemental security, and it tended immediately to develop the moral qualities of the people: hope, initiative, perseverance, self-reliance, self-respect.[40] The AISA member's prime duty was to campaign for hand-spinning and khadi. But more than this work in the social sphere, it was in the personal realm that he was primarily held responsible. In the villages where khadi work

[38] "Foreign Cloth Boycott", *YI*, 25 April 1929, *CWMG* 40: 281.

[39] "Letter to Satcowripati Ray", 19 May 1927, *CWMG* 33: 340–42.

[40] R.B. Gregg, *Economics of Khaddar*, 153.

took a foothold, the activists also initiated anti-liquor and sanitation campaigns. The spinning venture aided in forging bonds between activists and villagers. A khadi ashram at Vedchhi, a village in Gujarat's Surat district, initiated an anti-liquor movement.[41] Rajagopalachari's ashram in Tamil Nadu came to focus on many aspects of village reconstruction, communal sanitation, and basic personal hygiene along with their main work of khadi.[42] They were the by-products of the khadi movement.

Political Utility or Economic Proposition

Was khadi a strategy by the nationalist leadership to keep the masses engaged in some kind of peacetime activity during quiescent periods in the national struggle? Apparently not, for the constructive work of khadi was not just a preparation for aggressive phases of civil disobedience; it was an activity complete in itself. Gandhi was reluctant to concede a political character to the AISA.[43] He fiercely protected its non-political aims. He reiterated that the AISA was as much political as any endeavour done with a pure, progressive motive. In the preamble of the AISA, two things stood out in unequivocal and emphatic terms. First, it was unaffected and uncontrolled by politics, political changes, or political bodies. Second, it had an independent existence and power. Congress parentage and patronage of the AISA made it a target of governmental suspicion, espionage, and harassment. In the government's view the AISA had the potential

[41] "Notes: Self-purification among Chodhras", *Navajivan*, 27 June 1926, *CWMG* 31: 58.

[42] Referring to the report from the Gandhi Ashram conducted by Rajagopalachari, Gandhi wrote: "From the report read at the meeting it appears that round khadi as the centre, removal of untouchability and of the evil drink, rural sanitation and medical relief have sprung up" ("Byproducts of Khadi", YI, 19 July 1928, *CWMG* 37: 74).

[43] "Khadi Week", *Harijan*, 23 September 1940, *CWMG* 73: 46–48.

to organise civil disobedience. As a disciplinary measure, the government restricted its employees from contributing to the Khadi Fund. "How such an association could be called a political association, simply because it is an integral part of the Congress passes comprehension", Gandhi said.[44] His only objective, he said, was to abolish idleness. "I dare not think of land improvement and improvement in the methods of agriculture, for I know my limitations." There was no linkage of the AISA with civil disobedience, as it was to be organised independently, he asserted.

At the same time, civil disobedience was incomplete without the constructive organisation, as it not only broadened the base of the struggle but such a strategy was also mutually empowering based as it was on non-violence. "The constructive programme may more fittingly be called construction of poorna swaraj by truthful and non-violent means."[45] While imprisoned at Yervada, Gandhi who used to write a weekly discourse on various issues for the ashram was reluctant to send one on swadeshi as it was a political issue. "I feel that by writing on it I may violate to some extent my resolution to make no reference to political subjects", he wrote to an ashram colleague.[46]

The constant advocacy through a mix of political and economic reasons had transformed khadi into a "uniform of rebellion"[47]. During each of the rebellious crests, people vied to don the "uniform". If donning khadi was an expression of patriotism, then, Indians conscious of the cause of struggle were determined to buy it. The irony was that it was not the boycott movement that raised the demand of khadi among the conscious consumers. It was khadi's transformation into a freedom's fabric that brought

[44] "What is Political Association?" *YI*, 7 July 1927, *CWMG* 34: 126–28.

[45] "Constructive Programme: Its Meaning and Place", 13 December 1941, *CWMG* 75: 165.

[46] "Letter to Narandas Gandhi", 25/30 September 1930, *CWMG* 44: 186.

[47] Bernard S. Cohen, *Colonialism and its Forms of Knowledge*; 107

its surging popularity. It was therefore during the crests of the struggle that khadi touched the peak of consumption. In the period between 1919 and 1929, Gandhi worked hard in propagating and systematising khadi consumption and production. Meanwhile, in the interregnum, khadi had also changed its meaning. In 1919–22, it was the slogan for boycott through khadi that had mostly brought its popularity. But in the period 1929–32, khadi was worn more as a protest uniform than as replacement for foreign cloth. Its texture got interwoven with the rebellious mood of the times. Its wearer knew exactly why he was wearing it and the very act taunted the law enforcement authority.

In its twenty-second council meeting held just before Gandhi was leaving the ashram for Dandi, in March 1930, the AISA resolved to meet the eventualities that might occur in case the civil disobedience movement was launched. The council while permitting individual khadi workers to participate in the campaign ensured that the khadi organisation was not affected. Workers who joined the civil disobedience movement were considered to be on leave without allowance. The movement brought in its wake the arrest of almost all the officiating members of the AISA. In its twenty-third meeting held in October 1930, the council appointed a new set of members who were nominated by the preceding office-bearers.

Whatever its political ambitions, the AISA primarily fashioned itself as an economic enterprise catering to the poorest. Its ostensible aim was to provide an opportunity for earning a supplementary wage. In 1927, while on an Orissa tour, Gandhi offered to disengage khadi producers of the region from the need to market their products. He asked them to determinedly pursue the production goal alone. In the early 1930s, provincial branches of the AISA registered profits of varying degrees. It attracted the attention of the Income Tax Department which slapped a heavy penalty for the non-payment of tax. It was a penalty tax of over fifty thousand rupees for the years of 1935–36, though the AISA claimed that it was a non-profit organisation.

Khadi was a non-violent political weapon to establish nationalist hegemony over mass consciousness. By its silent work, the AISA attempted to produce a symbol of nationalist upsurge. Khadi was political in the sense that a simple gesture of wearing it transformed a person into a vehicle of assertion. By donning it one conveyed in a remarkably silent, non-confrontationist way one's break from the imperial chain; unobtrusively one announced one's shift in allegiance. Thereby it provided the meekest of individuals a banner to foist his/her freedom. But at the same time it also provided individuals an opportunity to shift their allegiance from a distant and abstract Empire to the neighborhood. Khadi was a visible, almost universal articulation of a shift in allegiance. It provided autonomy of choice. In doing so it empowered each individual to freedom of thought and action. The freedom Gandhi fought for was not only national but also personal. Khadi was the tale of personal empowerment. It conveyed a message to the people that "they were stronger than they thought and that the rulers were weaker than they imagined".[48] The campaign was not directly "designed to establish independence but to arm the people with the power to do so." Most of Gandhi's campaigns were, as Weber says, in a different context, "about reforming society and the self-reformation of individuals". There was a close linkage between the two. "Reform yourself and you have started to reform the world, reform the world non-violently and you will have reformed the self."[49]

CONCLUSION

"I am a man possessed by an idea", Gandhi spoke to Louis Fisher at Sevagram in the first week of June 1942, just before his

[48] Thomas Weber, 1997, *On the Salt March*, 472.

[49] Ibid., 472–73. 1

"Quit India" call. "If such a man cannot get an organization, he becomes an organization", he claimed.[50] The AISA was born from the obsession of one man; its creation and career embodied Gandhi's ideological conviction and passionate perseverance. Founded in late 1925, it was an effort towards the creation of a decentralised network. Gandhi called it a purely philanthropic initiative. One factor that catalysed its establishment was the lack of suitable workers in the service of khadi. The AISA, also, was a remedial measure for the existing problems of managing the subscription yarn. The AISA attempted to establish a permanent agency manned by dedicated and trained workers. From the perspective of voluntary work, with all the limitations that such work entails, the AISA's achievement was significant. The initiatives of the AISA are significant precedents for voluntary work. Even while it professed to be a philanthropic enterprise, it was run like any other commercial firm. To a degree it succeeded in fusing the discipline of commerce and sentiments of philanthropy together. But what in its early days was its crucial contribution, in a later phase came to stultify its growth. Gandhi's opponents were many and their sniping was in poor taste, but in some tragic way their prediction proved truer than Gandhi's optimism. Khadi lost out as a political weapon and was transformed into a commodity by sustained opposition from the Congress. But even its conversion into a commodity was not a profitable venture.

The AISA faced two problems. On the one hand it had a mass of illiterate, unskilled, famished, and secluded women as its producing agents. On the other hand it had to face the agony of constantly explaining its viability to sceptics. Its organising workers were lowly paid. Its buyers were discerning customers who complained of the lack of quality, durability, convenience, etc. Its spurt in sales only came when national

[50] Louis Fischer, 1944, *A Week with Gandhi*, 27.

struggles were launched. Despite its symbolic association with ahimsa, it was not a peacetime cloth. Inadvertently, it took on a rebellious hue that constrained considerably its commercial prospects. Government servants who were comparatively better placed on the capacity-to-purchase scale would not touch it for fear of being suspended. The government did not purchase khadi as it was reluctant to provide legitimacy to the nationalist entrepreneurship. It also became a cloak to hide one's inner impurity and gain outer acceptance. Those who wore it were not always with integrity, specially under the merciless scrutiny of the public eye, even when they were constantly harping on the symbolic "pure whiteness" that had positioned it in public perception as a value-laden cloth. Its association with a seemingly backward technology, which for the forward-looking, educated generation was unpalatable, restricted its appeal. What alternative they had for khadi's income distributional capacity and mass employment (even if partial) was not clear, but they were unanimous that the modern production system alone could obviate India's poverty. The Westernised and vocal section of Indians saw the khadi organisation as an attempt to cling to India's poverty. Nehru and other socialists often derided it. It was an instrument, they averred, for Gandhi to worship the god of poverty, Daridranarayana. They did not see it as having the capacity to eradicate Indian poverty. Indeed, khadi, in their perception, scuttled the real issue of class conflict and exploitation in Indian villages. Charkha could only spin a patchwork; it could never cure the real rural afflictions. Such an attitude of rejection made the AISA's work difficult.

Despite the spreading links and deepening roots, there was widespread belief that the AISA would down shutters once Gandhi was no more. Economists were sceptical of Gandhi's efforts. Many of Gandhi's opponents went so far as to sarcastically remark that Gandhi's mortal remains would be cremated with the wooden frames of so many of the discarded charkhas. Contrary to such impressions, Gandhi refused to concede that the charkha would disappear with his own earthly disappearance. He hoped that other members of the AISA would reciprocate his "matchless faith in khadi". While asserting that destruction is the law of nature, he scarcely believed that the country would dump khadi after his demise. "I do not find a single sign to suggest that khadi work will totally disappear from the country." Instead, he saw signs of increasing faith in khadi. There were people, independent-minded and who had sacrificed their all on the altar of khadi, who would not allow the AISA to be wound up, he said. It could be possible that the AISA might one day cease to function but it would not be an unceremonious end. Its identity could be merged into a bigger entity. "Destruction as such is no evil. The destruction of an activity which is sacred is as good as a revolution."[51] Further, being a donor-driven organisation, the AISA could not be wound up without their permission. In its fifty-sixth meeting, held in October 1946, it was mooted that the AISA should hand over all khadi production and sales work to the people's institutions and confine itself to auditing duties. This was not done. Within a decade, however, in 1953, after initial dithering, the AISA was wound up and merged with a larger Gandhian umbrella organisation called Sarva Seva Sangh.[52] With that came the end to its career of philanthropic commerce. With the post-independence government appropriating its agenda, it was soon reduced to a department within the vast governmental hierarchy.

To rate the khadi movement on the scale of cloth production and consumption would be futile. Moral progress it had undoubtedly achieved. Its material progress cannot be gauged vis-à-vis total cloth production in the country. As the movement

[51] "About the Charkha Sangh", *Navajivan*, 11 November 1927, *CWMG* 35: 279.

[52] Dhirendra Majumdar became one of the pillars of the AISA in its later phase and was also appointed as president after Gandhi's death.

progressed, khadi did become a brand. Its quality had also improved. But the achievement was dismal as a war measure. Gandhi did not expect dealers/merchants/mill-owners to court bankruptcy or forego profits for the country. "They will be the last, not the first, to wake up. To blame them on this ground is to blame human nature."[53] The onus for the fiasco was put on consumers. The consumer had been satisfied with a partial boycott. Neither did the consumers take to spinning. Only the poor took to spinning. Women could not reconcile themselves to the change as readily as men. The consumers were exhorted to spin and adopt khadi even if that meant bearing with heavy, unattractive clothes and paying a disproportionately high price. Mostly those driven by philanthropic or patriotic zeal purchased khadi as it was relatively dearer. But those who had no spare cash were not easily actuated by philanthropy or patriotism.

[53] "In the name itself, 'khadi', there is no magic. The magic lies in its virtues" ("Pitfalls in Swadeshi", *Navajivan*, 6 October 1921, *CWMG* 21: 255).

8 Quest for Freedom of the Lowest[1]

The Final Exit

The first indication to "leave Congress free to evolve a new programme" came to Gandhi from his old friend V. S. Srinivasa Sastri.[2] Gandhi, Sastri wrote "after much thought and destruction of several drafts", was not fit to lead India into the "fresh era". His khadi was leading India nowhere. "Leave Congress", Sastri wrote in August 1933, a full year after Gandhi's "epic fast" in September 1932 in response to the communal award. Sastri demanded suspension of the civil disobedience movement and adoption of "a new policy" aimed at the parliamentary path.

1 "Freedom must be judged by freedom of lowest but feel danger other issues obscuring only goal", Nehru telegrammed his opinion on Gandhi's impending fast on communal award (Telegram from Jawaharlal Nehru, 26 September 1932, *CWMG* 51: 134).

2 "Letter from V. S. Srinivasa Sastri", 27 August 1933, Appendix XIII, *CWMG* 55: 455.

Sastri spoke the Swarajist's language. Gandhi who had exhorted his opponents in 1924 to create conditions for his expulsion, now wrote to Vallabhbhai Patel, asking for an environment to facilitate his withdrawal.

Each constructive agenda and its laborious execution was an inch closer to India's swaraj and yet it had to struggle as much against the British imperialists as against the Indian nationalists. After his 1932 fast, Gandhi selected men, provided ideology and method, gave moral support, launched the multi-lingual *Harijan*, and forged regional organisations for the campaign against untouchability. It was from jail that he initiated, guided, and ran the movement. His prolific communication with various correspondents, his press interviews, his extracting of the right to undertake campaign while still in prison were all signs of his passionate belief in the cause. The anti-untouchability campaign had drawn the same passionate persona that just a while ago was engaged wholly in the khadi movement. Nationalist politicians saw Gandhi's fast and his campaign as diversionary; it might "indefinitely postpone the prospect of swaraj", they averred.[3] The news of Gandhi's fast caused "mental agony, confusion" to an imprisoned Jawaharlal Nehru.

The Congress respected his personality, not his politics. For instance, Subhas Chandra Bose thought "the Mahatma's popularity and reputation does not depend on his political leadership—but largely on his character".[4] The Congress relegated him to being a political relic, to be displayed for ritual observance. He protested against such insinuations of "intellectual decay". Gandhi's political marginalisation had begun soon after the Bardoli resolution at the beginning of 1922. But he fought on

[3] "Statement on Untouchability", 16 November 1932, *CWMG* 52: 4.

[4] Subhas Chandra Bose, 1935, "The role of Mahatma Gandhi in Indian History", in *The Indian Struggle*. (*The Essential Writings of Netaji Subhas Chandra Bose* 1997).

till about the end of his tenure in December 1925 as the Congress president. But, the halo his persona acquired was used to the advantage of the Congress when needed and dispensed with when it went against the established ethos of the original Congress. The marginalisation became more pronounced after the declaration of his fast in September 1932. With his campaign on untouchability, Gandhi was aiming for a bigger slice of the Indian consciousness. Thus it was necessary to urgently rein him in, as his subversive potential was enormous. Despite being the main beneficiary of Gandhi's politics, the Congress's concerns were never coterminous with his. Gandhi's attempts to engineer society from inside prison walls and by indulging in self-flagellation produced frenzied reactions but whose intensity waned equally rapidly. He was accused of bringing spirituality into worldly power politics. This was ironical as whatever success Gandhi achieved was more of a political nature than spiritual. Satyagraha Ashram, his spiritual warehouse, was disbanded following intractable problems, such as insinuations that inmates had contracted venereal diseases.[5]

Gandhi's politics was a double-edged weapon in the hands of Congress politicians. While they could accuse his politics, in Nehru's words, of "supporting a system which involves a continuous and devastating class war", they could also rely upon it to create a mass backing in their power tussle with the British ruling elite. He allowed himself to be used conveniently by the Congress, because he too used the political platform to further his own agenda of founding "Swaraj for the millions". But in the contestation of agendas, he was finally "defeated and humbled", and the conditions causing his ejection from his formal association with the political organisation came to a head. He remained a Congress figurehead for they understood their need for each other and played along. He founded many voluntary agencies

[5] "Letter to Narandas Gandhi", 5/6 May 1933, *CWMG* 55: 127

possessing nominal affiliation with the Congress to carry out his work for the social and economic regeneration of the Indian masses, which, according to him, would eventually lead to political liberation. Congress allowed such leverage not because it empathised with Gandhi's agenda, but because his name provided an aura while his work did not threaten its schema of seeking political power.

Gandhi was up against two adversaries. If the content of freedom was as indispensable a matter of principle as the achievement of freedom, the battle was to be led on two fronts. He founded a parallel stream of politics that had reluctant acceptance in the Congress. His activities around constructive work had failed to galvanise the Congress into action though the political organisation gained a mass base. "Congressmen, as a whole", Gandhi noted in a candid speech at the AICC meeting at Patna in May 1934, "have never taken kindly to purely constructive work, such as the charkha".[6] The Congress had a primordial craving for a share in political power, but this did not interest Gandhi. Such mutual disillusionment precipitated Gandhi's eventual withdrawal from the Congress. His presence, as Gandhi reflected in a sad note, "more and more estranges the intelligentsia from the Congress". "My remaining in the Congress", Gandhi wrote in a long letter to Patel, "...may interfere with free expression of those ideas, however distasteful some of them may be to me."[7]

Gandhi's stature had certainly dwarfed many of the people around him. He had "out-topped", Sastri wrote, all other leaders so long and so decisively that there was no one near his vicinity.[8]

[6] "Speech at AICC Meeting", Patna, *CWMG* 58: 10.

[7] "I feel that my policies fail to convince their reason, though strange as it may appear, I do nothing that does not satisfy my own reason" ("Letter to Vallabhbhai Patel", 5 September 1934, *CWMG* 58: 405).

[8] "Letter from V. S. Srinivasa Sastri", 27 August 1933, Appendix XIII, *CWMG* 55: 455.

In a poignant letter, Birla brought the fact to light when he wrote, "We are so much dazzled with your superhuman personality that we have almost lost self-confidence in ourselves."[9] Gandhi called the "dazzle of my presence" a "greater embarrassment" to his person than to friends who were victims of such "dazzling" impairment.[10] He came to conclude "that the best interests of the Congress and the nation will be served by my completely severing all connection with the Congress, including the original membership". He proposed "voluntary retirement" because "my doing so will rid it of hypocrisy."[11]

He was resigning, he said, because "the Congress had degenerated into an organisation dominated by my own personality".[12] In reality he was a demi-god who was past his prime. There were generous votes in favour of his resolutions, but when it came to their practical application they were ingeniously scuttled. It amounted to sabotage from within, all in the name of respect, loyalty, and greatness. The active allegiance Gandhi strove for was rarely obtained. But his attachment to the aim, despite all his reading of the *Gita*, was intense. As a last-ditch effort he proposed certain amendments that sought to strengthen khadi in the Congress hierarchy. It was his final bid before he bowed out. The Congress did not take kindly to Gandhi's attempts. He refused to withdraw his amendments and, as a consequence, Congress consented to his removal.

At the Bombay annual session of the Congress in 1934 where his withdrawal was finally permitted, Gandhi received some concessions. He extracted a commitment from the Congress to shift its annual session from a city centre to a village base. He added a new constructive organisation called the All India Village

[9] "Letter from G.D. Birla", 21 December 1932, Appendix XIII, *CWMG* 52: 436–38.

[10] "Letter to G.D. Birla", 27 December 1932, *CWMG* 52: 295.

[11] "Letter to Vallabhbhai Patel", 19 August 1934, *CWMG* 58: 329.

[12] "Statement to the Press", 17 September 1934, *CWMG* 59: 4.

Industries Association (AIVIA), with J. C. Kumarappa as its organising secretary, to his kitty of autonomous organisations such as the AISA. The idea of AIVIA was an outcome of the Harijan tours that Gandhi undertook in the aftermath of "the epic fast". During his tours, Gandhi found that khadi had become a lifeless symbol. He was also criticised for the absence of economic content in his "temple entry" campaign. In the new formulation, khadi retained its centrality, being called the sun of the solar system, but attention was now also laid on a number of other village industries, the planets.

In the immediate aftermath of his withdrawal from the Congress in 1934, a new organisation received the attention of Gandhi and his colleagues. It was the Gandhi Sewa Sangh (GSS), founded in July 1923 at Wardha while Gandhi was in prison. The founding members of the sangh were Gandhi's loyal political colleagues who had faithfully fought within the Congress to keep afloat his agenda of constructive work as the basis of freedom. They were collectively known as the "no-changers" whose rival "pro-changers" wanted the Congress to participate in the elections to the council. The Gandhi Sewa Sangh identified with the vision of national struggle through constructive work. In its formative years, its main task was to provide financial support to full-time workers and their families. Admission to the sangh was restricted to non-cooperators and to those who believed in constructive work. It gave membership only to those who had faith in the charkha with "wide interpretations". The organisation for a decade remained dormant after its establishment under the Registration of Charitable Societies Act of 1860. Gandhi's close non-political associates reactivated the moribund organisation in 1934.

Its moving force was Jamnalal Bajaj, the founding president. The organisation's finances came mainly from Bajaj. The control, guidance, and management of the sangh were vested in a board of trustees. Among the "no-changers", who were its founding trustees as well, were Rajendra Prasad, Rajagopalachari and Sardar Patel. Together they were called the "rightists". Each of them was responsible for the organisation of the sangh and its activities in their respective regions. Gandhi himself was not on the board. He kept a distance from its proceedings till the mid-thirties when the organisation was reorganised with changed priorities. In its new incarnation, the Gandhi Sewa Sangh held its first annual session in November 1934, a month after the Bombay Congress session where Gandhi had formally severed his membership from the Congress.

At its second annual meeting held in early 1936, the sangh decided to hold all its sessions in villages. Each session had an exhibition of local manufactures and crafts. The exhibition housed artifacts related to village economic life. The aim of such exhibitions was meant to imbue life in fast-dying rural industries. The sangh paid support money to its activists. It also decided to constitute a committee to compile and collate Gandhian thought. The third session of the newborn organisation was held at Hudli in Karnataka in April 1937.

In the popular consciousness, the sangh in Gandhi's post-Congress phase was seen as an alternative outfit to the Congress.[13] In the Congress, it was widely believed that if the Faizpur Congress belonged to Jawaharlal Nehru, the Hudli conclave of the sangh was Gandhi's response to it. Whether as an organisation the sangh could have rivalled the Congress base is left to historical speculation, but the frequency of its national meet did increase suddenly and Gandhi's attention on it increased in proportion to his distance from the Congress.

At Hudli, the air was laden with the perceived rivalry between him and Nehru. It occupied Gandhi's attention so much so that he devoted his entire opening speech to it. "It is a sin to imagine

[13] "Speech at Gandhi Sewa Sangh", Hudli-I, 16 April 1937, *CWMG* 65: 88.

even in jest that there can be any rivalry between Jawaharlal and me", he said. "The Gandhi Sewa Sangh is not opposed to the Congress." Yet, the very acknowledgement of rumours gave further credence to the perceived rivalry. The ideological division between Gandhi and Nehru had acquired a new, sharp dimension. Gandhi had helped establish a new wing of the Congress to undertake parliamentary politics. It could have been a counter to the emerging socialists who were critical of Gandhi's khadi-centric policies. Nehru no longer was dependent on Gandhi for his stature as a leader of the country. He now had an independent base and was no longer required to underline his filial affection for "dear Bapu". The journey from Lahore to Lucknow, where in 1936 he was again crowned with the Congress presidency, had established Nehru as a leader of a new block of socialists.

Gandhi tried to bury the rumour. "How could the Sangh", he asked "be opposed to the Congress when it was conceived in order to carry out the constructive programme of the Congress?" The Congress represented the country; the sangh members represented only themselves, he said. It was an organ committed to the Congress and its programme of constructive work as laid down in 1920. It was a voluntary institution unlike bodies such as the AISA or AIVIA, which were created under the Congress mandate. Whatever the objectives, its intention was to create and sustain an alternative cadre that could do what the Congress was now refusing to do. Just as Gandhi's agenda was an alternative to the Congress traditional wisdom of cooperation with the government, the sangh was an alternative outfit that would nurture his politics.

Gandhi's firm belief was that if the Congress, owing to the exigencies of its politics and compulsion of the constituting factions, left the constructive programme, it would be an pronouncement of its own death. It was the constructive programme that provided grassroots' support to the political work of the Congress. The sangh was founded to persevere with constructive work irrespective of the Congress. If the AISA was to develop the science of khadi, the sangh was to evolve the philosophy of khadi a little further. Because of the sangh's foundational moorings, the constructive work was its permanent agenda.

In 1937, the sangh's participation in elections was announced. It was at the behest of Gandhi that a Congress Parliamentary Board was instituted. Yet, initially, Gandhi was reluctant to allow constructive workers to participate in the elections. Gandhi had moved from being a non-cooperator to advocating acceptance of ministerial responsibility. Many of the political workers were members of the AISA as well as of the sangh. The sangh members had the most interaction with the electorate. Among members of the Gandhi Sewa Sangh, there was a tendency to deride political work and those associated with it, but Gandhi advised participation in the elections as he felt that suitable candidates could only be found in the sangh. The sangh members in the council could help further khadi. Gandhi was speaking a language reminiscent of the Swarajist's arguments in favour of their programme of council entry. The ethos had come full circle.

Most of the members favoured participation while at the same time many others saw the electoral endeavour as a diversion from the main vocation. There was a minor rebellion in the sangh when its president, Kishorelal Mashruwala, resigned owing to differences over the issue of participation in the election.[14] Kishorelal had felt that by going for elections the sangh was giving up truth and non-violence. His argument was that the parliamentary programme was full of temptations. Gandhi argued that the programme had created considerable enthusiasm among the members. The sangh members were permitted with approval from the Congress Working Committee to participate in elections

[14] "Speech at Gandhi Sewa Sangh", Hudli-III, 20 April 1937, *CWMG* 65: 116–34.

to the legislative assembly. Participation of the sangh members as candidates and campaigners in the election helped Congress emerge victorious.[15]

The sangh was the citadel of Gandhi's indigenous intellectuals. Most of the close comrades of Gandhi, his actual colleagues in his constructive work, are not to be found in the annals of Indian history. While his political colleagues who espoused the constitutional and political course got their share of historical limelight, his colleagues in constructive work were barely remembered. It was these colleagues that participated in the deliberation of the sangh. The AISA or AIVIA were action bodies with limited mandates and Congress affiliation. The sangh was the apex body of Gandhian workers. It was a mighty tree of which the AISA and AIVIA and other such offshoots were its branch.... Gandhi repeatedly asserted its voluntary status and disclaimed any rivalry with the Congress. But the frequency of sessions declined once it began to be associated as an alternative formation to the Congress.

Gandhi's indifference to political problems did not mean that he had turned his back on the fight for freedom. It was, he asserted, "a fight to finish", but it was a non-violent fight. The charkha was a "symbol of ahimsa". Nehru often accused the khadi workers of passivity. He regarded charkha-adherents to be fanatics lacking in "intellect". It was no discipline to spin like automatons, he said. Gandhi too often criticised the "Charkhawalla" for lacking enough faith to make charkha a "living image" that could induce change. But Gandhi did not admit that plying the charkha stunted the intellect.

The difference between Gandhi and Nehru on the economic aspects was, as Gandhi himself said, "difference...of emphasis". Nehru believed in industrialisation while Gandhi had "grave

15 "Speech at Gandhi Sewa Sangh", Hudli-II, 17 April 1937, *CWMG* 65: 99–106

doubts about its usefulness for India". Nehru was impatient with Gandhi's village reform programme. In 1936, Nehru, as the president of the Congress, visited a Khadi Bhandar in Bombay. The *Hindu* of 18 May 1936 reported that Nehru expressed doubts over khadi's economic utility.[16] He said that khadi might be a necessity in the present environment but it would scarcely solve India's poverty problem. He was for "big industry". His colleagues in the Congress such as Patel and Prasad were disturbed. Gandhi later mediated between Nehru and his aggrieved colleagues and effected a peace. In an article "A False Alarm", Gandhi said even if khadi did not receive unstinted support from Nehru, it had a number of confirmed believers. In response to Nehru's view, Gandhi argued on khadi's economic utility in another article titled: "Is Khadi Economically Sound?"

Nehru, moreover, believed in the inevitability of class conflict. Gandhi saw no such necessity. The difference was born out of Gandhi's faith in absolute non-violence. For Gandhi, non-violence was a matter of creed which it was not for Nehru. Nehru effectively said that Gandhi in the garb of non-violence was approving a system based essentially on violence. Of his differences with Nehru, Gandhi wrote to a common friend that "Jawaharlal's way is not my way. I do not accept practically any of his methods. My method is designed to avoid conflict. His is not so designed."[17] Gandhi expected "to convert the zamindars and other capitalist by non-violent methods", for, he argued, "if the toilers intelligently combine, they will become an irresistible power". The capital and not capitalist is "insentient".

When media reports insinuated friction between the "two rivals", Gandhi wrote in *Harijan* asking "Are we rivals?" It was said that Gandhi had averred that Nehru's policy had "ruined" his "life-work". Gandhi plainly refused that he ever had said

[16] "Letter to Jawaharlal Nehru", 21 May 1936, *CWMG* 62: 425.

[17] "Letter to Agatha Harrison", 30 April 1936, *CWMG* 62: 353.

such a thing. Gandhi admitted the difference of opinion on policies. His philosophy of life, he said, excluded the "possibility of harm to one's cause by outside agencies". "We remain the same adherents to the Congress goal that we have ever been." But just a month later, Gandhi was almost pathetically pleading with Nehru, "Why is it that with all the will in the world I cannot understand what is so obvious to you?" "Unfurl your own banner" was a distant memory. The 1930s was Nehru's decade, when he was twice elected the Congress president, and when he led the Congress to a substantial victory in the elections.

The distance was growing as is obvious from Gandhi's letter to Nehru on 25 April 1938. Gandhi wrote, "It hurts me that, at this very critical juncture in our history, we do not seem to see eye to eye in important matters." He was feeling lonely, just the way Nehru had felt in the 1920s, when he did not understand Gandhi's political manoeuvers. "Somehow or other everything I say and even perhaps do jars on you", was a pathetic plea to his protégé.

The distance kept on growing to such a degree that even in 1942, prior to the launch of the quit India movement, Gandhi was refuting insinuations of estrangement and declaring Nehru to be his "successor". "When I am gone he will do what I am doing now. Even if this does not happen, I would at least die with this faith."[18] Earlier he had written to B.C. Roy, "Jawaharlal is the only man with drive to take my place".[19] His influence over the country would depend on the extent he would be able to influence Jawaharlal. Ten days after his letter to Roy in which he declared Nehru to be his "successor", Gandhi wrote to Nehru that he would "observe complete silence" if the latter desired it. But even while he offered to surrender, he did not fail to mention that "differences in outlook between us are becoming most marked".[20]

18 "Speech at AICC Meeting", Wardha, 15 January 1942, *CWMG* 75: 225

19 "Letter to B.C. Roy", 12 October 1939.

20 "Letter to Jawaharlal", 26 October 1939.

For about ten years Gandhi remained obscured from the politics of the country, only intervening occasionally when he thought he could influence policies. He settled himself at Segaon, a small village near Wardha with a population of barely 600, which was later renamed Sewagram, the Village of Service, to live amongst the poor and "show them how to live"[21] and to develop "rural mindedness". For more than even one village, he spurned Birla's offer of financial help to undertake experimentation in rural uplift. It was not the extent but depth of work he was interested in, he said. He went back to doing what he had started at the very beginning of his career in South Africa—to build by doing. His decade-long isolation at Sewagram, his speeches, which were longer at GSS than at the Congress session, his occasional rejoinders on contemporary political issues, etc., made his stature within the Congress hierarchy a matter of speculation.

On the new crop of leadership his influence was limited. The ideological divergence had drawn a wedge between him and them. Socialism and communism, that the new crop of young leaders propagated, were making inroads and Gandhi's khadi was seen as an anachronism. Shapurji Saklatwala, a communist MP, protested against khadi by asserting that it was not a non-violent programme as it killed the livelihood of the Lancashire labour. Further, he saw that the khadi disrupted labour unity. "Unity can be achieved by working together in factories." Saklatwala proposed Gandhi's exclusion, ordering him to "lead us as we tell you." These young leaders, however, had no compunction in taking help from Gandhi to get financial help from Birla for the upliftment of their families, and yet they accused Gandhi of being influenced by capitalists. With regard to their allegiance to his ideology they were irreverent if not hostile. Jayaprakash, the leader of the new crop, was one of

21 "Interview to the Bombay Chronicle", 22 May 1935, *CWMG* 61: 86.

them. Gandhi had negotiated his monthly pay packet from Birla. Jayaprakash also kept a link with Gandhi through his wife, Prabhawati, whose father, Brijkishore, was the first to bring Gandhi to Champaran in 1918.[22]

Subhas Chandra Bose was another such person. In his regime, the National Planning Committee was instituted but Gandhi was kept completely in the dark about it and Gandhi had written to Jawaharlal Nehru seeking "light". That Nehru thought the National Planning Committee wished to invent an industrialised India, while Gandhi was involved in rural education and occupation-based economic activities was telling of priorities. In Gandhi's conception, any national planning that ignored the availability of labour was misplaced. Nehru wanted a socialised industrialism. Soviet experiments had caught the attention of India's future leaders. Gandhi's own view was that "evils are inherent in industrialism, and no amount of socialization can eradicate them." As he wrote to Kumarappa, "what we have to combat is socialization of industrialism."

As Gandhi faced socialist opposition he too became conscious of his weapon. Charkha was posited against the sickle; non-violence was pitted against red-rebellion. Gandhi thought that the programmes of the socialist party ignored Indian conditions. He found that there was a glaring omission of khadi in the socialist manifesto. It is "socialism of spinning wheel" that was workable in the Indian context, he wrote to Narendra Deva. Gandhi wrote that the implications of socialist principles were "intoxicating" but added, "I fear all intoxicants". The socialist party espoused "wholesale expropriation of the propertied classes". Gandhi's position was unequivocal. "All land belongs to Gopal,"

[22] "The present fight is not for people who have debts to pay and wish to discharge their responsibilities towards their brothers and sisters. This fight requires one to sacrifice one's all. ...Jaiprakash can remain in the present fight only if he is thus prepared to embrace poverty" ("Letter to Prabhavati", 23 November 1933, *CWMG* 56: 266).

he quoted a lore, and added, "Gopal… means the State, i.e., the people…. Land and all property is his who will work it." "Unfortunately," he added, "the workers are or have been kept ignorant of this fact".[23]

Gandhi seemed to be blind to the situation surrounding him, oblivious of winds blowing in the opposite direction and seemed to exist in isolation. As violence in all its variations encircled Gandhi, he increasingly advocated charkha as a symbol of non-violence, and the more he became determined to apply non-violence on a still larger scale. In December 1941, surrounded by gory violence raging internally as well as externally, Gandhi laid out the meaning and place of his constructive work programme. Communal unity headed the list and, yet, he called khadi the most controversial of the thirteen sub-heads in the list. It was his conviction that non-violence on a mass scale could only be applied by making people "usefully and knowingly occupied for the sake of the country". It was hand-spinning and its anterior processes that fulfilled the required criteria for such an occupation. Gandhi still desired to turn Congress committees into "a model laboratory and spinning and weaving institute for the organisation of villages".

The Congress on the other hand was steeped in a phenomenon that Gandhi called "internal decay". "The problem of purifying the Congress is a big one", he wrote in a letter to Vallabhbhai Patel.[24] Gandhi's main purpose in proposing the Congress's acceptance to govern in the wake of its victories in the 1937 election was to further the acceptance and implementation of the constructive agenda. But, soon power began to cause indigestion in the body of the Congress. Gandhi wrote in his "viewspapers" his opinion on the rapidly falling standards in the Congress. But rarely did anyone pay heed to it.

[23] "Speech at Exhibition Ground", Faizpur, 27 December 1936, *CWMG* 64: 192.

[24] "Letter to Vallabhbhai Patel", 21 August 1934, *CWMG* 58: 339.

A disillusioned Gandhi publicly admitted his inability to lead such "an army of civil resisters" if he was called upon in such a situation, for he saw only "anarchy and red-ruin in front of the country". But to many this "harsh truth" was not at all visible.[25] Subhas Chandra Bose was one of the people who attempted to force Gandhi on the warpath. For him, corruption in the Congress was manageable and not alarming enough to warrant deferring the launch of the movement. Gandhi did not agree with this interpretation. The Congress, Gandhi said, needed to be strengthened and purified "so as to make it an effective vehicle for launching nation-wide Satyagraha".[26] Gandhi was "decidedly against his re-election" at Tripuri which Bose won defeating Pattabhi Sitaramayya, Gandhi's sponsored candidate. Gandhi rejoiced in his defeat and said, "I am nothing if I do not represent definite principles and policy."[27] It was open defiance by Bose. He had come to believe what Sanketwala had jocularly insinuated that Gandhi could be imprisoned by the new-ideologues and his appeal could be jockeyed to fulfil ambitions contrary to his ideas.

Schisms became so obvious after Subhas Chandra Bose's re-election that the AICC had to reiterate its adherence to the old policy and leadership. In August 1939, Subhas Chandra Bose was disqualified from the Congress for a period of three years for his "deliberate and flagrant breach of discipline". "I dissent from you", Gandhi wrote to Subhas Chandra Bose in November 1939. "Your way is not mine. For the time being you are my lost sheep. Some day I shall find you returning to the fold, if I am right and my love is pure." Subhas Chandra Bose too openly claimed his difference from the Mahatma.[28] Subhas Chandra

[25] "Internal Decay", *Harijan*, 28 January 1939, *CWMG* 68: 320–21.

[26] "Its Implication", *Harijan*, 24 June 1939, *CWMG* 69: 361.

[27] "Statement to the Press", 31 January 1939, *CWMG* 68: 359.

[28] Speaking on "The Fundamental Problems of India" in an address given to faculty and students of Tokyo University in November 1944, Subhas

(contd.)

Bose's expulsion was no show of Gandhi's power. His words had begun to fall in the wilderness. His plea was a pathetic repetition of phrases told many times since 1920 and now it was falling on deaf ears. It no longer enthused the Congress.

In Gandhi's own assessment, he had till date failed to make the Congress spin. Now Gandhi desired the conversion of the Congress into a peace organisation and a Congressman into "a soldier of peace". During the war, Gandhi spoke of the end of the "age of cities" and going "back to the villages".[29] The psychological moment for the new programme had arrived with the outbreak of the war. "Back to the villages!" had become a necessity from every point of view. "Now is the time to decentralize production and distribution. Every village has to become a self-sufficient republic." The Indian village organisation, "congeries of republics", was constituted so as to remain undisturbed by the periodical visitations from barbarous hordes. Cities are an invitation to invasion.

It was Gandhi's ambition to build a band of non-violent soldiers. He wanted the right to conscript India's adult population in a non-violent war by engaging every one in "productive national service". The charkha was linked with ahimsa and therefore with swaraj. The Congress's chief weapon was to be the charkha, and spinning regularly was their "military" discipline. It was simply a withdrawal into private space, with each individual producing to meet another's immediate requirement. In such a private space, there were no vital instalments worth conquering.

(contd.)

Chandra Bose said: "In Gandhi there are two aspects—Gandhi as a political leader and Gandhi as a philosopher. We have been following him in his capacity as a political leader, but we have not accepted his philosophy" (*The Essential Writings of Netaji Subhas Chandra Bose* 316).

29 "Speech at Khadi Vidyalaya", Bardoli, 8 January 1942, *CWMG* 75: 203.

It was, however, soon decided that the Congress did not agree with Gandhi's definition of non-violence. The Congress Working Committee decided that they were "unable to go the full length" with Gandhi on the question of non-violence. It left Gandhi free to "pursue his great ideal in his way".[30] The Congress argued for adopting a path contrary to Gandhi's in dealing with external aggression and internal disorder. Rajagopalachari said that the Congress was a political organisation not working for non-violence but for the political ideal. He rejected the idea that non-violence could ever win India's freedom. Gandhi, he said, was impaired in his judgment owing to "too much brooding on ahimsa". Gandhi's insistence, Nehru said, incapacitated the functioning of the Congress. Gandhi in response insisted "that it is possible to touch power through non-violence".

Unlike earlier times, now there was rebellion from his coterie of close associates. The schism between Gandhi and the Congress eventually came to the fore. In its earlier occurrence, Gandhi took initiatives to remove the differences by unilaterally withdrawing from the Congress. But, now, the ideological difference was much more pronounced. Gandhi was seen as retrogressive and idealistic. If his views on industrialism hampered India's emergence as a modern nation, his creed of non-violence held up India's march to freedom. The formation of the Planning Committee with its focus on engineering India's industrialisation was a rebuff to Gandhi's khadi and his programme for village reinvigoration. His ultimate isolation was now proved by the Congress resolution which showed that its adherence to non-violence was merely tactical or, as Gandhi would say, a non-violence of the weak. Gandhi asked for a resolute demonstration of non-violence through adoption of the charkha. But he received an ultimatum to mend or end his informal association with the

30 "Both Happy and Unhappy", *Harijan*, 29 June 1940, *CWMG* 72: 194–47.

Congress. Sadly, the ultimatum was by people "whom he would not disown and who could not do without him."

Even when the Congress made a pretension of putting aside Gandhi's agenda of non-violence in order to gain independence in return for its war support to the British, it yielded meager results. Gandhi was brought back as the general of a confused army. He, with his individual satyagraha, compounded the confusion. The movement, launched with much idealistic fanfare, petered out without much effect on the morals of the British. As Gandhi had written to Viceroy Linlithgow, launching of movements had become an existential imperative for the Congress. Its self-imposed restraint owing to British engagement in the war could lead to self-extinction. Individual satyagraha was a survival strategy, a mock display of satyagraha, as much to the people of India as to the British rulers. Vinoba Bhave was chosen to be the first *satyagrahi* as he had no rival in perfect spinning. In his introductory note on the eve of launching the satyagraha, Gandhi wrote of Vinoba as one who believed that "real independence of the villagers is impossible without the constructive programme of which khadi is the centre." Charkha for Vinoba, Gandhi wrote, was the most "suitable outward symbol of non-violence".

Gandhi was reluctant to announce civil disobedience till the country's environment was more conducive to such action. "My standard of success is khadi, and unless it is achieved, I cannot venture to launch a civil disobedience movement." He resisted all pressures and even resorted to extreme measures such as suspension of Subhas Chandra Bose from the Congress owing to differences in method. He would wait till the country got "demonstratively non-violent and disciplined". He would not allow erosion of the "great moral prestige of the Congress" by resorting to civil disobedience at this historical juncture that may embarrass the embattled British. India needs to demonstrate the non-violence of the strong and be peaceful when her tormentor is in trouble. In Gandhi's conception of satyagraha, civil disobedience meant courting imprisonment and doing constructive work. It was for this reason that he would increase the pitch for khadi every time the spectre of struggle loomed large over the Indian political firmament.[31] With each passing day, he argued more passionately for charkha and its non-violent ideology. His attack on Congress for being "half-hearted" with regard to khadi and non-violence also became more passionate. "This terrible, suicidal war may perhaps show that khadi, the principle of self-reliance for meeting one's needs, is of universal application."[32]

In early September 1946 an Interim National Government was formed. The ministers met Gandhi in the Bhangi Colony where he was then putting up. The appointed day being his day of silence, he scribbled a brief, bald message for them. It ran: "Take to khadi."

Reorienting Khadi

The first reorientation in the khadi campaign was effected in the year 1934–35 when, after a decade of contestation, khadi, battered by Congress intransigence and harassed by government suspicion, was stripped of its political potential and turned into a commodity of philanthropic commerce. Because it was a matter of conscience it confounded the khadi discourse during the earlier decade. It was a decade during which the limitations of khadi dawned upon its aggressive protagonists. It was discovered that spinning gave abysmally low wages, it could not by itself bring about village reconstruction, and the path hitherto pursued was contrary to principles laid down. Many of the converts had turned into rebels asserting that khadi was most exploitative. The criticisms from insiders caused Gandhi's to think of

[31] "Not Yet", *Harijan*, 1 June 1940, *CWMG* 72: 103–5
[32] "Rentia Baras", 1 July 1941, *CWMG* 74: 136.

reorientation. His focus now veered to take into account the wages earned by the spinners. The AISA was an association named after spinners and ostensibly worked for their welfare, though the spinners, who constituted the majority of artisans, were paid the least. Spinners, by the very nature of their work and also by the ethical standards of the AISA, could not form unions to demand wage hikes. Gandhi was particularly worried about the low wages that were given to the spinners.

The AISA had stiffened into an establishment. It had become a worker-driven organisation that served the city-based consumers by paying starvation wages to producers inhabiting low-opportunity areas. Being worker driven restricted its expansion plans. Its producers could not afford to wear the cloth they produced. In February 1934, Gandhi wrote a letter to Vithaldas Jerajani suggesting reorienting the course of the khadi organisation.[33] Jerajani was told that the focus of spreading khadi must now shift from cities to villages. Khadi must find a local market, instead of catering to distant cities. A city-centric marketing strategy, though initially inevitable, had harmed khadi's long-term prospects. It needed to sell where it was produced. It needed to be used by the manufacturers themselves.[34] Khadi's measures of self-evaluation were not in the charts of profit and growth but in its contribution to poverty amelioration. Its economic theory was such that the prices when realised should be returned to the prime producers, the spinners, while others were given just the hire charges.

In October 1935, the AISA, at its Wardha sitting, resolved to raise the spinners' wage to give "clothing (20 yards annually) and maintenance in accordance with a scientifically prescribed scale of minimum food requirement". The wage was calculated

33 "Letter to Vithaldas Jerajani", 19 February 1934, *CWMG* 57: 178.

34 "Interview to Khadi Workers", *Harijan*, 21 September 1934, *CWMG* 58: 353–55.

on the basis of eight hours efficient work. A spinner's wage was to be an anna an hour. It requested all its associate agencies to permit a progressive rise in the wage scale. All artisans associated with the khadi-manufacturing process were implored to use only khadi for their personal and family clothing requirements. It was also decided to pay wages, a part or the whole of it, in khadi or other necessities of life. This was done to ensure the use of the wages for clothing and food.

Distribution was to be primarily confined to the province where it was manufactured. The sales in the cities was to be that of surplus khadi—producers were entitled to market their produce only after they had taken what they needed for personal use.[35] The affiliated production and distribution units were asked to restrict their activities within their local region. To avoid a glut in production, operations were restricted to only those spinners who were most needy or who were solely dependent on spinning for their livelihood during lean seasons. The associate units were asked to maintain an accurate register of all the spinners and other artisans employed by them. All associate agencies were also reminded of their duty to promote khadi as a means to self-sufficiency. The AISA asked its associate agencies to be "autonomous and self-supporting". It was a double-pronged strategy to help speedy expansion based on expertise and resourcefulness of entrepreneurs and to protect it from political vicissitudes and reprisals. In enforcing these policy measures the AISA was even prepared to stop khadi work.

But a significant dilemma that the protagonists had to face was the declining demand once khadi's price was raised to accomodate the enhanced wages for spinners. It was a sensitive issue as the AISA was producing in village centres and selling at city outlets. Its campaign was directed at potential urban buyers. In the eyes of its middle-class consumers there was always an

[35] "Three Questions", *Harijan*, 5 October 1935, *CWMG* 62:10

attempt to rationalise the price of khadi. Wage increase would make khadi dearer. It could sound the death knell for the nascent enterprise. The unilateral decision to raise the wages of the spinners was seen as giving the khadi movement a "decent burial". It was seen as a "blunder". There was opposition also from poor khadi wearers who were unable to buy dearer khadi. Gandhi ignored the protests, asserting that khadi sold even when its quality and variety were abysmally limited and it was also relatively dearer. His point was that "systematic propaganda" could help in retaining khadi's customer base even if the prices were raised.

The AISA being not an ordinary, commercial, profit-driven business concern, the rules governing the reduction in cost differed. The AISA tried to meet the raised cost of khadi production partly by making the production efficient and partly by increasing the sales price of khadi. Other measures were inducing producers to wear their produced clothes, cutting down the overhead cost, adopting coarse, unbleached khadi, as processing khadi added to its cost. It also simultaneously worked on improving the quality of khadi. It was hoped that more scientific knowledge would improve the capacity of hand-gins, carding-bows, and spinning wheels. The work by spinners must be more skilled and efficient. An attempt was also made to gradually eliminate middlemen by making khadi self-supporting and self-sufficing.[36] The AISA's resolve to pay eight annas for eight hours of work was oblivious of ground realities. It was met by rising stock, declining sales, and closures of production centres. This even when the Maharashtra branch of the AISA could pay only three annas; while the rest of the provincial branches was still paying the old rates, it dawned on the nationalist entrepreneurs, that despite all philanthropic and patriotic sentiments, the middle-class khadi buyers simply could not

[36] "Spinners' Wages", *Harijan*, 17 April 1937, *CWMG* 65: 90.

afford more than three annas to buy khadi, the price of which had increased owing to the rise in wages. It had reached saturation point. The ambition of giving an eight-anna wage for eight hours of work was downsized to three annas for the same amount of work.

Finding purchasers was becoming the greatest obstacle in the mission of the AISA. The moment provincial governments came under the Congress, the AISA implored them to buy its products indiscriminately. It asked the provincial governments to adopt legislative and administrative measures to support khadi. Gandhi wanted the provincial governments to regard the AISA and other sister organisations as their own expert, voluntary agencies. Gandhi added that in other countries, governments see that the goods produced under its supervision are given first preference in the market.

In 1941, Gandhi asserted that the AISA was the largest institution of its kind in India. The AISA was representative of the dumb and semi-starved millions of India, he said. It was the peak year of its activities when it had some 3,400 workers on its rolls. In 1926, the AISA had on its record 110 carders, 42,959 spinners and 3,407 weavers. They worked at 150 production centres catering to the needs of some 1,500 villages. In 1941, *Khadi Jagat*, published a record of the AISA's engagements.[37] According to it, the AISA's work directly affected some 2,75,146 villagers, including 19,654 Harijans and 57,378 Muslims, scattered in at least 13,451 villages. In 1940, a sum of Rs 34,85,609 was distributed among them for their work as spinners, weavers, etc. The spinners were largely women. But soon after, decline set in. Political repression played a role. But its expansion too had reached a plateau.

[37] *Khadi Jagat*, 25 July 1941, *CWMG* 74: 59–60. After the suspension of the trilingual journals of *Harijan*, Gandhi supported *Khadi Jagat*, a Hindi journal launched in July 1941. In this, Gandhi, articulated his belief through khadi.

It was in 1944, after the political dust raised by the quit India movement had settled, that the AISA met at Sewagram, presided over by Gandhi for taking stock. The AISA was meeting after a gap of more than two years. The world was still engrossed in the dangerous game of warfare, which had begun in the winter of 1939. India had undergone an upheaval of the last national struggle. It had taken a heavy toll. A large amount of the AISA property had been either destroyed or was in government custody. Many of its workers, having taken part in the quit India movement, now languished in jail. The scars caused by government action daunted Gandhi. He discovered that the "foundation of the AISA was so weak that the Association could be easily wiped out of existence". The years of work had not made it take root in the life of the people. The government could destroy it by imprisoning its leaders and impounding its property. This therefore was the year of confessions and introspection.

It was in this year of introspection that a new reorientation in the work of the AISA was introduced. It came to be known as *Charkha Sangh ka Navasamskaran*—the reorientation in the work of the AISA. On the basis of experience of a decade of khadi work (1935–44), during which wages for spinners were fixed in terms of the objective of a living wage, the sales of khadi rose to rupees one crore (partly doing to rise in price). The demand for khadi developed because of patriotic fervour and shortage of cloth during the earlier years of the war. Gandhi reviewed the khadi situation with considerable dissatisfaction over some of the emerging trends. In his talks and discussions with the trustees of the AISA at Sewagram in September 1944, he measured the khadi work against the objective of reaching 700,000 villages and found that very little had been achieved.

Although khadi was sold in the cities and work was thereby provided to villagers, it had not become acceptable in the villages, and the spinners hardly spun for their own use. In the reoriented approach to khadi, four aspects were intensively focused on: first, all efforts were to be directed towards self-sufficiency, that is towards spinning for one's own consumption; second, self-sufficiency was interpreted to mean allowing scope for some sale so long as the sale was in the nearby village or district or at most the province; third, khadi was not to be viewed as an occupation or craft merely to earn a living but as a means to uplift the villages and thereby generate in the people spontaneous strength for swaraj; and fourth, the objective was to rejuvenate village life as a whole, and this could not be done by khadi alone but through a rehabilitation of agriculture, dairy and all other village industries.

> Khadi was never meant merely for the townspeople.... They neither understood nor appreciated the dignity and value that its use carried. The fault was not theirs. The workers themselves did not understand. The town dwellers had to wear khadi and do the penance. They were willing to buy penance for a few extra rupees which they could easily spare and be called patriots in the bargain.[38]

Gandhi emphasised that mere pursuit of the social objective of providing employment to the people or the economic objective of producing khadi for sale was not the core of the khadi programme. "Today", he stated, "our main concern should be to lay the foundation for this [khadi] work as deep as possible and not merely be satisfied with the production of khadi and sale of khadi itself." The cardinal point in the above approach was to build up self-reliance among the rural people. Gandhi presented a draft of the proposal, which contained the following points.

1. The village is the centre for the charkha, and the Charkha Sangh can realise its highest ambitions only when its work is decentralised in the villages.

[38] "The New Plan", *Harijan*, 27 July, 1946.

2. The largest number of workers whose one passion is the charkha and whom the AISA approves should go to the villages.
3. The sales depots and production centres should be curtailed.
4. Training institutions should be developed and teaching courses enlarged.
5. The sangh should permit any province or district, which wants to be independent and self-sufficient to become so.
6. A standing committee composed of the members of the AISA, AIVIA, and the Hindustani Talimi Sangh should be formed in order to issue necessary directions in the light of the new ideology.

"We plied the Charkha", Gandhi complained, "but mechanically, not intelligently." The workers had not fully adopted the non-violent outlook. Gandhi had even thought of disbanding the AISA and distributing its property and funds among the people.

> There would then be no reason to fear government ordinances. Nor need we look to the rich for alms. We shall without effort become the centre of hope, and people will come to us of their own accord. Every village will become the nerve centre of Independent India... This is the real function of the Sangh. We have to live and die for it.

Conclusion

The AISA's workforce was mainly illiterate, poverty-afflicted women. Their main concern was to add, however meagrely, to their family income. This was not a question of utilising their idle hours for their life itself was idle in the absence of productive work along with their unskilled capacity. For many of these women spinning was not a supplementary occupation but the only occupation. These women walked miles to the AISA production depot to procure cotton, slivers, or spin there or take their wages in return for spun yarn. They were paid meagrely. It was concern for them that Gandhi attempted unilaterally to force a rise in their wages. Although, they were at the centre of the AISA organisation, ironically the consumers were the AISA's main concern; and not the spinners. It was for consumers that khadi was priced low and produced attractively. The rise in the wages of spinners was a recognition of this situation on the part of the organisers. But it resulted in surging production and stagnant sales; a recipe for financial breakdown and organisational collapse. Consideration for these women had restrained the AISA's search for the most suitable spinning inventory. A suitable charkha was one which could be made by village craftsmen; its design so simple that repair could be undertaken by the spinners themselves. Its production would not involve import of resources from outside the local village arena. It was a benchmark that exasperated many courageous souls. Educated India was impatient with Gandhi's vision to determine every step in accordance with the needs of the last man.

In the early twenties, Gandhi with extremely limited infrastructure for khadi production was exhorting Indians to boycott foreign clothes. If there was a famine of cloth, he advised, people should simply strip themselves to the bare minimum. "Indian weather", he said in innumerable public speeches, mostly delivered to his urban, middle-class audience, did not need a great amount of covering. So boycott could still be resorted to with an extremely rudimentary production base for handspun and handwoven khadi. In the mid-1930s, when he reoriented khadi to focus more on individual self-sufficiency in clothing matters, he asked his workers to organise khadi production in such a fashion as to bring an overlap of producers and consumers; that is to say, those who produced must also consume. At the same time he also raised wages of spinners as many of them, in his calculation, depended solely on spinning for their survival. Somewhere his calculations lacked clarity. If there were people depending on their spinning wage to survive, how could they be helped by the adoption of the self-sufficiency agenda? Food rather than clothing was their priority.

The formation of the AISA was aimed at ending the exploitation of artisans. It was thought that the artisans, in due course, would be conscious controllers of the AISA.[39] Instead, the AISA was accused of running a most exploitative occupation.

[39] "Instructive Figures", *Harijan*, 10 July 1937, *CWMG* 65, 379.

9 Epilogue

Many Histories: A Singular Oral Tradition

Jailok Thakur, till his death in 2001 at the age of eighty-four, was a doyen of khadi institutions in Bihar.[1] He was the chairman of the Zila Khadi Gramodyog Sangh located at Muzaffarpur in north Bihar and remained so till his very end. He had a sterling memory, remembering, almost down to the dates, his exploits during the quit India movement in 1942.

Gandhi, Thakur said, was initially not in favour of letting the khadi cadre participate in the politics of the freedom movement. "Khadi workers were to focus primarily on the constructive activities. But surely there was to be some political utility of a

[1] Personal interview was conducted by the author in 1998. I met him at Muzaffarpur, where he was the chairman of the District Khadi and Village Industries Association. Jailok Thakur clearly relished talking about his exploits during the quit India movement going by the details to which he went. Jailok Thakur not only had an agile mind but was acutely perceptive too.

cadre of disciplined, dedicated and trained khadi workers. Gandhi called them 'Reserve Force' or 'Soldiers in Barrack'. In 1942, when the call of 'Do or Die' was given, their utility was discovered."

At the commencement of "the last and the best war", Gandhi exhorted the constructive "reserve force" to consign their whole in the struggle. As a result, the khadi organisation came to be regarded as citadels of treason by the government. The government's suspicion resulted in imprisonment of workers, forceful closures of khadi production centres, sealing of retail shops, freezing bank accounts and many other disruptive measures. The government's vindictive action resulted in the total collapse of the painstakingly created khadi superstructure. In 1942, Jailok Thakur, then a 22-year-old lad was at Jamshedpur, working in a Khadi Bhandar.

"We used to receive some 300 copies of Gandhi's *Harijan* which was then published in three languages of Hindi, English and Gujarati. I used to stand outside the Khadi Bhandar exhorting people to buy *Harijan*. Jamshedpur is a multilingual town. At the time it was too anglicized. TATA officers used to get their clothes stitched in Calcutta. *Harijan*, however, was the best campaign vehicle for khadi sales. One who read *Harijan* immediately also bought khadi. Dadabhai Naoroji's grandson who worked at TATA was an ardent believer in khadi, although he was sceptical of the satyagraha.

"K.D. Dastur was another high-heeled Parsi official who wore stiff clothes. Once he passed through the pavement across the Khadi Bhandar. I approached him and said, 'Sir, this is Gandhiji's newspaper', thrusting a copy of *Harijan* in his hand. He took the newspaper off my hand and asked, 'How much?' 'Two annas', I said. Next day he came up to me to ask for a regular subscription of the newspaper. We were not in favour of annual subscription of the newspaper although such a provision did exist at the payment of five rupees. Annual subscription curtailed the opportunity to interact with readers and their family members—our potential recruits in the national struggle. I was in favour of personal contacts with readers. I took only eight annas from Dastur with the assurance that I shall drop the newspaper every week at his door. Dastur became a habitual khadi wearer. Later, after the police revolt at Jamshedpur, Dastur was arrested. TISCO went on a lightening strike. Even its furnace was shut down.

"It was on the tenth of August 1942 that the police strike broke out in Jamshedpur and TISCO became charged with excitement. It was the first such strike in the country. A police constable Ramanand Tiwari facilitated traffic near our Bhandar. He used to drop in at the Bhandar to read the *Harijan*. He became instrumental in organising the police strike. It was totally non-violent. The striking police personnel handed over their weapons to their superiors. Twenty-five people were relieved of their jobs. Gandhi had already sounded the bugle of 'do or die' on the eighth of August at Bombay. At Jamshedpur, the police action was swift. They clamped down heavily on khadi activities by sealing the Khadi Bhandar. Although there was a magisterial order for arresting khadi workers, police officials were sympathetic to our cause and we were allowed to flee. An arrest warrant was issued in my name. I fled to Jharia in Dhanbad district to work with Khurshidbehan Captain, sister of Dadabhai Naoroji, who was then organising coal miners there. Tommies arrested her too and soon I was on run again.

"This time to Simri in Madhubani. Ramdev Thakur was my cousin. He was a disciple of J.B. Kriplani. He had also participated in the Champaran satyagraha. He had his khadi-producing centre at Simri, which was burnt down by the government during the 1942 agitation. Ramdev had sent a message for me and we arranged to meet in the mangrove in Bathua village at Pusa. The village headmen were held responsible for any nationalist activity in their village. They had to report to the police of any such activities. News of our meeting at a mangrove was leaked and the police came to raid the place. However, we avoided arrest and escaped taking advantage of the dense mangrove. An arrest warrant was issued against my name at Pusa police station, too. Immediately afterwards, I headed southward, to Hazaribagh.

"Here, while I stayed in a *mohalla* inhabited mostly by Ansari Muslims, I got engaged in local college politics. Although, I had refrained from giving my real identity, my khadi clothes made my movements in the area quite conspicuous. I was also circulating cyclostyled pamphlets, using a machine owned by a Christian college principal. A plan to eliminate the DIG Tenbrook was made. In those days, Bihar had only two DIGs, one responsible each for south and north zone. As north zone DIG, Tenbrook had earned notoriety for being a brutal police officer. His elimination was an act in revenge.

"It, however, remained unaccomplished due to the infiltration of an informer in our ranks. My hideout in the Okani colony was busted. After much drama, on 3 January 1943, I was arrested. After an internship of eleven months at Hazaribagh jail, I was released on 30 November. Police gave me a ticket for Samastipur. I was a free man. But in reality, my real identity still had two arrest warrants issued against it. Instead of Samastipur, I headed for Ranchi. Luck would not be favouring me, though. I was recognised. Police found out my antecedents and I was arrested. This was a real arrest as here I was my real self. After a two-month and twenty-six days stay in Ranchi jail I was taken to Samastipur Jail. Here, I met Kapoori Thakur, later to become the Chief Minister of Bihar. In June 1944, I was released on health grounds. At Hazaribagh jail, I was given the first-class facility, given my status as a political prisoner. There the conditions were extremely conducive and my health improved. At Ranchi and Samastipur, however, I underwent a marked decline in my health.

"After the release, I went to Balughat at the bank of Budhi Ganddak to recuperate. It was here that the Bihar branch of the

AISA initially was headquartered. It was later shifted to Madhubani. While there, I tried reviving the place. For three years I was there."

Jailok Thakur's oral narration of his involvement with khadi and the freedom movement throws light on varied aspects of the campaign. His narration reveals an ambivalence in Gandhi's view of political participation of khadi workers. It also questions Nehru's assumption that khadi workers were much cocooned individuals, a de-politicised lot. As the career of Thakur shows, khadi workers did convert and recruit common people for the national cause. Their work itself was politics. Thakur's narration also shows that truth and non-violence was not always a policy even among khadi workers. Just as khadi faced competition from its spurious variety, khadi workers too impersonated and disguised their real identity during the struggle. But just as Nehru had repeatedly scorned khadi's economic utility, even while calling it the "livery of freedom", the educated too remained sceptical of values that Gandhi's campaign had invested in it. The biggest irony of the khadi movement was the fact that despite his aggressive campaign to recruit the educated, Gandhi not only failed in bringing them in but also faced a barrage of criticism from them. The educated instead of complimenting the movement continuously derided it.

Khadi fell short disastrously of its designed ambition. It did not win India her freedom, neither was swaraj won for India's famished millions. Instead, khadi, immediately after Gandhi's assassination or even in his lifetime, was set into an establishment, receiving government patronage by becoming one of its myriad departments. It was not as if such a course was a deviation from the path laid down by Gandhi. In fact, even while proclaiming khadi's autonomous existence, he had repeatedly demanded governmental patronage and protection to his khadi enterprise, more so, when the Congress formed provincial governments in 1937. Gandhi, during the two years of the Congress government

(1937–39) in the provinces, demanded the institution of a separate department for khadi and village industries. So, nobody could really accuse Nehru of betraying Gandhi's khadi after independence. Yet, it was during his prime ministerial tenure that the khadi institution became the dumping ground for inconvenient politicians. Its chairmen came to be political appointees who were shunted out of mainstream power battles when they raised too many questions on Nehru's "un-Gandhian" economic policies.[2]

[2] Most of the appointees were reluctant to accept the job as they were aware of its secondary importance on the power turf. Some retiring politicians were appointed as the position was seen as a post-retirement sop with built-in leverage of patronage. Some like Vaikunthbhai Mehta, the first chairman, were appointed to ward off their being a political threat to the powers that be. Otherwise, most, with few exceptions, were appointees who had outlived their political utility. Until Mahesh Sharma, one who specifically asked for the job because of his interest and prior involvement, the KVIC has had ten successive chairmen. They were men of varied characteristics; if Vaikunthbhai Mehta (1953–63) was christened the father of the co-operative movement, then Deberbahi (1963–71) was an institution builder who crystallised the structure of the KVIC. With Deberbhai ended an era of political inputs into khadi development. Its philosophical growth became stunted, never to achieve again any of its past glory. Khadi was the biggest casualty of Indira Gandhi's ascendance to power. In the battle of wits between the syndicate and her, it was khadi which lost political patronage that it so strongly had in the Nehru era. Most of the members of the syndicate belonged to the khadi generation. As they made an exit from the portals of power, khadi too eclipsed from the political pedestal and became something to be soldiered on with rather than shouldering responsibility. It was the most ironical finale of Gandhi's khadi. Indira Gandhi soon played a devastating role as mother to khadi organisations on her return to power in the 1980s by constituting the Kudal Commission to investigate their functioning and financing. She perceived their role in her defeat.

The third chairman, G. Ramachandran's (1971–74) only credentials, it is said in informed circles, was that he had received the Mahatma's attention to his queries on machines and technology. A student with

(contd.)

But importantly Khadi failed in its avowed mission. Its main objective was to "gain independence, not for the literate and the rich in India, but for the dumb millions…."[3] It was Gandhi's

---

(contd.)

exceptional intelligence, Ramachandran lived with Gandhi for some time at Sewagram. Ghanshyam Ojha's (1974–75) was a short tenure without any authority on khadi. A.M. Thomas (1975–77, 1980–86) was a product of Indira Gandhi's politics of appointing insecure people who shall be loyal to none, ideology included, but to her alone. His was one of the longest tenure of nine years. Although blamed for ad-hocism in polices, he was generally regarded as an able administrator. His tenure was particularly marked for parochial policies as his prime focus came to rest upon Cochin-centred development. Dislodged by the Janta government, which appointed Som Dutt (1977–80), Thomas staged a come back in 1980, with the return of Indira Gandhi. Som Dutt, who was squeezed in between the two tenures of Thomas, was a doyen of post-independence khadi organisation and was based in Panipat till his very recent death. A disciple of J.B. Kirpalani, he was with khadi since partition when he worked to provide relief to refugees through khadi works.

From 1986–88, Rajiv Gandhi did not have enough time to find a full-time chairman, enabling his minister of state for industries to take charge. The Rajiv Gandhi found his man-Friday in Laxmi Das, a comparatively young person. The tenure of chairmanship too was increased from three to five years. But luck would not be his as following tradition he resigned in the wake of Rajiv's defeat in 1989. Yashveer Singh, the next in league, was an Ajit Singh appointee. Ajit Singh, the industry minister in V.P. Singh's cabinet, took a unilateral decision without even consulting his prime minister. Yashveer Singh, a western UP landlord from Muradabad, was a Charan Singh protégé. From all accounts he was an unlikely appointee. A professor of biotechnology at JNU, he resigned from the university, as he said in a personal interview in his Nizammuddin house, to help realise the dream of "Kisan Neta" Charan Singh. Narasimha Rao brought in Naval Kishore Sharma, who kept his political ambition burning all through his tenure. Then there was a socialist ideologue, Surendra Mohan, known less for any administrative acumen. Then came, Mahesh Sharma, a BJP appointee with some experience in rural entrepreneurship development.

3 "Discussion with Dodd", 4 September 1934, *CWMG* 58: 401.

vehicle for achieving real swaraj for India's famished masses. It was a weapon to bring rural reinvigoration. It was strangely enough an apolitical process to politicise a long dormant rural population. It was a means taken from the traditional wisdom to introduce modern politics in a feudal populace. Freedom, and not just independence, was supposed to come in its wake. It was to become self-spreading, a "current coin". However, it neither become self-spreading nor did freedom come in its train. In the medley of factors that might have conspired to bring India's independence, khadi was nowhere in the picture. Transfer of power was effected largely because of gradual British loss of control on Indian administrative and military machinery. The British also lost to some extent control over the Indian mind; to that extent khadi did indeed contribute. But the important question is to what degree did the Indian mind rebel against British reign.[4] Indians retained "English rule without the Englishman", "tiger's nature, but not the tiger".[5]

It was left to one man to dwell upon khadi's futile future. In the decades after the non-cooperation movement, Gandhi's words fell upon deaf ears; there was no one to evince interest in what he was saying. He had been practically saying the same thing with which he had begun his Indian career somewhat tremblingly. The freshness that he had brought into Indian politics now was eons away. It was when Gandhi attempted to deepen his politics that the backlash became apparent. His words had a stultifying effect and were irritably stale for the Congress politicians. Nehru was to build his "modern temples" and khadi and the department he founded for it was to be a dumping ground for anyone who stood on his way to industrial glory.

[4] See Ashis Nandy's *The Intimate Enemy* for a study about the colonisation of the Indian mind.

[5] Anthony J. Parel, *Gandhi: Hind Swaraj*, 28.

ANALYSING PEOPLE'S MOVEMENT AND ITS IMPACT

Khadi was a people's movement. The people's movement seldom yields the targeted results. By its very nature, the people's movement, as a rule, is ranged against an established authority. The cause of the movement is generally either the insensitive misdemeanour on the part of the ruling caucus, or infringement of the given rights of the populace, or perceived wrongs committed by the authority. Therefore, more often than not, a people's movement only has a reactive agenda and therein lays its core limitation. Drawn by angry rhetoric and aroused passion, the phases of crests are short and, if the movement is long drawn, interspersed by long gestation periods. The movement is ranged against an establishment, confident of its coercive apparatus at its command, and it carries legitimacy until the contending hegemony tilts the balance away from it. Moreover, given the power and pelf that the authority wields, it can temporarily cause confusion among cadres of the movement through its self-serving propaganda. The people's movement, on the other hand, have loose organisational structure and an anarchic apex decision-making body, a reactive ideology and a set of powerful emotions, and is weighed down by the pressure of building a precedence. It is mired also in ideological controversies concerning objectives, techniques, and ideals.

By not yielding to the resistance offered by a people's movement, the authority sticks to its constitutional core that assumes that relenting to the movement, as in a climb-down, a governance failure. Therefore, clamping down is generally the preferred mode of response. An authority, which gets trapped in the climb-down or clamp-down dilemma, sows the seeds of its own extinction. While initially, in the face of the people's resistance, it steels itself against any climb-down, the very resolve robs it of its sustaining power and digs its own grave. The authority at some later date might roll back its policy or incapacitate a right-threatening legislation so convincingly brought into existence just a while ago. At the moment of denouement, however, a climb-down is perceived to be a suggestion of weakness and an invitation to greater insurgency. Therefore, the cost of clamp-down or even of a protracted face-off, in terms of the financial, rights violation, and the authority's own erosion of longevity and legitimacy is disregarded at the altar of short-term, repressed peace.

The 1905–07 resistance against the Bengal Partition and the 1918 satyagraha movement against the Rowlatt Bills are two such historical instances that help explain the dilemma in action against a spontaneous people's movement. Both the announcement of partition and enactment of a coercive legislation ignited the hitherto dormant but simmering sentiments of national hurt and slight. Both brought a spontaneous people's movement to the fore as a nationalist response. Both policy decisions were made ineffectual, not seemingly by the people's movement as the colonial administration claimed, but by the authority's own belated recognition of its folly. The Bengal partition was annulled not in 1905, when the movement against it was at its peak, but in 1911, when the resistance had substantially subsided. Similarly, the Rowlatt Bills, seen draconian in contemporary nationalist perception, though pushed through in the face of active opposition of the people was allowed to lapse unimplemented even for the three-year period that it existed in the statutory book of the government. The government found it hard to acknowledge that the people's opposition had dictated its climb-down.

The anti-partition movement laid the foundation for a more active phase of the nationalist agitation.[6] By 1907, the air of Calcutta was swirling with issues far beyond that of the annulment of partition. That was the success of the movement as it stretched itself to a domain hitherto unexplored. Similarly,

[6] Sumit Sarkar's masterly study of the anti-partition movement makes a listing of the types of the various ideological and methodological trends prevalent under that umbrella (Sarkar 1973).

though the violence that broke out in response to the satyagraha made Gandhi suspend the anti-Rowlatt Bill agitation, succeeding events overwhelmed the demand for repeal and the country got drawn into issues that laid the foundation for the non-cooperation movement. The underlying idea beneath the stubborn government's attitude was "not to give anything unless it is absolutely" essential. But its responses had given enough ammunition to the people's movement to gain strength and move onto new pastures.

During instances of local skirmishes, such as at Champaran and Kaira, the people's success in forcing the authority into a meaningful compromise was sheepishly disowned rather than acknowledged.[7] The outmanoeuvered authority was reluctant to acknowledge concessions (their climb-down) wrung by Gandhi. It was later claimed that Gandhi was given the velvet glove treatment, firstly, owing to the government's desire for domestic tranquility at the time of war and, secondly, owing to his image of "social and humanitarian activist". It is true that Gandhi succeeded in achieving tangible results in all the local skirmishes that he got involved in prior to the declaration of the non-cooperation movement. From the evidence available, it is obvious that he achieved his successes at a time when he was less a threat to the government. But in the aftermath of the Punjab atrocity following the Jalliainwala Bagh massacre and its "plain, deliberate shielding of the officials", Gandhi's words took on tones of a battle-cry which hardened the government's own approach towards him.[8]

[7] The authority's argument was to nullify intervention both from Gandhi and other educated Indians and claim that these agitations "did not in any way affect the course of action" ("Sir Sankaran Nair and Champaran", *YI*, 27 August 1919, *CWMG* 16: 63).

[8] "Speech on Hunter Committee Report", *Navajivan*, 4 July 1920, *CWMG* 17: 513. He negotiated his deals with impeccable facts collated by his team's painstaking grassroots, documentation of grievances, be it at

(contd.)

Gandhi never again succeeded in getting a concession from the government,—not even the abrogation of the much abused salt law,[9] and, as a school of historians say, not even independence, which according to them was more a negotiated transfer of power made exigent owing to extraneous factors than the internal pro-freedom movement. A recent book by Patrick French gives credence to the Loss of Control theory.[10] All governments, colonial, imperial, or domestic, have a similar attitude towards a people's movement. They rarely yield to them. What the people's movement is certain to achieve is a cautious authority, with the authorities wary of taking anti-people measures. In this lies the importance of the people's movement, in deepening democracy and reining in power wielders. Through oscillating responses to the people's movement from quick clamp-down and belated climb-down, despite its semi-democratic claims, the colonial state dug its grave and lost control over the governing apparatus and also legitimacy in the eyes of the governed populace. It is this that makes indigenous governments in independent India think first of co-option rather than resort to clamp-down or climb-down. The confines of this paradigm explicates the role of the khadi movement in the achievement of India's independence.

More than Gandhi's countrymen, however, the government, though confounded in action, understood the real intent of Gandhi's khadi campaign. Gandhi, in launching the khadi

---

(contd.)

Viramgam, Champaran, or Kaira. The government showed no repentance and, as is evident from its response, considered the offending officials as "distinguished servants of the crown".

[9] The salt law could not be removed even by Nehru's interim government. It was done only after India gained independence and its abrogation was one of the first administrative decisions of the Nehru government. Nehru perhaps took the decision to humour an ideologically distanced Gandhi.

[10] *Liberty of Death*: *India's Journey to Independence and Division.*

movement, brought into being a parallel system of the ruler-ruled discourse, alternative to that established by the colonial government. He was not opposing nor was in a protracted struggle against the colonial regime, but was attempting to establish a communication with his countrymen in a space autonomous from that of the government. In the colonial system, fear and subjugation were dominant themes; the participation of the people in governance was minimal. Gandhi's programme was for the enfranchisement of the millions of Indians by recognising the necessity and the value of non-violence. It was for this that the khadi movement was a non-violent programme of action. In its own limited but powerfully articulated way, khadi was an attempt at severing the economic relationship that defined colonialism. Beneath its constructive agenda, khadi was a subversive force against British supremacy.

Gandhi's was the politics of the periphery. By focusing on anonymous individuals he somehow negated the presence of the citadel. Masses and not mediation was his political weapon. It left many of his Congress comrades confused. Gandhi's simultaneous espousal of India's freedom from British domination and India's reconstruction through self-purification processes irked many ardent nationalists, who were not very sympathetic to the linkage and saw it as delaying India's tryst with her freedom. For Gandhi, India's reconstruction was a vital process as, according to him, it was the Indians who had fallen to temptation offered by the British. He regarded his package of constructive activities as constituting the road to freedom. It was this agenda of reconstruction of national self that eventually added to his isolation even when it was also the pursuit that gave him unparalleled mass appeal. His agenda was seen as a long-drawn project. As Nehru had noted quite acerbically that if India was to first achieve universal acceptance of khadi before she could knock at the freedom-door, she would have to wait "till the Greek Kalends".

TOOL OF MOBILISATION

Khadi was a tool of mobilisation, an "instrument of instruction", employed in a deeply divided society, with entrenched poverty, inequality, and powerlessness. It was chosen by Gandhi to be his politics. It was part of a larger package and yet was the pivot of the politics of constructive work.[11] The charkha was revived as a tool of mobilisation. Gandhi was at pains to explain the non-political aim of charkha. He reiterated its economic and spiritual aspects and explained away its political aspects, because it was above the mundane, was lofty, and above the contention of power politics. It was in understanding this agenda of khadi that Nehru failed when he accused khadi workers of being a non-politicised lot. The political class showed impatience with the khadi programme. Socialists emerged as the most organised group of opponents to Gandhi's politics. Since 1921, the Congress had a flag made of khadi and the wheel occupied a central place on it. Yet, no other constructive activity was so much ridiculed and denounced as khadi. The rapid stride in mechanisation of the textile industry added much to the intellectual contempt for hand-spinning.[12] Its stiffening into an establishment proved its unviability of which it was accused throughout its career.

Gandhi's other problem was the alliances he attempted for fulfilling his agenda. It is somewhat strange that in each of his battles, constructive or political, he sought allegiance from people whom he held responsible, at least partly, for the state of affairs he was fighting against. "The poor folks would seem to have been born in order to toil and moil for us! We have been guilty of a heinous sin, and it is time we expiated it." Or when he said: "Unless we discharge our debt, Hinduism will perish."[13] He squarely laid the blame on a specific section of society and

[11] "Constructive Programme and Government", *Harijan*, 25 January 1942.
[12] "Is Khadi Economically Sound?", *Harijan*, 20 June 1936.
[13] "Speech at Harijan Colony", Delhi, 2 January 1935, *CWMG* 60: 46.

asked it to perform remedial sacrifice. So it was not the village people, who were more distanced from British imperialism, but the educated, urban, and connected who were asked to make sacrifices. It was not the village people themselves but urban representatives and activists who were the fulcrum of village reconstruction. It was not the dalits but dvija castes on whose shoulders fell the responsibility for the eradication of untouchability.

Gandhi's ingenuity was in linking khadi, a process and a commodity, with politics. It was not as if he invented khadi. It was there before him; it was there even during the time he took up its advocacy and the full-blown brand-building exercise. His contribution was not in revival, however intangible in real terms, but in linking national subjugation in the hands of foreign power to that of internal decline and not external superiority. He argued not for adoring the body with self-woven fabric but for rebuilding the shattered self through industry, discipline, and penance. Khadi was a tool, an important part of the tool-kit called the constructive programme. Or, as he said, khadi was the sun of a solar system of the constructive programme. It was the richness of the indigenous craft of cloth-making that had attracted the avarice of the alien traders, who later took to territorial ambitions. It was this fine craft of weaving that enriched rapacious rulers or, in later times, the collaborating middlemen. This was the craft that had attracted colonisation. This was the craft that alone shall lead to deliverance of India from its sad state. "The very thing that was a cause of our slavery will open the door to our freedom."[14]

[14] "Speech at AISA Meeting, *Khadi Jagat*, December 1941, *CWMG* 75: 176.

Bibliography

Primary Sources

AISA. 1925–30. *Khadi Guide*. Ahmedabad.

AISA. 1930–44. *All India Spinners' Association Annual Report*. Ahemedabad.

Gandhi, M.K., ed. 1933–40. *Harjian*.

Gandhi, M.K. 1964. *Reorientation of Khadi*. Tanjavur: Sarvodaya Prachuralaya.

Gandhi, M.K., ed. 1919 onwards. *Navajivan*. Ahemedabad.

Gandhi, M.K., ed. 1919–30. *Young India*. Ahmedabad.

Govt. of India. 1958–84. *The Collected Works of Mahatma Gandhi*. 90 vols. Delhi: The Publication Division.

Khadi Jagat

Gopal, S., ed. 1976. *Selected Works of Jawaharlal Nehru*. New Delhi: Nehru Memorial Fund & Orient Longman.

Books and Journals

Alter, Joseph S. *Gandhi's Body: Sex, Diet and the Politics of Nationalism*. Philadelphia: University of Pennsylvania Press.

Amin Shahid. "Gandhi as Mahatma: Gorakhpur District, Eastern UP, 1921–2", in Ranjit Guha ed. 1998 *Subaltern Studies III: Writings on South Asian History and Society.* Delhi: Oxford.

Argov, Daniel; *Moderates and Extremists in the Indian Nationalist Movement.*

Arnold, David. 2001. *Gandhi: Profile in Power.* London: Pearson Education.

Arunachalam, K. 1974. *Khadi Economics—A Few Aspects.* Madurai: Koodal Publishers.

Bakshi, S.R. 1987. *Gandhi and Ideology of Swadeshi.* New Delhi: Reliance Publishing House.

———. 1988. *Gandhi and the Mass Movements.* New Delhi: Atlantic Publishers.

———. 1988; *Gandhi and Concept of Swaraj.* Criterion Publications.

———. 1989. *Swaraj Party and Gandhi.* New Delhi: Atlantic Publishers.

———. 1996. *Gandhi and the Congress.* New Delhi: Sarup & Sons.

Bandhu, Deep Chand ed. 2003. *History of Indian National Congress,* 1885–2002. Delhi: Kalpaz Publications.

Banker, Shankerlal G. 1969. *Gandhiji Aur Rashtriya Pravrittiyan* (Hindi). Varanasi: Sarva Seva Sangh.

Bayly, Christopher. 1986. "The Origins of Swadeshi (home industry): Cloth and Indian Society, 1700–1930". In *The Social Life of Things: Commodities in Cultural Perspective,* edited by Arjun Appadurai. Cambridge: Cambridge University Press.

Bean, Susan. 1989. "Gandhi and Khadi, the Fabric of Indian Independence". In *Cloth and Human Experience,* edited by Annette B. Weiner and Jane Schneider. Washington, D.C. and London: Smithsonian Institute Press.

Bernays, Robert. 1931. *Naked Fakir. London*: Victor Gollancz Ltd.

Bhatia, B.M. 1963. *Famines in India: A Study in Some Aspects of the Economic History of India, 1860–1945.* New Delhi: Asia Publishing House.

Bhattacharya, Sabyasachi, ed. 1997. *The Mahatma and the Poet: Letters and Debates between Gandhi and Tagore, 1915–1941.* New Delhi: National Book Trust.

Bose, Sisir K., and Sugatha Bose, eds. 1997. "Democracy in India". In *Essential Writings of Netaji Subhas Chandra Bose.* Delhi: Oxford University Press.

Brown, Judith M. 1972. *Gandhi's Rise to Power, 1915–22.* Cambridge.

———. 1990. *Gandhi: Prisoner of Hope.* Delhi: Oxford University Press.

Chakrabarti, Mohit. 2000. *The Gandhian Philosophy of the Spinning Wheel:* New Delhi: Concept Publishing Company.

Chakrabarty, Dipesh, 2001. 'Clothing the Political Man: a Reading of the Use of Khadi/White in Indian Public Life'. The Institute of Postcolonial Studies.

Chandra, Bipan. 1966. *Rise and Growth of Economic Nationalism in India; Economic Politics of India National Leadership, 1880–1905*. New Delhi: People's Publishing House.

Chandra, Bipan et al. 1989. *India's Struggle for Independence, 1857–1947*. Delhi: Penguin Books.

Chatterjee, Margaret. 1983. *Gandhi's Religious Thought*. London: Macmillan Press.

Chaudhuri, Nirad C. 2000. *The Autobiography of an Unknown Indian*. Mumbai: Jaico.

Cohn, Bernard S. "Cloth, Clothes, and Colonialism: India in the Nineteenth Century". In *Cloth and Human Experience*, edited by Annette B. Weiner and Jane Schneider. Wasington, D.C. and London: Smithsonian Institute.

———. 1996. *Colonialism and its Forms of Knowledge*. Princeton: Princeton University Press.

Dalton, Dennis. 1993. *Mahatma Gandhi: Non-violent Power in Action*, 16. New York: Columbia University Press.

Doke, Joseph J. 1967. *M.K. Gandhi: An Indian Patriot in South Africa*. Delhi: Publications Department, Government of India.

Dutt, R. Palme 1970. *India Today*. Calcutta: Manisha.

Fischer, Louis. 1944. *A Week with Gandhi*. Bombay: International Book House.

———. 1962. *The Life of Mahatma Gandhi*. London: Jonathan Cape.

Fox, Richard G. 1989. *Gandhian Utopia: Experiments With Culture*. Boston: Beacon Press.

French, Patrick. 1997. *Liberty or Death: India's Journey to Independence and Division*. New Delhi: Harper Collins Publishers India.

G.B Jathar & S.G. Beri. 9th edition 1949, first 1928. *Indian Economy: A Comprehensive and Critical Survey*, vol. 1. Oxford University Press.

Gandhi, Arun, 2000; *Kasturba: A Life*; New Delhi: Penguin Books.

Gandhi, Maganlal. 1924. *Charkha Sastra*. Sabarmati: All India Khadi Information Bureau.

Gandhi, Rajmohan. 1995. *The Good Boatman: A Portrait of Gandhi*. New Delhi: Viking.

Ghose, Sankar. 1973. *Socialism, Democracy and Nationalism in India*. Bombay: Allied Publishers.

Ghose, Sri Aurobindo. 1994. *India's Rebirth*. Paris: Institut De Recherches Evolutives,

Green, Martin. 1993. *Gandhi: Voice of a New Age Revolution*. New York: Continuum.

———. 1998. *The Origins of Non-violence: Tolstoy and Gandhi in their Historical Setting*. New Delhi: Harper Collins Publishers India.

Green, Martin., ed. 1987; *Gandhi in India, In his Own Words*. England: University Press.

Gregg, Richard B. 1928. *Economics of Khaddar*. Madras: S. Ganesan Publisher,

———. 1957. *Which Way Lies Hope?: An Examination of Capitalism, Communism, Socialism and Gandhiji's Programme*. Ahmedabad: Navajivan Publishing House.

———. 1958. *A Philosophy of Indian Economic Development*. Ahmedabad: Navajivan Publishing House.

Gregg, Richard B. & Maganlal K. Gandhi 1926. *The Takli Teacher*. Ahmedabad: The Technical Department, AISA.

Guha, Ramchandra. 2001. *An Anthropologist among the Marxists*. Delhi: Permanent Black.

Hardiman, David. 2003. *Gandhi in his Time and Ours*. Delhi: Permanent Black.

Harold Coward, ed. 2003. *Indian Critiques of Gandhi*. New York: State University of New York.

Heredia, Rudolf. 1999. "Interpreting Gandhi's *Hindu Swaraj*". In *Economic and Political Weekly*, 34, no. 24 (12–18) June.

Jajoo, Srikrishnadas & Anna. B. Sashrabuddhe.1962. *Akhil Bharat Charkha Sangh Ka Itihaas; Uday Se Vilay Tak* (Hindi). Varanasi: Sarva Seva Sangh.

Jajoo, Srikrishnadas. 1958. *The Ideology of Charkha: A Collection of Some of Gandhiji's Speeches and Writings about Khadi*. Varanasi: Sarva Seva Sangh.

Jha, Jagdanand. 1990. *Khadi and Village Industries in Economic Development*. New Delhi: Deep & Deep Publications.

Jha, Sadan. 2004, "Charkha 'Dear Forgotten Friend' of Widows: Reading the Erasures of a symbol", In *Economic and Political Weekly*, 39, no. 28 (10–16 July).

Jha, Shiva Nand. 1955. *A Critical study of Gandhian Economic Thought*. Agra: Lakshmi Narain Agarwal Educational Publishers.

Joseph, George Gheverghese. 2003, *George Joseph: The Life and Times of a Kerala Christian Nationalist*. Delhi: Orient Longman.

Joshi, Nandini. 1992. *Development without Destruction: Economics of the Spinning Wheel*. Ahmedabad: Navjivan.

Joshi, Sanjay. 2001. *Fractured Modernity: Making of a Middle Class in Colonial North India*. Delhi: OUP.

Kamath, M.V. & V.B. Kher. 1993. *The Story of Militant but Non-Violent Trade Unionism: A Biographical and Historical Study*. Ahmedabad: Navjivan.

Kaushik, Asha. 2001. *Politics, Symbols and Political Theory: Rethinking Gandhi.* Jaipur: Rawat Publication.

Kaushik, P.D. 1986. *The Congress Ideology and Programme, 1920–85*. Delhi: Gitanjali Publishing House.

Kosambi, D.D. 1996. "Problems of Science and Technology in Underdeveloped Countries". In *Science, Society and Peace.* Delhi: PPH.

Kothari, M.M. 1996. *Critique of Gandhi.* Jodhpur: Critique Publications.

Kothari, S. 1996. *Whose? The Displaced as Victims of Development. EPW* (15 June).

Kripalani, J.B. Acharya. 1946. *Politics of Charkha.* Bombay: Vora & Co., Publishers.

———. 1970. *Gandhi: His Life and Thought.* New Delhi: Publications Division.

Krishna Das. 1928, *Seven Months with Mahatma Gandhi: Being an Inside view of the Non-co-operation movement (1921–22)*, volume I. Madras: S. Gaṇesan.

Krishnayya, U. Venkata. 1951. *25 Years Contact of Mahatma Gandhi with Khaddar Samsthanam.* Jogannapalem: Gramaswarajya Peetham.

Kumar, Dharma. 1982. *The Cambridge Economic History of India vol. II, 1757–1970.* Delhi: Orient Longman.

Kumarappa, Dr Bharatan. 1946. *Capitalism, Socialism or Villagism?* Madras: Shakti Karyalayam.

Kumarappa, J.C. 1935. *The Philosophy of the Village Movement.* Kovvur: Published by Sanivarapu Subba Rao.

———. 1948. *The Economy of Permanence, I & II.* Wardha: AIVIA.

———. 1949. *Why The Village Movement? A Plea For A Village-Centred Economic Order In India.* Wardha: AIVIA.

———. 1954. *Planning by the People for the People: Being a Collection of* Bihar Khadi Gramodyog Sangh. 1971. *Essays on Sarvodaya Planning.* Bombay: Vora & Co., Publishers.

Laxminarayan Smriti-Granth. 1971. *Bihar ka Khadi Andolan aur uska Vikas.* Muzaffarpur.

Lohia, Rammanohar. 1978. *Marx, Gandhi and Socialism.* Hyderabad: Rammanohar Lohia Samata Vidyalaya Nysa.

Mahadevan, T.K. 1977. *Dvija: A Prophet Unheard.* New Delhi: Affiliated East-West Press.

Marx, Karl. 1976. "The Eighteenth Brumaire of Louis Bonaparte" in K. Marx, F. Engels, V. Lenin, *On Historical Materialism: A Collection.*

Mehta, Ved. 1977. *Mahatma Gandhi and His Apostles.* Middlesex: Penguin Books.

Menon, Visalakshi. 2003. *From Movement to Government: The Congress in the United Provinces, 1937–42*. Delhi: Sage.

Moon, Panderel. 1968. *Gandhi and Modern India*. London: The English Universities Press.

Nanda, B.R. 1965. *Mahatma Gandhi: A Biography.* London: Unwin Books.

———. 1985. *Gandhi and His Critiques*. Delhi: Oxford University Press.

———. 1990. *In Gandhi's Footsteps: The Life and Times of Jamnalal Bajaj.* Delhi: Oxford University Press,

———. 1998, *The Making of a Nation: India's Road to Independence*, New Delhi: Harper Collins.

Nandy, Ashis. 1983. *The Intimate Enemy: Loss and Recovery of Self under Colonialism*. Delhi: OUP.

Narayan, Shriman. 1960. *Principles of Gandhian Planning.* Allahabad: Kitab Mahal.

Nehru, Jawaharlal. 1990. *The Discovery of India.* Delhi: Oxford University Press.

Pani, Narendar, 2001. *Inclusive Economics: Gandhian Method and Contemporary Policy*. New Delhi: Sage.

Parekh, Bhikhu. 1999. *Colonialism, Tradition and Reform: An Analysis of Gandhi's Political Discourse*. New Delhi: Sage.

Parel, Anthony J., ed. 1977 *Gandhi: Hind Swaraj and Other Writings.* New Delhi: Foundation Books.

Polak, H.S.L., H.N. Brailsford, Lord Pethick-Lawrence.1949. *Mahatma Gandhi.* London: Odhams Press Limited.

Prasad, Pradhan H. 1994. *Gandhi, Marx India: An Alternative Path of Progress.* New Delhi: Manak Publications.

Prasad, Rajendra. 1927. *Economics of Khadi*. Muzzaffarpur: Bihar Charkha Sangh.

———. 1949. *Satyagraha in Champaran*. Ahmedabad: Navajivan Publishing House.

Prasad, Shambhu. 2001. "Towards an Understanding of Gandhi's Views on Science". In *Economic and Political Weekly* 34, no. 39 (29 September–5 October).

Pyarelal. 1959. *Towards New Horizons.* Ahmedabad: Navajivan Publishing House.

Ramagundam, Rahul. 1996. "Spinning off Track". The *Economic Times*, New Delhi (30 June).

———. 2001. *Defeated Innocence: Adivasi Assertion, Land Rights, and the Ekta Parishad Movement.* New Delhi: Grassroots India Publications.

———. 2004. *Khadi and its Agency: Organizing Structures of Philanthropic Commerce. Social Scientist* (May–June 2004).

Ramanathan, A. S., 1947. *Gandhi and the Youth.* Bombay: Thacker & Co.,

Ramanathan, S., Pattabhi Sitharamyya, & N.S. Varadachari. 1931. *The Superstition of Khadi: A Discussion.* Erode: The Kudi Arasu Publishing House.

Ranga, N.G. 1945. *Four Crore Artisans Hail the Gandhian Plan.* Bombay: Hind Kitab.

Ray, Prithwis Chandra. 1927. *Life and Times of C.R. Das: The Story of Bengal's Self Expression.*

Rolland, Romain. 1990. *Mahatma Gandhi, The Man Who Became One With The Universal Being.* Delhi: Publications Division, Government of India.

Roy, M.N. 1999. *Politics, Power and Parties.* Delhi: Ajanta Publications.

Roy, Ramashray. 1985. *Self and Society: A Study in Gandhian Thought.* New Delhi: Sage Publications.

———. 1996. *Understanding Gandhi.* New Delhi: Ajanta Publications.

Roy, Tirthankar. 1996. *Cloth & Commerce: Textiles in Colonial India.* Delhi: Sage.

Rudolph, Lloyd & Susanne H. Rudolph. 1999. *The Modernity of Tradition: Political Development in India.* Delhi: Orient Longman.

Sarkar, Sumit. 1973; *The Swadeshi Movement in Bengal, 1903–8.* Delhi: People's Publishing House.

———. 1983. *Modern India: 1885–1947.* Madras: Macmillan India Limited.

Schumacher, E.F. 1993. *Small is Beautiful: A Study of Economics As If People Mattered.* London: Vintage.

Sheean, Vincent; 1949. *Lead Kindly Light.*New York: Random House.

Shiva, Vandana. 1989. *Staying Alive—Women, Ecology and Development.* New Delhi: Kali for Women.

Sitharamyya, Pattabhi. 1931. *On Khaddar.* Madras: Natesan & Co.

Srivastava, Hari Shanker. 1968. *The History of Indian Famines and Development of Famine Policy, 1858–1918.* Agra: Sri Ram Mehra & Co.

Steger, Manfred B. *Gandhi's Dilemma: Non-violent Principles and Nationalist Power.*

Tarlo, Emma. 1996. *Clothing Matters: Dress and Identity in India.* New Delhi: Viking.

Tendulkar, D.G. 1951. *Mahatma, Life of Mohandas Karamchand Gandhi.* Vol. I. Delhi: Publications Division.

———. 1957. *Gandhi in Champaran.* New Delhi: Publications Division.

Terchek, Ronald J. 2000. *Gandhi: Struggling for Autonomy.* Delhi: Vistaar Publications.

Thomson, Mark. 1993; *Gandhi and His Ashram.* Bombay: Popular Prakashan.

Trivedi, Lisa N. 2003, "Visually Mapping the 'Nation': Swadeshi Politics in Nationalist India, 1920–1930". In *The Journal of Asian Studies* (February) 62, no. l.

Varadachari, N.S. & S.V. Puntambekar. 1926. *Hand Spinning and Hand Weaving.* Sabarmati: AISA,

Weber, Thomas. 1997. *On the Salt March: The Historiography of Gandhi's March to Dandi.* New Delhi: Harper Collins Publishers India.

———. 2004. *Gandhi as Disciple and Mentor.* Cambridge: Cambridge University Press.

Wolpert, Stanley. 2001. *Gandhi's Passion: The Life and Legacy of Mahatma Gandhi.* Oxford.

Zaidi, A.M. 1985. *A Century of State Craft in India: A Study of Political Resolutions of INC Adopted During the Last 100 Years.* New Delhi: Publication Department, Indian Institute of Applied Political Research.

———. 1985. *A Tryst With Destiny: A Study of Congress Economic Policy Resolutions Passed During The Last 100 Years.* New Delhi: Publication Department, Indian Institute of Applied Political Research.

Zealey, Philip. "Comments on Khadi". In *Gandhi Marg*, journal of the Gandhi Peace Foundation 2, no. 4: 295.

Index

A

B

H

I

R

S

W

Y

Z